Frances E. O. Monck

My Canadian Leaves

An Account of a Visit to Canada in 1864-1865

Frances E. O. Monck

My Canadian Leaves
An Account of a Visit to Canada in 1864-1865

ISBN/EAN: 9783337187705

Printed in Europe, USA, Canada, Australia, Japan

Cover: Foto ©Andreas Hilbeck / pixelio.de

More available books at **www.hansebooks.com**

MY
CANADIAN LEAVES

AN
ACCOUNT OF A VISIT TO CANADA
IN 1864—1865.

BY

FRANCES E. O. MONCK.

LONDON:
RICHARD BENTLEY AND SON,
Publishers in Ordinary to Her Majesty the Queen.
1891.
(All rights reserved.)

LEAVES
FROM MY JOURNAL
IN CANADA,
1864—1865.

Ship "Asia," Monday Evening, Cabin 67, May 16th, 1864.—You will like a journal even begun in this terrible hole of suffering humanity. I think so much of you all and of lovely Ryde. Blayney will tell you all about us *—of our fog between Holyhead and Kingstown when we stopped in the middle of the sea and nearly ran down a brig, of our friendship with Mr. Maguire, the M.P. for Dungarvan, and of my meeting with Dick. Dear F. was so pleasant in London; he advised B. to pretend he was going to enlist in the Federal army and he would get over for a shilling. Mr. Maguire travelled from Dublin to Cork

* My horror of the sea is such that I was so ill from fright that I was left at Ryde with my people, but I travelled night and day, and caught my husband up at Queenstown.

with us. Conway and I were the only women in the train. You may see by my writing how the ship rolls. How lovely Queenstown is! It wasn't a bit like Sunday, all seemed to be amusing themselves. I never shall forget the horror of the train from Cork to Queenstown, the spitty Yankee in the carriage, and then the most terrible of tug boats which rolled horribly, and the work of rushing on board this hole of misery, the gangway jumping and slipping away with the awful rolling. Dick was enchanted to get me. I never could describe to you the horrors of last night and half of to-day; every one on board was sick—the rolling never ceases for one minute—and *this* is called a splendid passage, because there is always a roll on the Atlantic. I am now getting accustomed to it, but I lie down on the floor all day and night on a mattress and bed clothes. The steward and purser come in when one is in bed. I was sick for about six hours yesterday, slept like a top all night. I never knew before (except the Rotterdam night) what sickness was, I never could express it. The untruths people told me about the passage are *glaring*. Holyhead and Calais passages are pleasure trips compared to this never ceasing roll, roll. Thank God, it is, on and off, better; we have had much rain and darkness, which of course frightened me. I pretend we are close to land, and as I have not seen the sea I can pretend it. I think of Linnell's pictures of sheep and hills. Eating is never ceasing, and it is the only thing to do. I had coffee and toast for breakfast (the first thing that did me good): and beef tea for lunch; and soup, boiled chicken, potatoes, and a delicious fricasée of something, and grapes for dinner. I made myself eat at first, and now I like it. Dick is very ill, C. much better; Dick struggled through dinner. Our places are kept at the captain's table. Col. Carter (63rd), wife and five children, and two nurses, are on board, also the Hon. J. Young (Canadian M.P.P.), and a young officer of the 17th. There are some very quaint American women next cabin to us, their talk is my diversion. The child of one of them came down saying what a good dinner she had had with apple pie, and the answer was in a long drawl, "You never get sweets at home. What will you do when you get home? I never give anything but bread and butter for dessert." Fancy a ship being a scene of pleasure. One of these women said to the other (they are friends), "The thing I don't like about Jiney (the child) is the way she treats you (the mamma); wait till she goes to school, and then her troubles will begin." I like them because they have been arranging with the purser about telegraphing when they *land*, and one said, "When you see your *folks*, all your sickness will be forgotten." I envied them meeting their "folks." They make so free with the purser; he told one of them she was looking "very jolly." The fog-whistle is sounding so often. They say we shall stay several hours at Halifax where we can land, and it is only thirty hours on to Boston, but we shall not get to Halifax on Sunday.

Tuesday Evening.—Such a day of horrors! A fresh breeze in our favour, and all sails up! Oh, such misery! I cried with terror, and was sick besides. How I *longed* to be at home again, God only knows. The morning Psalms for this day (17th) describe me exactly. At last the wind is going down, but the sea is still awful. I ate a very good dinner all the same. Conway is as happy as a queen; it took her four hours to-day to dress and to get to me. There are five French priests on board. The Yankee women amuse me so; they are great fun; they have made friends with me. One of them cried with fright last night when the ship rolled and the light went out, and Dick had to go and comfort her. She said she was sure something was happening to the ship, and said to Dick, " Thank you, gentleman." They call me " Mrs." No more to-day.

Wednesday.—Last night and to-day most horrible. Even the sailors called it rough. Last night one of the Yankee women said, "I guess I shall lose my senses," and Dick had again to comfort. Please God, if I ever get home safely, I will never cross the Atlantic again! I never could tell you what it is, and a thousand times I have wished that I had never come. A Yankee man said to the 17th officer last night, "I am neither pig nor bustard, that is, neither sick nor well." He also said, "I have just paid my tribute to Nep-*tune.*" One of the Yankee women told me, " My poor husband's dead body is now crossing the Atlantic in a sailing-vessel with my boy," and she is going on to make preparations for the funeral. She is a Mrs. Robin*son*, and her friend (the coward) is Mrs. Richard*son*. The former told me that she didn't think the Prince of Wales "anything of a smart boy." She also spoke of "your Victoria." They say on board that on Saturday (D.V.) we shall reach the banks of Newfoundland, and shall then be in smoother water. We go there, they say, to avoid the icebergs. It is very cold now. A lady nearly died on board from sea-sickness, but is now better. Dick met Captain Legge and Colonel Earle in London, who both thought it a pity I was not going to Canada, so I must write and say I am gone. How I wish I was safe at home. Let no one ever grumble at anything on dry land.

Thursday.—It was calm all the day till after dinner, and I was one of the five ladies who dined at the table d'hôte; I send you a bill of fare. After dinner it got very rough, and was so nearly all night. I can't sleep with terror. Since the first night my nights are maddening. I advise no one for love or money to cross the Atlantic. I sat next the captain at dinner. The faces at the table are worth a study. We have three newspaper correspondents; one a Yankee who writes for the *New York Herald.* We have a German man who has crossed the Atlantic seventy-nine times!!! Also ten Southerners who are going to run the blockade, and quantities of Yankees, some English, Scotch, and French.

Friday.—To-day has been calm all day, and I have lunched and dined upstairs and am now writing in the saloon; it is getting rougher. Dick and many others have been playing games on deck all day—a sort of croquet, only different, and now they are playing a game with a ring, and great row is the consequence. *On dit* that General Hastings Doyle always comes down at Halifax to see the passengers land, if it is in the daytime; I should like to see him again. Mr. Young advises us to go to Quebec by Montreal and the river. We have passed three ships and a *whale*, none of which I saw. I haven't seen the sea *yet*; the bulwarks are so high, except you go on the top deck, you need not see it. It is odd to hear the man calling the people every morning, as if on land.

Saturday Afternoon.—The captain did not dine to-day as he is asleep preparatory to coming near the Banks and Cape Race, when he must be up all night. We expect he must be up to-night. If the weather is clear we are all right; but in fogs the icebergs are dangerous. Thank God, it is now calm. This is said to be a splendid passage. What must a bad one be! Conway makes me laugh much; she announced to-day that a young Canadian man on board had said to her that those that loved scenery would be happy in Canada. "Ma'am," he says, "there are quantities of French people, and beetles, and (h)umming birds." She very properly would not tell me about the saloon of this ship being once washed away in a storm; but I told her, and she said she would not have let me know it. We have discovered that one of the newspaper correspondents is Mr. Stephen Lawley, who wrote those beautiful letters for the South in the *Times*. He is so handsome, with silvery hair. The other is Vizitelly, of the *Illustrated London Times*.

Monday.—Yesterday was a *very* rough day; I stayed all day in bed. We passed quantities of icebergs, and got through them safely, thank God: they are very dangerous things. There was quite a panic on Saturday night among the females about them, and my Yankee friend wanted not to undress that she might be *prepared* if anything happened! These women now have a Yankee called Captain Edwards in their room, though they are *in bed*. I have made acquaintance with a Mrs. Legh, widow of the late Colonel of the 77th; he greatly distinguished himself in the Crimea, and afterwards went to India, where his wife and two children joined him just in time to see him die of sunstroke; she

CHURCH SERVICE.

is going to her family at St. John's; she is a lady, and so pretty looking. Conway went to the service on board yesterday, and said it was so nice, except that they carefully avoided anything connected with Trinity Sunday. The doctor read, and the purser led the singing, the captain and all the passengers present joined; both singing and responses were very loud and nice; none could *move* off their seats, or they would have fallen! The icebergs were *grand*, Dick said. Last night was very rough and foggy. The sailors are singing a loud chorus now. Last night some ladies and men sang psalms round the funnel! The cold is intense; Saturday, two degrees of frost. Yesterday there was ice on deck, and to-day it is four degrees below freezing. I don't like the stewardess. The steward said last night was "a very nasty night." The 17th officer is a Mr. Aylmer. It is said we shall get to Halifax (D.V.) to-morrow night. There is a fresh breeze in our favour to-day, so I shall stay all day in bed. Oh, how I trust every one will write to me, and tell me every little thing! Mr. Aylmer and I had great fun on Saturday; he told me he was at dinner with Vizitelly, Lawley, etc., and an old Spaniard with "a wall eye," and they call him for fun "Mr. Walleye;" he is perfectly unconscious of the joke, and goes on so civilly; when they pressed him to have more wine, he said, "I am drunk." I wish I was going home with my letter!

Tuesday.—I did go up yesterday, it got so lovely; we had the American sky, which is as blue as the Italian. We saw a whale spouting. Do you know we were in danger for two nights, Saturday and Sunday, and many of the gentlemen stayed up all night, and were much afraid. One night it was the icebergs, the next Cape Race; both nights we had fogs. Sunday night, the captain said, was a dreadful night, *a black fog, lightning, torrents* of rain, and a shifting wind. His manner was quite different yesterday, from his relieved feelings. God is very good to bring us safe. I never sleep now; we had a very rough night last night, and I was quite idiotic. The Yankee women call Conway "May-rye;" she answers to the name, though her name is Julia. We are expected to land to-night or to-morrow at Halifax (D.V.).—Ever yours, F. E. Q. MONCK.

Revere House, Boston, U.S., Friday, May 27*th.*—You see we are at last on land again; thank God for His great mercies in bringing us safely. That night I wrote to you about (Monday) was a terrible night; I heard about it afterwards; the sailors were up to their knees in water, and the ship shipped three awful seas, the sails could not be put up for fear they would be torn to pieces with the wind, and salt was nearly to the top of the funnel. On Tuesday we had a poor little attempt at keeping the queen's birthday; we had three flags up (the wind would not allow more), we had *two* cannons fired, and Colonel Carter was made to propose the queen's health at dinner; it was very touching to hear the tremendous cheering (three times three, and one more), and I nearly cried; you know cheering always upsets my composure. The toast was well received even by the Yankees, but the Frenchmen at table all sat down, and well were they worried afterwards by Mr. Vizitelly and an English bag-man (a Mr. Stone), who made them tremble in their shoes. "The captain, officers, and crew of the good ship *Asia*," was the next and *last* toast; no more were allowed, for fear of the Americans. Mrs. Carter was at dinner that day; I like her very much, she looks so young and so gentle, and seems so good. Colonel Carter says, "What do you call 'em," every instant when in a fuss, and never explains more than that; this amuses me. Explaining a journey to me, he said, " Then you start from what do you call 'em, and go on to what do you call 'em," etc., and never made it clearer. I like Mrs. Legh extremely; her sister is married to Mr. Moodie, A.D.C. to Mr. Gordon, who was staying at Spencer Wood; her father is a judge at St. John's. I made acquaintance with two more men, one Mr. St. George, who is settled at Toronto, and speaks English like a Frenchman; the other a Mr. Beswick, a Quebec merchant; they introduced themselves. Then there was a Mr. Rimner, a Montreal wine merchant, who introduced himself to Dick, and was marvellously civil; invited him to his shooting lodges in August and October, and said he would only have Guardsmen to meet him! We had also a Mr. Pell on board, a pleasant old man, who had one son in the Northern and the other in the Southern army. There was also a great Yankee publisher of Boston, who came over to England to purchase all Dickens's works; he was very civil to me, when another Yankee was very rude, a Mr. Croker, one of the great men out here, and a *hater* of England; this man tried to take away a cushion from me—all the gentlemen were so angry, and the publisher rushed with another cushion. We tried that night (Tuesday) to get up some singing, but failed. That was an exciting night; we were nearing Halifax, and rockets were sent up and guns fired. I went up near midnight on the high·deck to see the northern lights, and the moon rising like a ball of fire; the night was lovely and calm, and the sky was exquisite. At last we stopped, and oh, the joy of it! It was midnight, alas, so no fun could be had. News of a great battle came on board, and the excitement of the Americans was marvellous. Wretched Mr. Croker was in bed, and some one rushed in and awoke him, saying, "There's great news; General Lee has marched into Washington." The man was like a maniac, he rushed ashore, and never stopped till he found papers which he sat up reading. At 5.30 a.m. my Yankee woman had a gentleman to call her whom she begged to *come in*. I got up and made Dick get up (I had only lain down dressed), and we sallied out to see the town; we walked for more than an hour; every poor man was Irish; I never was so glad to hear the brogue. Halifax is not much of a town; we saw the citadel from a little distance and Government House. The houses are mostly built of wood, and look pinched up; the 16th and 17th (2nd battalion) are quartered there. We lost seventy passengers there, and some of the nicest went, viz. Mrs. Legh and a charming Mrs. Anderson who was going with her husband to St. John's; he was to be Adjutant-General of Militia to Mr. Gordon, and she was so good about it; she evidently did not like going (as it may last for ever), but would not say so; she had three nice children, and she had such a sweet face like a picture of people's great-aunts, with little fair curls; every lady on board raved about her; she was like a Sister of Mercy, and kept all the children on board amused on Sunday with stories, and gave them tracts and texts. A great many Southerners left at Halifax. We set off at eight again, and had a smooth passage till yesterday, when it got very rough, but we were, thank God, near Boston. The entrance to Boston harbour for miles is most remarkable, a succession of forts out in the sea. We saw two Russian frigates. The fog came on, and we ran a good chance of not getting to land last night, but, thank God, in torrents of rain, we got to land at last. The Yankee widow told me she was in such a fuss about passing her dead husband's dress suit (a new one) through the Custom-house.

She also told me she was very unhappy, and was suffering "chiefly from dirt," as she had not changed her clothes since she left Liverpool; by some accident her box had been put in the bottom of the hold, and she had no clean clothes. The passengers fraternized a good deal as we neared land. Mr. St. George, to whom I had spoken but three words, gave me "Guy Livingstone," insisted on my taking it, and said it was "a very nice book" (?) All the Yankees walk about leaning on perfect strangers, and two oldish English spinsters walked around leaning on Yankee men. There was great playing of games on deck the last two days. Dick was the wonder of the ship at throwing rings on a spike. The amount of betting among the low men was frightful. The rudeness of these low men to each other was past telling, but seemed to be well received. For instance, "You're an arrant coward," "You're a fool," "I did so and so," "No, you didn't," and such like phrases were the constant things one heard. We were met by a letter from the Governor-General, a very kind one which came through the Chief Agent of the Cunard Company, who was there to meet us, accompanied by the English Consul. Mr. Rose (a great Canadian man) invited us through the G. G. to stay at his house at Montreal, but the G. G. refused for us. We got our luggage through the Custom-house without anything being opened, through this Mr. Bates, who was civility itself; he said it was a thing he never did (to help people), but when he was written to by "such high authorities as Lord Monck and Mr. Rose he gladly did it." The Consul gave me his arm, and took me to a sort of drawing-room to wait; then Mr. Bates gave me his arm to conduct me to a carriage, in which we drove to this hotel. We went in the carriage across the ferry, and I never knew we were on the water till we were just across! I thought we were under an archway all the time. Mr. Aylmer went on before, and got us rooms, and we were very comfortable. Oh, the *enchantment* of a clean bed and a bath! Land felt very *stuffy* after the ocean. We had hot supper; we dined on board before we left, when it was getting very rough. This hotel (or *House*, as they call it here) is like a French one with English comforts. We had several fellow-travellers at supper last night, all in great excitement, as one of the passengers was taken up as we landed. Dick was talking to him last night; he is with a detective; he was charged with wanting to run the blockade. They were on the lookout for two more on board. He says he is unjustly treated, and is going to bring an action against them. He is a Canadian. We are going to drive out and see the town, and we start to-day at 5.30 for Montreal in the sleeping cars. Mr. Finlay, a railway official, has just been here; very civil. He heard of our arrival through the Governor-General, and is going to do his best to make us comfortable. My head aches so horribly, and the heat is so great. Captain Middy Seymour is to get us rooms at Montreal. —Ever yours, etc., F. E. O. MONCK.

Government House, Quebec, Sunday, May 29th, 1864.—I am so delighted to be able to write so often. I must go back now to Boston, and tell you of our time there, etc. After I sent my letter we went out driving. Mr. Aylmer went with us. I was nearly mad with heat and headache, so the first part of the drive was torture. We saw Longfellow's house, quite a house for a poet; yellow, and so surrounded with lilacs that you could scarcely see the house. We passed the Cambridge of Yankeedom; I think it is also called Cambridge. We went then to the best sight at Boston, viz. the churchyard! Mount Auburn is the name of

2

it. It is the most beautiful and cheerful churchyard I ever saw. There is a "Chapelle Mortuaire" in the grounds with a very wonderful window in it, very gaudy and bright coloured. This churchyard is divided into a hundred beautiful pathways, called after the names of different trees and flowers: for instance, " Snowdrop Path," " Azalea Path," and so on; one was " Hazel Dell." The almost total absence of crosses was remarkable. When the person buried was old, the monument was *very* large, when young very small, and on some children's tombs were little marble lambs, the size of toy lambs — so very quaint! One tomb was sacred to "*Joseph Lucifer;*" we also saw Spurzheim, the phrenologist's, tomb. The view was lovely, and the day cleared up and got cooler when we were there, so I got better. We then went to Bunker's Hill, where is a ridiculously ugly monument in honour of a victory gained by the Yankees over the English! (1775); it is a frightful sort of tall obelisk, without inscription of any kind. We drove all about the environs of Boston, and rather pretty they are. I saw so many curious old Puritan names on the shops as we drove through the town. Then we had dinner, and later set off for Montreal in the "sleeping cars." The G. G. had written about us to the railway people (most kindly), and we were presented with a *free* ticket through the States. Dick did not know what this meant, and took tickets; but the conductor hopes to refund the money, about £3. We were provided with a not uncomfortable partition in the cars, Mr. Aylmer with us. We went in a most disgusting omnibus, or "stage," from the hotel to the train—such bumping and knocking about, very small horses, and a large "stage," and really we were nearly squeezed to death and suffocated. When the night came, the conductor arranged our beds, and I laughed till I cried at the whole thing. Dick and I were in one bed, made of cushions and with pillows. Conway slept over our heads in a berth let down from the ceiling. A bride and bridegroom slept opposite to us, and Mr. Aylmer over their heads, opposite to Conway. Another married couple was further on in another bed, and so on. When Mr. A. asked where he was to be, the man said, "I'll fix you up, right away up there," pointing to the top berth. Between weakness and amusement I laughed till the tears rolled down my cheeks. The conductor was very civil, but a true Yankee, slapping us both on the shoulders. We had "the bear" to cover us, as Mrs. Carter had warned me against the blankets and quilts, and we would not have the curtains down. Fancy, washing in a train! Conway laughed so that she could not sleep. I slept very well, considering the awful jolting; we travelled from 5.30 p.m. on Friday till 10 a.m. on Saturday. I lived on one biscuit, an orange, and some wine and water, during all that time. We stopped at one place for breakfast, but I was not hungry. We passed through Ver*mont*, New Hampshire, and Massachusetts; some of the scenery is very beautiful, Lake Champlain is most grand, and the vegetation is wonderful; by that I mean trees and underwood, for there is not the slightest sign of cultivation anywhere. We passed Manchester, a large manufacturing town. The river Merrimac is very fine; we went along its banks most of the way. We were thankful at last to get to Montreal; we had to get out of the train when we came to the Canadian frontier, and we had to change again from the cars to a ferry steamer at Montreal. Dick was addressed by name on landing, which surprised us, but Mr. Beswick had gone on and announced that he was coming at the St. Lawrence Hall, the great hotel. We were glad to be clean again, and to have a first-rate breakfast; Mr. Aylmer was with us. The hotel looks very grand. Dick saw Mr. Lane Fox at the hotel, and told him to tell "Seymour" we were come, and soon a Fusilier orderly came to Dick with a note from him. I can't tell you the bliss of seeing a Guardsman in this land! Soon Captain Seymour came, and was so cordial. He arranged to come for me at three, and take me a drive in his waggon round Montreal. Dick and I then went out to walk; we saw the Roman Catholic cathedral; it is very enormous, but not handsome; it had the same bright-coloured windows I remarked at Mount Auburn church. At three Captain S. came in his waggon, with two horses; one of them, he said, was a "melancholy mare," and nothing would cheer her up. Montreal is such a pretty town, like a French town; we drove for more than two hours, Dick sitting up behind. Captain S. showed me where every one lived. We drove round the mountain, the show drive here; there were nice green lanes, and everything looked nice. We saw the skating rink, a wonderful place. We dined at the hotel, and sailed at seven for Quebec. Mr. Aylmer again joined us. He had gone to the 60th mess, and he said that Dick's fame as a racquet-player had preceded him. The St. Lawrence is a magnificent river, and the views lovely; all the houses being roofed with tin, makes them look like burnished gold and silver when the sun shines. The sunset was gorgeous. There were no amusing passengers on board. We were treated with great honour by the captain, who gave us supper at our own hour, and said we should have a *private* room, which turned out to be the *pantry!* We slept that night on board; the boats are very fine, three storeys high, and like floating hotels: they shake very much, and the lamps swing with the motion—not agreeable. We arrived about six a.m. on Sunday. We were met by Sergeant Lambkin (the orderly), and an open carriage from Spencer Wood. The view of Quebec from the river is most beautiful, and the day was perfect. We had got up at 4.30 to see the views. We had a pretty drive here, and oh, I felt so sad, it all seemed so weird and odd, the Monck liveries, and everything like home, and to think we are across the Atlantic, at the other side of the world, from B. B. and you all; it is not easy indeed to think about it! The trees are very little out here, and yesterday was bitterly cold except the sun was hot in the middle of the day. Spencer Wood is a lovely spot just over the river. My room was all done out with leaves and wreaths with "Welcome," etc., by Fraulein Denneler and Fan. They were all very glad to see us, and we to see them. When they all went to church, Dick and I took a little walk. I was quite worn out after the long journey, but got better, and went to afternoon service, leaving before the sermon. St. Michael's is a nice little church, and the walk through the woods very pretty. We had tea in the verandah at six; it was charming.

May 30, *Monday, Spencer Wood.* — L. drove me in her phaeton to the R.A. Band at Quebec in the afternoon. There were many officers and girls there. It is not a bad Band, and the view is pretty. Oh, the beauty of this place! I can't describe it, and such views everywhere!

Tuesday.—The Lindsays arrived before breakfast for a ten days' visit. The party is as follows: General L., Lady Sarah, three girls, and Captain Seymour, Brig.-Major and Captain Eliot, A.D.C. L. and I went to the Band again that day (the 62nd). It is a very good one; Captain Retallack and

Colonel Gordon were both with us. Many people have called on me, but I am always out when they come, so I have seen no one. Lady S. and I are to go, and return our visits together. I was made to sing " The Irish Jaunting Car," in the evening, which much amused every one. Dick looks very nice in staff uniform. My head aches so I can scarcely write sense.

Wednesday. — Mrs. Adamson (wife to Parliament Librarian) lunched to see me, she is so quaint with fat *shells* of black curls resting on her face. She said to me, " Now I hope you will walk a great deal, for people are apt to be bilious after a journey"!! She is Irish. Aunt L. and I took a long walk to see the cemetery, which is very pretty, just over the St. Lawrence, and kept like a nice garden. Dinner-party. I sat between General L. and Captain Eliot; both were so pleasant.

Thursday. — Got delightful home letters telling me of my darling B. B.; letters are *such* a comfort. We breakfasted early, and went off to the 17th inspection. It was on the plains of Abraham, so lovely with the blue river and hills and green fields, and trees and banks. It was so wonderful to think of how short a time (three weeks) since we were looking at the 26th being inspected at Southsea. After lunch we went to the 17th Band. Old Chief Justice Bowen was introduced to me. We saw a few Quebec young ladies there. We went then to the racquet-court, and saw Mr. G. and Mr. Gream (62nd) play. The view from the gardens where the Band plays is exquisite. (The G. G. is just come in to show me a letter from Sir Fenwick Williams to invite me and Dick to stay a week with him, at his Island, when we have seen Quebec.) Dinner-party. I sat next Col. C. (on the staff at Montreal), he does the Emperor, and tries to look like him; he has been all over this world. Major Brice amused me in the evening by saying he was sure Mr. Aylmer liked my being afraid in the ship, "because it is some occupation between breakfast and luncheon trying to reassure ladies!" General L. is charming. Lady S. is so kind, and I like the girls.

Friday (to-day). — The 62nd are being inspected to-day, I did not go to see them. I wanted to write, and the sun is so hot though the wind is cold.

Saturday, June 4th.—Lady Sarah, and Captain Retallack (ex-Mil. Sec.) went yesterday to return our visits. We went first to

"Chief Justice Bowen, the Misses Bowen, and the Misses Webster." They live in a nice large house, and have a garden.

Saturday. — A grand cricket-match, the 62nd and R.A. (one officer) against the 17th, household, and R.E. The 62nd won, I am sorry to say. Dick caught out "the best player" on the 62nd side, who had had fifty-five runs. The scene was beautiful beyond description, it is just that view scene in the photo, heightened in beauty by colouring. All the cricketers had lunch in the verandah. It was a very hot day, and I sat all the afternoon on the cricket-ground. Captain Seymour left, to our regret, and Col. G. came to stay. Dinner-party "according to list," mostly ministers, and Miss Mountain, the late bishop's daughter. Sir E. Taché (the Premier) took me in. Mr. Godley made me talk French to him; he is a nice agreeable old man. Sir Etienne is the only Queen's A.D.C. in Canada or America. He met Captain Eliot with the Prince of Wales, when he was here, and said to me that Captain E. is "un bien joli garçon." The mosquitoes were dreadful at dinner, they have never been so bad as this year, because the winter was mild. Sir E. told me one was on my shoulder, and the servant behind me stepped forward, slapped my shoulder with a napkin, and killed it on the spot! In the evening M. Dorion was introduced to me (an ex-minister); he is very agreeable, but just as I was talking to him, Captain P.'s little brute of a dog jumped on my lap and upset my tea all over my dress! Captain P. says he will give me a new one.

Sunday.—You ought to be getting my first letter in a day or two. Lady S. and Captain S. told me so much of the Bishop (Fulford) of Montreal; he lives in the poorest way because the cathedral is in debt; he is moderate church, and does so much good.

June 6th, Monday.—We went to afternoon service yesterday, and walked back through the woods. Tea in the verandah is very charming except for the mosquitoes. I am much bitten, and so is nearly every one; it is a funny sight to look up the table at dinner and see every one with their hands in an attitude of defiance, killing all round. Some dogs came into church, and one of them fought with the sexton. We had a stupid and flowery sermon. There was Thunder and great rain last night, which, thank God, I did not hear. It is cooler to-day, it was eighty in the shade yesterday;

they say we are to have a cool summer. The gentlemen dine at mess dinners to-day and to-morrow. They have sent us back the railway money from Boston, £3.

Spencer Wood, Monday, June 6th.—I have not very much to tell you this time. I am longing for letters, but no mail is in. After I sent your letters we had a small Thunderstorm, and I was much afraid and went to the cellar with Conway; the cellar is a very large one; General Lindsay says I go there to "liquor up." I sit in the middle with bottles all round me. The evening was lovely after the storm; it grew so cold that we have taken to fires and warm clothes again; there was ice on Lake St. Charles and frost. When it cleared, Lady S. and I went out in the phaeton to pay visits. Then I took a lovely walk with Dick about the place, and then we had severe tea, as the gentlemen were dining with the 62nd. I sang a good deal in the evening. My box, in which the music is, was by some mistake of Dick's left at Boston, and had only just come.

Tuesday.—Some of us went to hear the 62nd band; it is a good one. P. and I then drank tea with Mrs. Godley at her pretty cottage. The gentlemen all dined at the 17th mess. Dick said the 17th officers were gentlemanly and nice, and everything except the band nice.

Wednesday, June 8*th.*—Very Cold and windy. We went to a field-day of the 17th, 62nd, and R.A.; it was very pretty. Dick acted Brig.-Major to Col. Ingall (62nd). I hate him in a cocked hat. Lady S. and the girls left after lunch. Captain and Mrs. M. (R.A.) came; she is very pretty, and has five children, the eldest seven! Then we had tea severe at 6.30, and the gentlemen dined at the R.A. and R.E. mess. Some of us went to the House of Commons at Quebec. I was a good deal amused for a short time, but we stayed too long (till near eleven), and the debate was not interesting. Col. Gordon took care of us. I had a long talk with nice Mr. Rose. It is wonderful the way the M.P.P.'s abuse and contradict each other. Sometimes they throw pellets of paper at each other. The speaker looks like a priest with a priest's hat. M. Cartier was introduced to me! That most quaint-looking McGee was also introduced, he looks like a wild Indian. We got home about twelve, it was so hot and stuffy. Canadians hate air.

Thursday, 9*th.*—Got my letters. Letters are a marvellous comfort out here. When we go to Montreal, Lady S. is going to give a dinner, to which colonels of regiments are to be asked, also the Bishop and Mrs. Fulford, and the mayor; and the officers' wives are to be asked in the evening. Then the general is to have a review of the Guards, 60th Rifles, 30th, and R.A. I trust nothing will happen to mar all this fun, and that it will be cool. This is a regular wet day. The Governor of Prince Edward's Island, Mrs. Dundas, and her brother, Mr. Atkinson (secretary), come this week, and then we are to have excursions about the country. There is to be a dance on Thursday next. Mr. Levi, the man who was taken up on the *Asia*, is let out again; he was going to be married. The general and Captain E. left after lunch. I paid some visits with Captain Pemberton, A.D.C., and then went to the 17th band for a short time. Colonel G. dined and slept. Got more letters. There are fifteen dogs and seven cats in this house. There are thirty windows on each side of this house, and the rooms are some of them large. The servants' rooms, kitchen, etc., form a sort of wing. The cold is intense now. My hands were quite numbed with cold, and my face *blue*. The Guards are not to go home till October.

Friday, June 10th.—All here are going to-night to hear " Il Barbiere," by an Opera Company now at Quebec. I mean to stay at home with Dick, as my head aches. We have had great hail and rain to-day. Dick and I have just been out visiting colonels' wives at Quebec.

June 11th, St. Barnabas' Day, Spencer Wood.—I have so far very little to say, and yet I begin. I wish I had gone to the Opera last night, as the gas was not very hot. Dick and I read the papers, an undertaking here, when they come so many together. This morning before breakfast the Dundases arrived. They travelled here in the Prince of Wales's "sleeping car," and Mrs. D. slept well, not easy, I think, in a shaky car. After lunch, Aunt L., Mrs. Dundas, and F., and I, took a lovely drive all along the coves at the bottom of this place, through a wooden village, surrounded with rocks and banks of trees, at the side of the St. Lawrence, which was covered with rafts; it is a curious place, and most picturesque—so thoroughly Canadian. We came up and down the most awful hills I ever saw, quite straight. Mr. Atkinson took me in to dinner that evening, and was very pleasant. He and I agreed that one learns geography by crossing the Atlantic. For instance, we both talked of Halifax, St. John's, etc., as being in Canada before, and now we know where they really are. Mr. Rose dined, also Mr. Lake (62nd).

Sunday, 12*th.*—A most tiring day. I got up to go to early service, and as we were rather late we found all the gates on the way through the woods locked, and we could not have had time to go round by the road. I was so vexed. We trudged off to the eleven-o'clock service. Dick and I sat at the open church door, and came out before the sermon, my head ached so. At afternoon service we had a baptism and a sermon of thirty-four minutes, from Mr. Dodwell, of Lennoxville. We all walked back through the woods. After tea I went into the greenhouse to see a humming-bird. It is so very like a *slight* bee, and makes a pretty hum; such a little treasure. Mr. —— dined; he is the *image* of a cat, no difference.

Monday, 13*th.*—We have just been at a review of all the troops on the plains of Abraham. It was in honour of Mrs. Dundas, who *loves* soldiers. The G. G. rode, also Dick in his nasty cocked hat. It was a pretty sight—the review, I mean, not Dick. After lunch we all go for a long drive to see some view. I believe Colonel G. is to drive me in his waggon. Mrs. Dundas's maid is called *Towell*, and the valet's name is *Sword!* What quaint names to be in the same family.

June 13*th, Spencer Wood, Monday.*—We were just going out to drive when I left off. Colonel Gordon and I drove in his waggon to Cap-Rouge. Some of the others drove in the carriage; but we never saw them at all during the drive. Oh, I never could tell you the beauty of the drive through the bush, which really looked like a gentleman's park. Then glimpses of the deep blue St. Lawrence, and the blue hills and green woods; it was all too beautiful. It was very warm. Colonel G. was so pleasant. Cap-Rouge is pronounced "Carouge," or "Cawrouge," as the Canadians say. We stopped to rest quiet at a summer-house or tea-garden at Cap-Rouge, but we did not get out of the waggon. That night there was a dinner-party, and I was taken in by Mr. Hillier Cameron, M.P.P., and a great Orange man! He is a good speaker, and a very agreeable man. He told me two horrors about my voyage, which it was a blessing I did not know at the time—the *Asia* is celebrated for her *rats*—"the *Asia* rats" is a phrase;

and that Mr. Young is considered so unlucky to travel with (having been shipwrecked twice), that when people hear he is going to sail in a vessel they won't go by it. Fancy my having come in for this horror and not knowing it, though I must say I told Mr. Y. I was afraid of him. After dinner I talked to Mrs. H. Cameron; she is pretty, and very pleasing—comes from Bal*timore*. I showed her B. B.'s photo, and she was astonished at his size.

Tuesday, 14*th*.—We drove to the band in the afternoon. The heat was unbearable; I felt quite idiotic, and found myself repeating words and making foolish remarks. Some officers dined. One of the 17th told me a brother officer dreamt a week before the Derby that Blair Athol won, and that General Peel was second; they were afraid to put their money on it because it was only a dream.

Wednesday, 15*th*.—We are going to a lake to-day, a great excursion, and I dread the heat so. I have on a blue calico dress, and am covered with *leaves* down my back and inside my bonnet. A ministerial crisis, so the G. G. can't come.

Thursday, 16*th*.—We went our expedition yesterday to Lake Beauport. We set off at twelve, and were not back till nearly seven.

Most of the party went in covered waggons, but I went in an open one with Col. Gordon. I found my leaves keep out the heat uncommonly well. I had also a dust-coloured cloak and an umbrella. Most of the gentlemen wore straw hats, and Mr. Godley had a green veil, and Col. G. a blue one. They looked so odd. Col. G. had two strange horses that kicked and would not pull together, with *no* mouths, so I was afraid very often. He said, "If you are afraid, sit still!" It is a fourteen-mile drive there, and we got there before any one. I was a little disappointed with the lake, it ought to look much wilder so far off and in such an unlived-in part of the country; but the woods (which cover the hills all round it) look so very civilized, and so do all the wildest woods here, as far as I have seen. We had a very rough narrow road to get to it, and one wheel was constantly up on the side of a bank, and the other low down on the road. We also bumped over "corduroy" bridges, *i.e.* bridges made of *logs of wood*. The working men here all wear red shirts which look pretty. Dick drove Mrs. Dundas, and Mr. Dundas and her Ex. went together. When we arrived at the hotel (which is a verandahed cottage on a grassy hill), we all sat under the trees near the lake till lunch was ready. We then ate an enormous lunch in a small room in the inn; nearly every one had three helps of meat. After lunch we went out in boats on the lake; Mrs. Dundas, Fan, and I, chose the biggest boat, and got into it, and were rowed by Dick and Mr. Atkinson. The others paired off in other boats. The lake was very rough, and I longed to be on shore; our boat leaked, and was by degrees filling with water. When we landed we got lemonade, and then drove home. Col. G.'s horses kicked and rushed so at starting. It was lovely driving home. I got some home letters—enchanted to get them. This house might have been burnt down yesterday only that God's goodness saved it. C. gave the alarm, and they stopped it, a spark caught the roof, which is of wood, and so dry now that the least thing might set it off. They got water and put it out. This morning, Captain Hope and Captain Crichton (Gren. Guards) arrived from Montreal for the dance to-night. We ladies have been making wreaths all the morning for the dancing-room; fancy *me* making a wreath for the wall! I made nearly two, and was said to do them very well, stupid as I am with my hands.

VICEREGAL BALL.

Friday, 17*th*.—We made quantities of wreaths and garlands yesterday, and I must tell you mine were particularly admired, although Mrs. D. said *she should know my odd ones anywhere*. We got the maids in to help later, and Col. Gordon came also. Mrs. D. said to her maid, "Towell, did you make a nice wreath?" "No, ma'am," was the answer. The room looked lovely, for the garlands were all over it, and they were green mixed with bright flowers. We were so exhausted that Mrs. D., Colonel G., and I, went out and strolled about. The heat had been stifling all day, but the nights are cool here. The verandah was veiled in with a hundred and eighty yards of fine white muslin, nailed down to keep out the mosquitoes and insects, or "bugs," as the Yankees call them. The 17th band was outside the curtain. The verandah was lit up, and all the soldiers and their lights looked so very pretty. We assembled in her Ex.'s sitting-room, and then all walked in in procession. Then the presentations began, and lasted a few minutes. The dresses were very good, and a few of the girls nice-looking. They all bowed *very* low to her Ex., and two people backed out of the room. I danced all night, and enjoyed myself much. It was nice walking in the verandah between the dances. Fan went in to supper with old Sir E. Taché, and Louise with old M. Cartier. Mr. J. A. Macdonald took me in. When every one was gone but our own party, Cartier, and Colonel G., I sang "The Cure," and most of the gentlemen danced it. Cartier jumped higher than any one. This morning we were all pretty tired. The day we went to Lake Beauport, the thermometer was ninety-two degrees in the shade at the cool citadel. They are playing cricket to-day in this awful heat. Major B.'s dancing is never to be forgotten, hopping with his thumbs *en l'air*.

June 17th, Friday, Spencer Wood.—The heat is very dreadful every day now, and it is impossible to go out till near sunset: ninety-two and ninety-five in the shade. It makes my head ache much. We were thirteen at dinner for the second time. We sat out on the verandah after dinner. We had sat looking at the cricket under the trees before dinner.

Saturday, 18th.—Cricket again. We looked on, and were well broiled. I was so giddy from the heat. There was such a look of Thunder that I would not go in to dinner. Some ministers dined. We had a pleasant evening, as we sang choruses; first a Canadian song, and then the Christy Minstrels; I also sang two solos. M. Cartier sang the solo of the Canadian song. Our choruses sounded very pretty. The G. G. introduced Mr. Brown to me. He is to become a new minister, and is very nice-looking, tall and greyish, with a Ponsonby face. M. Cartier is the funniest of little men!

Sunday, 19th.—Dick and I went to eight-o'clock service. I was nearly dead with heat and fatigue. We had had a hot night, for a wonder, and you have a twenty-five-minutes' walk to get to Church. It was nice and quiet in Church; only eleven people inside, besides the sexton and clergy. At breakfast some of us agreed we could not face the furnace of heat, so we arranged that Dick was to be clergyman in a chapel of ease in the cellar, and Mr. Atkinson was to be clerk and sexton. He said, "The sexton always goes out of church," so he would be him. We went to inspect the cellar, and found it so smelly and cold we changed our minds, and had service in L.'s sitting-room. Dick read, and we answered the responses, and were very devout and quiet. Dick read a short sermon. I did not go to Church in the afternoon either.

After tea in the verandah, Dick and I walked to the summer-house over the cliff, where we met Captain Pemberton and Mr. Atkinson, and stayed looking at a wind-storm coming up the river. Mr. Rose dined. We had a little distant Thunder in the night.

Monday, June 20*th.*—A cool wind-storm blowing to-day. Mrs. Dundas has asked us to Prince Edward's Island, and we should much like to go if it can be managed. Their plan for us is this. The admiral—Sir J. Hope—is supposed to be coming up here soon; they want us to try and arrange to make him take us in his ship down the St. Lawrence, and through the Gulf to Prince Edward's Island, pay them a visit, and then go on (twenty-four hours' sea) to Halifax, and stay with General Doyle. It will be great fun if we can manage it when her Ex., etc., are gone home. I don't know what I shall do when they go home; I shall miss them so.

Tuesday, 21*st.*—Went to hear 62nd band.

Wednesday, 22*nd.*—We all went to see the Ursulines' Convent and the Laval College at Quebec. The nuns are cloistered, but the G. G. has a right to go to the convent, and he can allow people to go. Col. G. came also, and every one was in uniform.

The poor nuns were in great excitement; they teach most of the young ladies of Quebec, and make them accomplished, and give them good manners. We went all over the convent, and the girls sang "God save," etc., and played on many harps and pianofortes, and were all dressed in white. The G. G. and her Ex. would not go. Dick chaffed the poor nuns, and told them he knew they were longing to get out, and offered to take one out for a drive; they were amused, but pretended to be shocked. I asked one nun to show my husband her bedroom or cell, and after a little hesitation she said she would show it. "The Prince of Wales had seen it, and he was not married;" one of these poor things had been in the convent for twenty or thirty years! Vicaire General Cazeau showed us over the convent; he calls the nuns "St. Charles" and St. Pierre, etc., never says "Ma Mêre." I did not admire the pictures in the chapel which they thought very fine. We then all went into a room where we sat in a solemn semicircle (Mrs. D. in the middle of the semicircle), and were regaled with raspberry vinegar and water and lemonade. Wine is not allowed, except in case of illness. Then we all went to the Priests' College; it is a fine college, and the library is very good; they have also very fine botanical and geological collections; you all know I know absolutely *nothing* of botany; but I played my part so well examining each specimen so carefully with my eye-glass that a priest remarked to me, "Madame" seemed to have a great love for botany, and that whenever she liked to come and study they would be proud to admit her at any time she liked. I smiled benignly and thanked him. F. laughed so at my grave face and earnest studious manner. We all climbed up to the flat roof of the college, from which the view is most grand—you can see miles and miles round. Dick then began "chaffing" the priests, and told them they ought to give a ball in their college. The good-humoured Vicaire-General said, "Ask the bishop; but I am afraid he is too *ardent*." After a time we parted from the priests, and were very very tired when we got home, the convent was so stuffy and the day hot.

Thursday, June 23*rd.*—Dundases left, to our great regret. Dick and Captain P. went to see them off, and on board the steamer, by accident, Mr. D. sat down on an old woman's head, thinking she was a seat.

Saturday, 25th.—Slight Thunder-storm and rain, rather cold. I always fly to the cellar when the Thunder begins. You may remark that I always write Thunder with a big T, this is from *awe* and *respect*.

Sunday, 26th.—The most appalling darkness came on after breakfast; no one could account for it. I hear at Quebec many people ran out of church terrified; I was quite distracted, and thought the end of the world was come; of course I did not go to church, and Dick stayed with me. The others bravely went. It turned into a Thunder-storm with much rain. I believe it all came from the fires in the woods, which are always going on now, and the atmosphere being very heavy. The smoke could not rise or blow away; it was stifling, but there was no smell of smoke.

Monday, 27th.—*Himalaya* arrived with the 25th Regiment on board.

Tuesday, 28th.—A warm day. I drove into town to see them disembark and march in; they have a pretty band.

Wednesday, 29th.—Hot. We went to see the *Himalaya*. There was a school feast at Spencer Wood. The children have little or no manners, and are very independent, but are improving.

Thursday, June 30th. Cooler. Parliament prorogued. We all started for Lennoxville, the Eton of Canada.

Mountain House, Memphamagog Lake, July 3rd.—I left off when we were just starting for Lennoxville. We ladies drove into town and met the gentlemen on the wharf, where we were to cross for the railway at Point Levi. I entered the ferry on the arm of Mr. Galt, Finance Minister. Mr. Galt and Mr. McGee (Minister of Agriculture) were with us all the way. We walked out of the ship in procession, as we went into it, I on Mr. Galt's arm! We had the Prince of Wales's car, and you never saw such luxury and comfort in a railway carriage—a large sitting-room, two bedrooms, and a smoking-room. The servants had a car to themselves. We had lamps, armchairs, and sofas. Dick had ordered wine, sandwiches, and cakes, so we had food enough, and we were all very pleasant. Of course, Dick and Capt. Pemberton were in uniform. The journey is rather pretty, through pine woods, but very flat. It was raining a little, and nice and cool. We read the papers and talked. We stopped at one place after dark, where there was a great crowd, and much cheering, and letting up of rockets. It was called Rich-

VISIT TO LENNOXVILLE.

mond. The G. G. was asleep, and one of the gentlemen said, "I think we must wake up the Gov. Gen., as some gentlemen are coming in here to speak to him." Vice-Chancellor Hale (of Lennoxville College) got in here, and Mr. Rawson, our Lennoxville host. The former gave me his arm, and walked me about the station-house and platform. The fireflies were lovely. Mr. Rawson is a very nice kind man. Arrived at Lennoxville, there was great excitement. We had left Quebec about two, and we reached Lennoxville about eleven p.m. There were to be a great many addresses presented here, and a torch-light procession of schoolboys, and a guard of honour of boy volunteers. We all went into the station-house, and you never can imagine the curious weird scene there—more than a hundred torches blazing away, boys without end, and a mob of people, boys in rifle volunteer uniforms, and old men shuffling about to be ready with their addresses. Three addresses were presented, and the G. G. made very suitable answers. He was immensely cheered, and the torches waved, and the volunteer band played a whole set of Scotch airs, meant, I suppose, to be Irish. Some gentlemen were presented, and after some time Aunt L. went off in Mr. Rawson's open waggon, wearing his B.A. cloak to keep her from the rain! The horses were frightened at the waving torches. I think most of the people had never seen an English carriage before, and they were almost as much excited by the Gov. Gen.'s carriage as by himself. Fan, Louise, Mrs. Godley, and I drove in the shut carriage, and were escorted by volunteers and boys with torches, who ran beside the carriage. The G. G., Staff, and Mr. Godley followed in the open carriage. He was loudly cheered, the houses were decorated outside with pine or fir branches, and there was a triumphal arch, and people standing on the balconies waving their handkerchiefs, even to *our* carriage, for fear they might make a mistake in the dark, and not bow to the G. G. The Rawsons' house is a charming Gothic house, quite like an English home, and they are very nice people. We were received by Mrs. R. and her daughter, and Mrs. Williams, the Bishop of Quebec's wife. We were soon shown to our rooms. Dick and I slept in a schoolboy's room. Captain Pemberton was next door, in another boy's room, with a balcony between our rooms. We were so glad to get supper, and about *two* a.m. we went to bed. It was *very* hot, and when we opened our little cross-barred windows *swarms* of insects flew in and drove me quite wild.

Friday, July 1*st.*—Some of the ladies went to early service at the College chapel at seven. I did not. Mr. Rawson has two married daughters—Mrs. de Winton, married to Sir Fenwick's A.D.C., and Mrs. de Chair. Both have been married since Christmas. Mr. Dudley de Chair is an Oxonian, and is very nice-looking, and only twenty-two. After breakfast some of the ladies went to church again! The G. G., Captain Pem., Mr. Godley, and Mr. Rawson went to Sherbrooke, where there were more addresses presented, and a cavalry escort, and good decorations. I laid down and rested, the heat was intolerable. After church we got ready and drove in three detachments, Dick with us, to the pretty red college, just like an English college, with such pretty grounds, and a river called *Massawippi*, meaning "river of pines" in Indian. The thought *would* strike me, what a delicious name for a river near a school, it could so easily be turned into "Master whipped me." There we walked in the grounds, broiled by sun, to the river banks, where the boys had swimming-matches, and diving-matches, and boat-races, and canoe-races. It was nice sitting under the trees looking at them from a bank. The boys are more like English boys than any I have seen out here, and pride themselves on their English cheer. They seem to have the same love and respect for their college as Eton boys have for Eton. We then went back to the college, and dawdled about in the sitting-room till lunch was ready, to which we went in procession, headed by Aunt L. and the Chancellor of the College. Fan and L. went in with the Bishops of Montreal and Quebec, and I with Dr. Nicholls, the Principal of the College. The G. G. had arrived in the meantime. I think he took Mrs. Nicholls in. We had very good food, and the G. G. made an excellent speech. We were waited on by niggers. The dining-hall is a fine large one, and was wonderfully cool. One or two people asked me about my coming out to Canada, and seemed to know all about my flight after Dick. I met Mr. Young (the Jonah) there, and we were so very glad to meet. Lennoxville is the Eton of Canada, and it is a charming and civilized place; the boys seem very gentlemanly and well looked after. After lunch we all marched in procession (except the G. G.) to the hall, where degrees were

SPEECHES AND PRIZES. 49

to be conferred, and we mounted up on a dais behind her Ex. Then the G. G. was made an LL.D., and several degrees were given, and there was much cheering, and some extremely good speeches were made. The G. G. spoke very well on education—his speech was thought quite an essay. A Mr. Irving (head-master) spoke most beautifully; he is an English clergyman of great talent. You will have all the speeches in the paper, so I will not enlarge upon them. The hall was crammed, and it was very hot; I was not sorry to get out of the tremendous crowd into the cool geological museum and chapel. The college is called Bishop's College, having been founded by the good Bishop Mountain of Quebec. We went home and dressed for the conversazione. We dined at the Rawsons' first; I sat next the Bishop of Quebec, who was very agreeable. Then we went off in different detachments to the college, where from a dais we saw boys get prizes and heard them recite poetry. The B. of Montreal spoke so nicely to the boys. After all this was over, we walked into a large hall where there were presentations to "their Exes," and music; some glees were *roared* too loud with fine voices. Nina would have been quite bewildered with all the clergy in their gowns. Dick had to present some of the people; he *seemed* to do it very well, but forgot some of their names. At last we went away, I on the Chancellor's arm! Next day, Saturday, the 2nd July, we breakfasted very early, and then a swarm of waggons came to the door, and with great difficulty and packing, off we drove in the following order:—Mr. Galt, her Ex., and Louise in one waggon, the G. G., Fan, and I, and Mr. Rawson (part of the time) in another, and in a large open sort of van were Dick, Mr. McGee, Captain Pem., and Mr. de Chair. The Godleys were in another waggon, and all the servants in another. You will read in the papers Mr. McGee's account of the journey; it is a full and true account, to save us writing long letters on the journey. He is a most amusing man, a former Irish rebel, but now no one is so loyal as he is. He looks like a nigger with an Irish peasant's mouth and a fine brogue. He tells capital stories, but I hate his puns; all puns depress me. The day was very very wet, and we were not sorry to reach *Hatley East*, a village where we stopped to dry ourselves and lunch. It is a very Yankee place, though in Canada, and the wooden inn we stopped at reminded us all of " The Wide Wide World;" we expected to see Miss Fortune, and the near ox. We had a scrambled lunch at this little inn, and much fun and laughing. Mr. McGee was in great force. The scenery during all our drive was most lovely "through the forests primeval," like parks, and up and down wonderful hills tearing along in the waggons. There is a most curious sect in this part of the world called "Universalists," they believe that every one will be saved! Judge Day once sapiently remarked it was a very happy religion, as whether we believed in it or not, we should be saved! In this part of the country they have their burial-places at the side of their houses, every family its own burial-place. We saw such quantities of "snake fences," wood laid together in a zig-zag fashion. It is curious to see the "clearings" in the woods where trees have been set fire to, to make space; burnt stumps everywhere—they look very desolate and weird. Towards nightfall we neared Georgeville, at the side of Lake Memphramagog. The drive was too beautiful, the angry wind-clouds over the deep deep blue mountains, the dark green "forests primeval," and the blue lake; it was all like what one might dream of in an inspired moment, but rarely see in real life. The lake is quite surrounded with mountains covered with forests, and at the foot of one of the highest of them stands the Mountain House, or inn, the only house for miles round. It is wooden, and built with galleries all round it, and it is very picturesque-looking. The lake was rough, and they said "there was quite a sea on." I was not happy at this. The G. G. was very well received at Georgeville, and we embarked, having parted with regret from Messrs. Rawson and de Chair. After more than an hour's steaming in the *Maid of the Mist*, we got to the Mountain House; a crowd from the hotel was assembled in the dark night to see us land. We had great fun at dinner; the knives would not cut, and such hacking you never saw. It was a rough clean inn, and we had a floor to ourselves.

Sunday, July 3rd.—This was a peaceful, heavenly day; the silence of the air round, not a sound but rippling water, and at night the croaking of frogs, was to me quite oppressive, and I longed for noise again. I would not let myself think how far I was from home; one could so well realize it there. We had a very nice young clergyman sent from Lennoxville, and we had service in the ballroom of the inn at eleven.

The visitors at the hotel came to it, and happened to be musical, so we had nice singing, and everything was done in the right way, even to the surplice and sermon, a very good one. In the afternoon we had service in another room, with a piano and no sermon. We chanted Gregorians, which sounded very well. Dick, Mr. Galt, and Captain Pem. had gone up the Owl's Head mountain, at the foot of which this inn is; Mr. G. and Captain P. failed, but Dick triumphed. I send you a wild flower he brought from the top. The Owl's Head is very high and steep, and the day was so hot. It was very nice sitting reading in the summer-house, or sitting talking on the hill-side. At lunch, I forgot to say, we had scarcely enough to eat, and Mr. McGee and Dick went and peeped in the presses to look for food. At last a tart was in triumph produced. In the night, after dinner, we all sat out near the lake edge, and looked at the stars and fire-flies, or "lightning bugs," as the Yankees call them. Conway said to me, "I wish I could catch one, and send it home to my mother in a letter." Some Yankees were singing hymns at the hotel in chorus; it sounded so pretty through the open windows. One hymn was a new version of

"Nearer, my God, to Thee." Captain Pem. wanted to row me about the lake, but I was afraid he might upset me in the dark; or Dick *said* I should be afraid.

Next day we breakfasted before seven a.m., and were off to Newport in the steamer at 7.30. The 4th of July is a great day in Yankeeland, and Newport is a Yankee town. The ship was crowded and top-heavy. I was afraid, so made heavy Mr. McGee sit by me and not leave me, to try and balance the ship! The captain forbad such rushing to the side of the ship as took place every moment. They received the G. G. very well at Newport. Several quaint old men were presented to him and her Ex. on board the steamer. A large coach and *six* white steeds met us, followed by another large coach and four brown steeds, and Mr. Knight, the M.P.P. for Stanstead, the border town between Canada and the States, was to convey the rest of the party. I begged to be taken by Mr. Knight, as I dreaded the fiery steeds. He was delighted to take me. The town was gay with flags in honour of the day, the sun shone brightly, and everything had *un air de fête.* There was a great crowd on the wharf, who cheered *lustily.* Mr. Galt, Dick, and I went in Mr. Knight's nice waggon, driven by him. The drive was some of it very pretty. There is a school-house to every five houses in this part of the country, and they are distinguished by having their window-sashes painted red. I forgot to say the servants brought up the rear in a shut waggon. Sergeant Lambkin was on the box of the yellow coach, and his red uniform looked very gay. We drove nine miles to Stanstead, where there was great excitement, flags flying, a band playing, and great crowds of people. There was an address presented, but we ladies remained in the carriages to save time, and because of the crowd. At one house, a Mr. Pierce's, there was a monster bull brought out for the G. G. to inspect; it was called General Grant, and had flags on its horns. Of course I forget its weight. Ladies waved their handkerchiefs at all the carriages, and *we all bowed*. Stanstead is the border town, and one house is built half in America and half in Canada. We saw it on our way through the town. At last we arrived at Mr. Knight's house; it is beautiful. "Walk about, and make yourselves quite at home," said Mrs. K. I got Miss K. to talk to, and she amused me much. The youngest child was named Ulysses S. Grant, after the general, and he had a burning desire to speak to the Governor-General. Miss K. said, "There are quite a number of ministers here," and so there were, parsons to the right of us, and parsons to the left of us! No Church of England clergyman, but every other sect was represented, even the Universalist. At last lunch was announced. The G. G. and Mrs. K., and Mr. K. and her Ex., of course led the way; Fan and Louise followed, and to my joy I fell to the lot of *Tomkins*, the Wesleyan minister! In my happiest dreams I never aspired to share a crust with a Tomkins, and it is just the sort of a name Dickens would give to a Wesleyan minister. Maids and a kind of waiter attended us; the waiter and Tomkins seemed to be on very friendly terms, so I suppose he was a clerk or sexton; they conversed together. I forgot to say that *all* the ministers were introduced to us before lunch by Mrs. Knight, who each time forgot all our names, and had to ask us them every minute. Tomkins said "Ma'am" to me every moment. He left Herefordshire, his birthplace, in '27. I made a lucky hit by remarking to him how much the country we had driven through reminded me of Herefordshire; he agreed, and then told me it was his birthplace. There were some speeches at lunch, and then we had to clear out, as all our servants had to feed in the dining-room on what we left. After lunch we started for Coaticooke, where we were to meet the special train for Montreal. Captain Pem. and I drove together, with Dick on the box of the waggon; we tore through beautiful woods, and up and down hills, scarcely touching the ground, shaken and bumped, and laughing at it all. Some of the places we stopped at on Saturday for loyal subjects to present addresses were most rough and ready places, one a booth literally, with seats raised a little for the gubernatorial party, and decorated with the everlasting fir branches, and there were always crowds of people in the pours of rain. Luckily to-day was fine; but we passed no village from Stanstead to Coaticooke. Near the latter town we were met by a band of musicians in a sort of van, which preceded us to the village. We felt rather like a menagerie or travelling circus. This had been the custom whenever we were nearing villages, but this van and band were the grandest. There was an address presented at Coaticooke, and much cheering, and we went "aboard" the special train for Montreal. We stopped several times for addresses and presentations, and the G. G.'s hands must have been dirty —he had to shake hands with the most dirty-looking men, some of them looking like hodmen; one in particular, I remarked, was covered with whitewash. We had a very pleasant journey to Montreal. We passed over a drawbridge where a most frightful accident had happened a few days before. The bridge, by some carelessness, had been left open, and a train full of poor German emigrants went down into the river, and a hundred were killed. It gave me a thrill of horror to pass over it. We had got papers somewhere, and Mr. McGee saw in them the death of his old friend, Smith O'Brien, which distressed him and brought back old days. We had been travelling for twelve and a half hours a day on Saturday and Monday, thirty miles in waggons one day and twenty-nine the next. I never felt tired except in the mornings. It was great fun arriving at Montreal at 8.30 p.m., and being met by a guard of honour of the Grenadier Guards, General Lindsay and Captains Seymour and Eliot. We had a very grand dinner at the St. Lawrence Hall, where we were lodged, and were very comfortable, one floor to ourselves, and sentries and orderlies of the

Grenadier Guards. The orderlies in the passage, always with their bear-skins on, looking after the visiting-books. Everything looks so warlike at home that perhaps we shall have to go home; this is only a supposition!

I left off at our arrival at Montreal on Monday night. Next morning early we set off in two carriages for the Champ de Mars, to see them "trooping the colours;" there were a good many people there, and I was much excited by the "dear Guards." Mrs. Godley and I were in one carriage. After this sight, we went to Notman's (the photographer's), where every one was photoed except me. He is about the best photographer in the world, so report says. Then we all got ready to go to Monklands, the convent where her Ex. was to give prizes to the girls. Mr. Godley and I drove there together. The heat and dust were horrible. We were received by nuns, and soon we all walked into the hall where the prizes were to be given. The mayor conducted her Ex. first, Sir Fenwick Williams took me, General Lindsay Mrs. Godley, F. went with Mr. McGee, and L. with a nun. There were front seats for us all. I sat with Madame Cartier, Mr. McGee, and the mayor. Her Ex. gave the prizes most gracefully, and the G. G. made a very good speech, as usual. You will see the account of the proceedings in the paper—they are too tedious to tell; there was playing and singing and acting, and one girl was dressed as a squaw, and they recited and got prizes and wreaths, and presented her Ex. with a bouquet, and made a speech to her, and bowed and curtsied and smiled—there is a resumé of it all. The heat was very great; the large "salle" was *crammed* to suffocation. The mayor, who is French, remarked to me, "How chaste the young ladies look." They were all in white muslin. It seemed so odd that Generals and their staffs should be there amongst nuns and priests and schoolgirls. Madame Cartier said to me that the reason the girls were so good was because "no *bachelors* were admitted there," except, of course, on great days. Then, when all was over, and it lasted a very long time, we returned to the nice cool hall, and had food, cakes, and wine. My friend Mr. Young was there, and introduced his wife to me; they have twelve children. I also made acquaintance with pretty Mrs. de Winton and her husband, and we met Miss Symes, the great R. C. heiress, *such* a nice face and manner.

Mrs. Godley and I drove home together, and tried to get some tea, but failed. Her Ex., F. and L., and Dick had gone to tea at Lady Sarah's. Then Dick, the girls, and I went to see a cricket-match between the officers of the garrison. There I made acquaintance with Colonel Moncreiff, Fusilier Guards, who painted most of St. Luke's Church here. We only stayed a very short time at the cricket-match, and went home to dress for Lady Sarah's dinner-party. General Lindsay had sent me a message that if I came I should have a cellar fitted up for me in case of Thunder. There were only four ladies at dinner, Lady Sarah, her Ex., Mrs. Fulford, and I. There were several gentlemen, Sir F. Williams and A.D.C., the colonels of regiments, Captain Pem., Captain Eliot, and the husbands of the ladies. Now I must make a diversion, and say that I am in a great fuss about the war; we hear such accounts from England of expected war, and I am very anxious; now that I *am* here, I should rather not go home yet; I want to go to Prince Edward's Island in August, and I want to go to Niagara. Now I return to our mutton. The Bishop of Montreal took me in to dinner, and General Lindsay was on my other side, so I was well placed; the bishop is both handsome and agreeable, and his wife is a dear old lady. There was a "drum" in the evening, and a very nice set of people, military and otherwise. I sat in the verandah with different people and listened to the band. Col. Hawley (60th Rifles) was introduced to me, and asked me to a picnic on Friday at the Island of St. Helens, where his regiment is quartered, opposite Montreal. The 30th band played so sweetly in a tent outside. Gen. Lindsay's house is so very nice, with a large ballroom, and people were very well dressed. Lady Sarah so kind. People were presented to her Ex.

July 6th.—To-day (Wednesday) was to have been the review at Logan's Farm, but of course it rained. Her Ex. and the girls lunched with Lady Sarah and Sir Fenwick and staff, and Mrs. de Winton, lunched at the hotel with our party, also Col. Hawley. Then we agreed to go and have ourselves photoed on tin for twopence-halfpenny a piece; the day had cleared. There was much excitement "on the street" (as they say here) at seeing the G. G. and staff, and Sir Fenwick and staff walking about. The tin-man was a most funny character, and made us laugh much. I do think the photos, some of them, excellent. Mrs. G. and I called on Mrs. Bramston, and then returned to the hotel, where we all got into carriages and drove a long way to where we were to embark for the Isle D'Orval, Sir F. Williams's island. At last we got to La Chine (the embarking-place), and embarked in the General's barge, and were rowed across to his heavenly island by ten Grenadier soldiers. The island is almost all covered with primeval forest trees and green grass, only one road on it. Primeval trees are generally very thin tall trees; but these are fine ones. The house is a red-brick cottage with four bedrooms in it. Most of the gentlemen were in tents, and the four maids slept in one outhouse room together. The Gen. is civility and kindness itself. Dick and I had Captain Lane Fox's room, covered with boots and harness and coats. On the wall hung my bonnet, Dick's gold belt, and Captain Fox's harness! there being also a very nice white felt wide-awake with brigade riband on it, which I ventured to wear next day, as I had no hat of my own, and the glare was so great; Captain Fox allowed me to wear it. The General had a *horn* blown every morning to call us to breakfast; it sounded so funny. He gave each of the ladies a rosebud every morning; was he not gallant? He has a wonderful parrot, of which I was in terror; one day it pulled Col. Conolly's long nose!

July 7th.—This was my day of misery, for we were to have a sail in the yacht!! Some of us hated going, and oh, horrors! we were told with joy, " That a nice little breeze was getting up." Dick and Captain Pem. rowed all the morning till we started. We all went in the yacht but Captain Fox and Mr. Godley, who went to some races at Montreal. We went in the barge to the yacht. I have not felt so wretched since the *Asia*, except in Thunder-storms and darkness! I behaved tolerably well. Kind Sir F. did not perceive my misery, and went on saying, " Delightful! is it not delightful?" and trying to impress on us how the breeze would get up; but, thank God, it would not get up. We tried to get to St. Anne's, celebrated by Moore's Canadian boat-song, but the wind fell instead of rising, so we got home in two hours, finding that we had only succeeded in sailing round the island. We had a very good lunch on board, and the last part of the sail was not unpleasant, as we were so near home. Later Dick and Captain Pem. rowed me in an outrigger, and I steered so beautifully! Anything was nice after the yacht. The Guards' Yacht Club is on the opposite side from the island. After late dinner we groped about on the grass looking at the St. Lawrence and the stars; the island was always cool, sometimes cold.

July 8th.—We were under weigh very early for Montreal; Dick and Captain Pem. rowed me across in the tiny boat, and I steered. We had a long procession of carriages driving in. Then Dick and I went out to buy hats like Captain Fox's, and then we dressed for the picnic, and drove to the embarking place. The row was very cool after the awful heat of Montreal. St. Helen's is a lovely island, twice the size of the general's island. First we walked about, and soon it was time to go to luncheon, which was laid on a very long table under the trees. After lunch old Commodore Magruder and his daughter (a pretty widow) were introduced to me by General Lindsay, for me to tell them about my meeting Lady Abinger in London; the commodore's old eyes filled with tears, and he said, "Every one likes her." Then we walked about and looked at a game called "knock 'em down." Then the G. G. and party were to go, so we walked down to see them embark; it was a long way, but under trees, so that the sun was not so hot. After parting with them, we walked back and joined the Bramstons' party, and played "Aunt Sally" till all the pipes were broken! Then dancing was to begin on a board under the trees with the band near; it looked like a scene in a play. We stayed for a few dances and then went away. It was almost pleasanter sitting and talking than dancing, as the ladies' dresses flew about so. We were to go and stay with the Roses. Mr. Rose, Captain Seymour, Dick, and I walked to the boat together. The evening or night was too beautiful, the reddest of sunsets and the water so very blue. The lights of Montreal with its mountain at the back also looked very well. We rowed across, and then drove home with the Roses, Mr., Mrs., and Miss. The latter is a very handsome girl. They have such a nice house on the mountain, and they are very hospitable to the officers, who are in and out all day and night. He is one of the M.P.P.'s for Montreal, and a well-known man in England. After supper we soon went to bed. I have views of Isle d'Orval, and I am going to get a view of this pretty house.

July 9th.—Miss Rose drove me in her

pony-carriage into town to see Lady Sarah, who was out. Dick met us at Notman's, and I was photoed. After lunch some officers came to play croquet. You know I detest croquet, so Dick and I, and Mr. and Mrs. Rose soon went out to drive, and drove to the churchyard, which is even prettier than Mount Auburn at Boston. In the evening several officers dined. I must stop now, and will tell the rest next time.

Sunday, July 10*th.*—The heat was terrible, so Miss Rose and I stayed at home, young Mr. Rose having allowed his mother to go to church on condition that she would not "growl" about the heat. Dick went off at ten to La Chine with Captain Seymour, first to church, and then to sail on the river, and they were nearly upset. Some officers came to lunch. Colonel Moncrieff came early, and at 3.30 he and I and Miss Rose set off in the close carriage, with Mr. Rose on the box, to St. Luke's Church. It is a sweet pretty little church, painted by Colonel M. and Mr. Baker, of the Fusiliers; there is a pretty organ and good chanting. There was only the Litany, and one hymn from the "Ancient and Modern." Then we returned home, and sat in the verandah talking for some time. There is a hammock slung up in the verandah, and a lovely wild vine grows all over the verandah and makes a sort of curtain. The flies were something I never could express; we breakfasted in the verandah, and lunched in the dining-room with closed shutters, but wherever we went we found the table *perfectly black* with these little beasts of house-flies; it is one of the miseries of a Canadian summer, and is like one of the plagues of Egypt. At last Dick came back, and I was not sorry to see him. More officers dined. Great American news came in, and they were in such excitement. I am so stupid; I know nothing at all about the war, and never *shall* understand it; all I know is that the rebels (?) are supposed to be marching on Washington.

July 11*th.*—We talked a good deal, as it was too hot to go out. Miss Rose went off to the States on a visit after lunch. There was a Thunder-storm, and the unkind servant refused to let me into the cellar, and seemed quite surprised at my asking to be admitted, so I shut myself in a dark room with Dick till it was nearly over. Mrs. Rose and I had a nice cool walk after the storm, whilst Dick, Mr. Rose, and the son played "fives." Mr. Crichton dined. He photos so beautifully, and is very amusing. We were to have left that day, but General Lindsay said he would try and have a field-day on Tuesday, so we waited, but alas! he was not able to manage one.

July 12*th*.—Mrs. Rose, Dick, and I drove to the rapids of La Chine; such a pretty drive—the rapids are so curious, like a rough bit of sea going downhill. In the afternoon we two and Mr. and Mrs. Rose scrambled up to the top of the mountain, and had such a view as I could not easily forget of the whole country round, the variegated town of Montreal looking very well at our feet. Mr. McGee is M.P.P. for the Irish part of Montreal. I was so hot and tired, toiling along, but Mrs. R. was up on the top before any of us. We sat and rested, and admired the view, and soon went home, had some tea, and left per seven p.m. boat for Quebec, which we reached at six next morning. We were in the same boat as last time, and the civil little Captain Labelle remembered us, and was so kind, and let us have supper by ourselves—I mean with him, but away from the crowd. He said the next best thing to having the G. G. on board was having his brother.

Spencer Wood, July 13*th*.—To-day was very hot, and my head ached so that when we drove to the 25th band at five I had to sit in the closed carriage; I could not venture to stay in the sun. The band played at the camp in the Rink Field, and it all looked so pretty; the band is lovely, and the soldiers sang in one piece. Colonel Fane had chairs arranged with flags for our party.

July 14*th.*—My clothes arrived all safe last night, and being directed to Dick, Sergeant Lambkin said they were "uniforms," so I had no duty to pay. Intensely hot. At home all day. The bill at Magog was so cheap, two and a half dollars a day per head, and the servants one and a half dollars. I have nothing more to say.

Spencer Wood, July 15*th.*—This will be but a dull letter, as I have nothing to tell you. Heat very great.

July 16*th.*—Intensely hot. Yesterday it was ninety-six degrees in the shade at Quebec. We are some of us ill from the heat. L. has a heat-stroke; the G. G. is ill, and so am I. Dr. B. came to inspect us to-day; he said he must recommend us to go "down below," which does not sound pleasant! But I discovered it meant Rivière du Loup or Tadousac on the river below this, or he advised my going to Prince Edward's Island, where,

Mrs. Dundas writes, it is quite cool. Colonel Gordon came, and he, Dick, and I took a walk to try and get cool, but only got hotter.

Sunday, 17*th*.—A great wind-storm in the night, which gave us a nice cool day. The "invalids" did not go to church, and Dr. B. came again, and urged me to go "down below," even for twenty-four hours; but I detest the steamer and river, so I won't go. On Sunday Mr. Lyulph Stanley arrived with a letter from his father, and so he was asked to stay; he has "strong Northern proclivities," has been travelling all over the North, and has much that is interesting to tell. He gave a frightful account of the way the South treat their slaves, and showed a photo of a slave's back frightfully lacerated, which I scarcely saw, it was so horrible. He says he saw some emancipated slaves, some of them *brutish* still, but some happy. We went to afternoon service, and happily the clergyman's house took fire, and there was a fuss, which made our sermon from Mr. Dodwell only fourteen and a half minutes instead of thirty-five minutes, like the morning. Colonel Fane was in church, and came to tea. There is a good company of actors here now, and the 25th soldiers are to sing at the theatre to-morrow, but the G. G., I fear, won't go. Colonel Fane saw that the cat, Tom, was a favourite; he said, "Shall I pull its tail?"

July 18*th.*—Oh, the heat! There is nothing to do but to groan and grumble. Mr. Stanley amuses me much.

July 19*th.*—Mr. Stanley went to the Saguenay for two days. Mr. Dodwell (the clergyman) lunched; he is pleasing. The heat is worse than ever. Dick and I drove out late to visit.

July 20*th.*—We had a Thunder-storm in the afternoon, so I went to the cellar. It got cooler after floods of rain, and we drove into town. The country looked so green and fresh.

July 21*st.*—Thank God, it has got quite cold, and we all feel so much better; it is charming to be able to wear a silk dress and shiver. Fan and I took a walk after lunch, and we sat out looking over the coves where all the rafts are, and where lumber is prepared for the loading of the ships. Mr. Stanley arrived in time for tea. A lady at tea flattered him so dreadfully; at last he said, "I'm not listening to you—go on flattering me." We went to the 17th band; it is not a good band, but plays very pretty things. Some officers dined here, and Mr.

Dodwell, also Mr. Cartier, and Captain Ballantine of the s.s. *Peruvian*. Her Ex., etc., are going home in her. Captain B. sat on one side of me at dinner, and amused me much; he is a regular character, very broad Scotch; his mouth is always open. He calls his wife "the auld hen;" he was once a common sailor. He told me that he had heard all about my running after Dick to Queenstown; he thought it "*splendid*." He said to Mrs. Godley and me just before grace after dinner, "Did you ever chance on a Scotch tabby?" (travelling). We were just able to restrain our laughing till after grace, and then instantly burst out laughing. Poor Mr. Dodwell, who said grace as fast as possible, thought we were laughing at him, and I had to explain about it. Captain B. then told us he had had "a Scotch tabby" in his ship once who made a revolt among forty ladies in the ladies' cabin; she made them all think that the captain was going the wrong way to "Canaday" (as he calls it), and that as "Canaday" was south of England, he ought to steer *south* and not *north-west*. At last they met a steamer, and some one suggested that they must be right as they were so near a steamer coming from Canada. After some thought, she said she had found them all out. It was the time so many thousand pounds were offered for the discovery of Sir J. Franklin, and she said she knew they were just going off to look for him in the Arctic Regions, and that the other ship was doing the same. This idea was put into her head by seeing icebergs! In the evening we sang choruses and played squails. Mr. Cartier is so funny. He screams and whoops at the end of some of his Canadian songs. Mr. Cartier and Mr. S. danced "The Cure," Cartier shouting it at the top of his voice all the time. Mr. Stanley jumped higher than any one I ever saw. Mr. Dodwell's face during "The Cure" was a study, neither exactly laughing nor crying.

Spencer Wood, July 22nd.—We went on Friday afternoon to see the *Peruvian*; she did the voyage in nine days to England. Colonel Gordon, Captain Retallack, and the Godleys were of the party, not Mr. S. We were met by the captain dressed very grandly, in great force. She is a fine ship, very long and narrow, the cabins not so large as in the *Asia*; she is built for speed. The smells and misery of seeing the cabins made me quite sick and depressed. The captain took us into his cabin and showed us a caricature Major Lowe (Grenadier Guards) did of one of the passengers; he said he was sure I was not sick at sea, and said to Dick, "She does not look *balious* (bilious)." Oh, the misery of being on a ship again! We returned home to tea. After tea some of us, including Mr. S., took a walk to Mr. Gibbs's place close by, and on to Mr. Le Moyne's place. Mr. Le M. is a naturalist, and has a collection of stuffed birds; he also has a sweet little live owl, such a little soft pet. The birds are very pretty, all Canadian; and he has also a good vinery. Col. G. dined, also the Dean of Leighlin (Lauder). He was Dean of Ontario, and has exchanged now with the Dean of Leighlin; he has fine dean-like legs.

Saturday, 23rd.—After lunch Mr. S., Fan, M. F., and I took a drive, and paid some visits. One person we wanted to visit was a "Mrs. A. Patrick." No one could tell where she lived, and they rarely put their addresses on their cards, so Mr. S. proposed that we should go to "Mrs. T. Patrick," whom every one knew, and ask if Mrs. A. Patrick lived there, and if she was at home. It succeeded very well, and we found her out. It was getting very dark, between smoke from the woods on fire and clouds, and the heat had returned. Just after tea a great Thunder-storm came on, and such rain. You could not see your own hand, it was so pitch dark, mostly from smoke. I was so afraid, and rushed to the cellar. At last it got fine. Captain Hope, 25th K.O.B.'s, came to tea. He told me he never could forget Frank's appearance when he first saw him at Malta—a very large white umbrella, blue spectacles, and the highest deep violet hat in the island!! Sir G. Le Marchant said no one should appear without high hats in the streets, so F. got the highest he could find. Mr. S. left. There was tremendous summer lightning after dinner and such rain.

Sunday, 24th.—Went twice to church. After tea Dick and I strolled down to walk over the river. Every sail was reflected in the water, it was such a dead calm; this is always a sign of coming bad weather.

Monday, 25th.—Cricket-match here. To-morrow the R. C. school children come to tea here; and Wednesday we go an excursion for ten days to the Saguenay in the Government steamer. It is cool now.

Spencer Wood, 25th of July.—On Monday we had a cricket-match between the 25th and the garrison, which consisted of some of the 17th, two R.E. officers, one R.A.

officer, Captain Pem., and Dick. The 25th were beaten. We sat out looking at it for a long time. It was nice sitting cool under the trees, looking at the St. Lawrence and the cricketers getting hot! Mr. Cox (17th) was with us, also his two little Irish dogs; one called "Whisky," and the other "Intoxicated," or "Toxey," for short. Whisky ran away once to the 62nd, so Mr. Cox cut off some of its hair in the shape of D to punish it.

Tuesday, 26th.—A school feast for the R. C. children, and Mr. Cazeau, the Vicaire-Général, came with Colonel Gordon, also some soldiers' children. I never saw so nice and orderly a set, with such nice Irish-Canadian schoolmistresses. The children were half Irish and half French-Canadians, some of the latter looking like Indians, almost quite black, with such round Indian eyes. M. Cazeau was so funny. He said such odd things to the children and to the mistresses. He said, "How are you, my good child?" everything literal. He is very pleasant, and played so nicely with the boys. Colonel G. blindfolded himself, and played with the boys, and his coat was nearly pulled off. At last, before they left, one little girl in white muslin put on a wreath, and with a brogue read out a speech of thanks to her Ex.

Wednesday, 27th.— Henry arrived from Eton, looking so fresh and well. We are going on our expedition to-day at four. I think of it in fear and trembling. We can only be a week away, as there are going to be grand cricket-matches here next week between Montreal and Quebec garrisons. I must tell you some Yankee slang while I think of it. "O.K." means "all correct;" they put it in telegrams. "I am exercised" means "I am put about." If I can I will write from the Saguenay. I wonder if you saw a picture in the *Illustrated News* of the tug at Queenstown going to meet the steamer.

Ship " Queen Victoria," Laval Bay, Friday, July 29th.—I must go back to Wednesday, 27th, when we started from Quebec. I chose to drive from Spencer Wood with Mr. Wilkinson in the waggon. His spasmodic attempts at driving amused me much. He told me that he was a coward at driving, but would "try his hand." Of course, we knocked hard against a pavement, and nearly broke the waggon. Mr. W., with a rein in each hand (*à la* Yankee), was a funny sight, speaking loud with the agonizing jerks he

A FISHING EXPEDITION.

gave the reins. We went to the office, where he made Dick take his place,—happily for me, for down those hills it would have been awful to go with Mr. W. Colonel Gordon and the gentlemen met us at the wharf, and we embarked in this nice ship, which the Prince of Wales and Prince Alfred went in when they were here. It was covered with flags, and looked very gay. I was miserable that evening, there was a good deal of wind, and it was so unpleasant. We passed the Isle of Orleans, and a most beautiful range of hills, which the setting sun made quite purple. We passed also Montmorençi Falls and St. Anne's in the distance, not Moore's St. Anne's, but another where are beautiful falls and mountains. We passed some ships, the people in them waved their hats and handkerchiefs. We are arranged thus : A ladies' cabin, where two of the maids sleep. Out of it two cabins, where some of the ladies are ; outside there is a cabin, where the G. G. and her Ex. are ; out of the saloon there are many cabins, containing all the gentlemen and her Ex.'s maid, and I am in one of them with Dick ; he dresses in Captain Pem.'s cabin, and the G. G. dresses in another. F.'s dog is on board, and Sergeant Lambkin brought his dog also. Oh, the beds are so hard! We had capital tea on deck that day, and fresh bread and butter. We went on to Rivière du Loup, where we anchored for the night. The next day, Thursday (28th), was very dark and calm happily, and my spirits rose instantly. R. du Loup is not pretty from the ship. We disembarked there, and the Monck family and Miss F. went in waggons to see Stanley, five miles off. The Godleys asked Col. G. and me to join them, and drive to see an Indian settlement a few miles off. Mr. G. and I went in the most primitive of waggons, followed by Col. G. and Mrs. Godley in just such another. We passed through the village of R. du Loup, rather pretty; past some rather pretty falls. The Indian settlement is most interesting, and well worth a visit; the people are *bonâ fide* Indians, almost black, very deep copper colour, with thick lips and round eyes, and the blackest hair you can imagine. They were squatted on the floor in "wigwams," and looking so wild; the men were very handsome, the women, all but one, frightful. They were making lovely baskets with bark and wood: Mr. G. gave me two things; they only cost a few pence. These people talked Indian, and it was hard to make them understand anything. We then drove to look at the R. C. church, a fine, big, bare place with odd light painted windows, dice of blue and red. Mr. G. told me that Col. P. used to patronize the R. C. churches they visited; whilst the people were praying, he used to stand up with his arms akimbo, saying, in the loudest voice, " Well, upon my word, this is rather a fine building," etc., etc. It rained so much on our return to the ship that we got wet, and had to change our clothes; it is so very cold on the water, we wear winter clothes. After a long time the G. G., etc., returned. When they embarked, we steamed off again, and soon got to the mouth of the Saguenay; it is so very beautiful, just the scenery that I admire,—wild bold rocks and water, with many small trees, and no cultivation of any sort or a living being to be seen. All the party went in boats to a wild shore except Miss Frend, Mr. Wilkie, and I; it was raining, so we wisely remained in the ship—it really *poured*. They brought sticks and made two nice fires on the shore, and had tea; we had tea in the ship. The scene looked very pretty to us from the ship, the people and fires being a great addition to the landscape. The gentlemen fished, and between Dick, Mr. Godley, and Col. Gordon caught eleven trout. We enjoyed the fish much at dinner. We steamed back three miles to Tadousac, a village near the mouth of the Saguenay, where we anchored for the night. Capt. Pem. disembarked, and went on shore to see some friends of his—Col. Hawley and Major and Mrs. Churchill. Col. H. came and paid us all a visit on board, bringing with him a fisherman called "Joe," to tell us where the best fishing was to be had. "Joe" arranged to come next day at 3.30 a.m., with two canoes, and go with our party; he was engaged by some other people, so it was very wrong of him to give them up. We steamed off at five a.m. for Laval Bay, which we reached about breakfast-time to-day, Friday. The water here is salt, it is like glass, and so very lovely, and the weather fine and cool. Several of our party feel ill from drinking the river water. We set off, soon after breakfast, in two canoes and two boats for Laval River. I went in the boat with Dick, "Pem.," and Mr. Wilkie, with Colonel G. tied to us in a canoe. All the gentlemen are wearing veils because of the mosquitoes, and they looked so funny. Colonel G. had on a mosquito-guard which looked like a baby's crinoline, covered with gauze, to wear over the head and face. Dick and the G. G. have green veils. I felt so wretched when we found we had to row seven miles to the river and seven back, instead of one and a half, which was what horrid Joe led us to believe. Joe is a French-Canadian. The scenery was perfectly *exquisite*, but so lonely (although covered with grass and trees), you never see the face of a human creature. We met twenty horses *alone* on the shore, and they ran down to meet us. We also met a king-fisher and a wild duck. There were lovely wooded and rocky hills all around the bay and river. The water is so clear you can see the bottom, although it is very deep. The moment we landed we found we had no luncheon, and we were landed on an arid shore with no standing-place even, except bushes and slippery stones. That horrid Joe had misled us as to the distance, so, after a discussion, to my delight, it was found best for the ladies to re-embark and row to the ship, which we all and Mr. Wilkie did. It was most enchanting, rowing back on the smooth sunbeamy water. We then sent back the boat to the gentlemen with lunch, and some of the servants went in it for the pleasure of a row. I am now writing to you on deck, as we lie at anchor. We are all better now, I hope. The gentlemen bathed in the sea yesterday. Tadousac is a very pretty-looking village, where is the first Christian church built in Canada; we anchor there to-night, I believe.

Saturday Night, Saguenay.—The vessel is shaking so that I can hardly write. The gentlemen came back, having caught only about two fish, Joe showing himself even a worse humbug than we imagined. Some men came over in a canoe from the village of "Saults aux Cochons," one very wild looking and handsome, with an old fur cap on. They brought fish, and would only take meat and bread in exchange; money would be of no use to them in their wild place, where they never see meat. There are falls at the village which looked pretty in the distance. Some of us tried to make the captain take us to see them in a boat, but he feared the difficulty of landing on this "unknown shore," so steadily refused to let us go, at which I secretly rejoiced, for the perils of landing are great and, to me, very disagreeable, and I felt far safer "aboard." Soon we heard singing on the water, and saw the gentlemen returning in their boats; the boatmen were singing Canadian boat-songs; it sounded so pretty on the water. The gentlemen were not cross, and we had passed a very pleasant quiet day. That night we left for Tadousac, where we were met by quantities of people, Col. Irvine and daughter, Col. Rhodes, Col. Hawley, etc. It was written outside the hotel that the G. G. and party had arrived, "and were all well, and that Col. Irvine had received us on the shore." (If they only knew how ill some of us felt!) Musicians played "God save," etc. The people told us that the hotel had been illuminated the night our ship arrived; we never found it out. But I must stop now, as this letter must be put in at R. du Loup to-morrow. We got letters from home to-day, so pleasant. I will write more by next mail (D.V.). We have had Thunder and lightning to-night; oh, horrors!

Ship, July 30*th.*—I am going to finish telling you of Saturday. Major Churchill and Captain and Mrs. Utterson (17th) came on board at Tadousac. The ship is shaking so I cannot write; it is a screw, and shakes more than the *Asia*, but I like the movement—a screw feels more real and earth-like than smooth paddles.

August 3*rd, Wednesday Evening.*—I am at last on land again. I now go on with Saturday. These people came on board after our stay at Tadousac, where we remained about an hour. Most of our party went to see the R. C. chapel, which was built on the site of the first Christian church ever built in Canada, two hundred years ago, by the Jesuits. The priest gave her Ex. a bouquet. I just looked in, and then went to look at the hotel, with Dick, Captain Pem., and Henry. It is a very big hotel, lately built, and does not look at all substantial; there is a large bowling-alley attached to it. There is nothing to do at any of the Canadian watering-places. We then sat on a grassy mound and surveyed the sands, water, and people; the rest of the party went to see Jacques Cartier's cave, but we were too lazy to tramp through the sands. You know, perhaps, that Jacques Cartier was the discoverer of Canada two hundred years ago! Mrs. Utterson is a nice little woman. Captain U. is clever and observing, and does caricatures. We steamed on through a part of the Saguenay to Bay St. Etienne, a lonely wild spot where not a living creature was to be seen; we there disembarked in boats, and one boat got all right to land; the second, in which I was, stuck on *sand banks*, and had to be shoved off ever so many times. We were constantly nearly upset, and I was afraid. At last we had two alternatives—either to be carried by the men to land, or walk in the water barefooted; we wanted to do the latter, when at last, with violent shoves, we got near enough to the land to put boards across on which we perilously stepped: I slipped, and had a struggle with Mr. Wilkie before I could be dragged on to the shaking boards! L. went wrong in some way, and upset the boat so that F. was terrified, and in the water till the boat righted itself! None of the gentlemen landed, but the discreet Mr. Wilkie; he and Sergeant Lambkin, and the captain's little boy and I made a grand fire with sticks. There was a fisherman's "shanty" near the shore, but uninhabited. It was all very romantic: the wonderful Canadian woods all round us so thick that it was dangerous to venture into them for fear of being lost, the sandy shore, the lovely salt river, and the rocky and wooded hills all round us and stretching back far behind us. Henry soon joined us, not having good sport. Mr. Godley and Dick were in a canoe with nasty Joe, whose fault it was about our landing, as he said there was water enough, and really the tide was too low. You never saw so grand a fire as we made. It reminded me of our day long ago in the woods near Bonn am

Rhein. Mr. Wilkie found the bottom of a bottle in the grass marked "Bass's Pale Ale," left by some fisher, I suppose, but it spoilt the romance of the place a good deal with me. Soon we heard thunder rumbling all over the hills, and I happily found that Mrs. Utterson was afraid, and Mrs. Godley did not like it. I meant to embark in a boat and go to the ship, which, being iron, was the safest place. However, it went off for a time, so we had our tea very warm and snug on a log of wood, which did beautifully for a table. We then heard that the tide would not be *haute* till eight, and the boatmen and Sergeant Lambkin said they would carry us into the boats. We walked through swamps a good way into the river with the aid of planks which Mr. W. and the boatmen put down, and at last, with a great effort, we succeeded in getting into the boat by planks on a rock; so we escaped being carried. They caught very few fish; Dick and Mr. G. caught about a dozen trout. Soon the Thunder began, and very vivid lightning. We were at dinner on deck under an awning. I could not eat one bit, of course; it did not last long, thank God. The summer lightning went on for a long time. The hills were covered with fires, and round one of them P. and I said we saw the witches dancing hand-in-hand; it all looked so wild and pretty. At last we got to Tadousac, and the guests left us. Captain Pem. heard that there had been a *dreadful* Thunder-storm at Tadousac, and also an awful one at R. du Loup, so I was very thankful for missing the bad part. We went on that night to Rivière du Loup, where we arrived early on Sunday morning. We had to go in boats to get to land, and we went up and down very unpleasantly; of course I was afraid. It was so hot on land after excessive cold on the water. Dick and I and Mr. Wilkie drove in a gig to church, and the others all went in different waggons and gigs. We found the clocks so different that we got in for the second lesson! it began at 10.30. We disturbed the people a good deal; people turned out of their seats to let us in, and we were scattered all over the church. The service was very badly and carelessly performed, and the clergyman, who is very old, read so horridly, leaving out half his words— it sounded *just* like when you open and shut your ears during a conversation and hear bits of the talk. We had not a bad sermon of twenty minutes by some one from Montreal. We then all ascended into our gigs, and

Dick, Mr. Wilkie, and I went to see the Indian encampment on our way to Stanley's house, five miles off. The Indians are all Christians now all over Canada, though they are called, and call themselves, "Les Sauvages;" they looked quite Sunday-like, not working, and sitting about doing nothing; of course they are R. C. I saw the copper-colour baby of four months old; its mother is dead; such a sweet little thing it was. They asked us to buy a canoe, but I said not on Sunday; they seemed to understand quite well. We then went to Stanley's wooden white house. We hear that his house is called Government House, and where the Bishop of Quebec's boys are lodged is called "The See House." The sun was broiling hot. We had lunch, etc., a regular picnic affair; cold water was brought to the table in a china tea-pot!! Dick and Captain Pem. were at a side table, and oh, they ate so much! After lunch some of the party returned to the ship, the G. G. read the evening service at Stanley's house after a time, and then her Ex. and I drove with Colonel Gordon to see the Indians—she had not seen them. We had the waggons and gigs in waiting all day. "Gordon the Good," as I call him, then left us, and went to the ship, and we had delicious tea at "Government House," and then returned to the ship. We got there all right in boats. We steamed on to the mouth of the Marguérite River (out of the Saguenay) in the night, and found ourselves anchored in a most lovely bay on the morning of Monday, all surrounded with rocky and wooded hills and sands. The gentlemen were off before seven, except Gordon the Good, and the G. G., and Mr. Wilkie. The noise they all made was dreadful: they rowed to the shore, and had breakfast there, and a fire; and after breakfast we all rowed to shore, and found they were catching such quantities of fish. Dick, Henry, and Captain Pem. were wading in the water nearly to their waists, quietly walking along all dressed, with boots and everything, and even *gloves* to keep off the flies, and Capt. Pem. wore a dark-brown veil. We sat about on the shore, and I read the *Times*. Some of the ladies tried to fish, but they only caught one each. Of course I did not fish. The servants came on shore and laid an enormous fire, and arranged lunch on some planks near the bank and on the shore; and we had a grand lunch of trout, just killed, and wild raspberries and blueberries, so good. Félix fried the trout in a pan over the fire; they smelt very good. We sat on logs, and had our plates on our laps. Very soon after lunch I got so afraid, as Thunder was coming on, and darkness. I asked kind dear Henry to help me to get to the ship in a boat (Dick was deep in the water). Henry arranged it all, and insisted on coming with me himself. The only way we could do it was that I sat in a canoe, and was almost carried by men and Henry across the shallow parts to the boat; then the same thing was done with Conway, and we were rowed to the ship, and were so tossed up and down, I was terrified. Félix would row, and made me more afraid, and the water was coming in at the bottom of the boat. The sailors and Henry were so kind to me. I sat on the deck reading and talking to the captain, whose name is Pouillot, pronounced here "Pouillote;" we all like him. He told me about the Prince of Wales and Prince Alfred being on board the ship: Prince A. gave him a pencil-case in the shape of a telescope, and a compass in the shape of a cocked hat, for ornaments for his chain. He was very kind to me about Thunder, and said there would be very little. The rain came down in *torrents;* it was what the Yankees call "quite a rain-storm." I was afraid of the rain and the darkness, but the captain reassured me. I was very thankful to be dry on board ship and not in the tent on land. The lady part of the land party came back in good spirits. The gentlemen turned up later, having caught a hundred and sixty-two trout! They were in high delight at their sport. The rain that night was truly *awful*, and the deck was swimming, so we sat in the saloon, and played squails. The next day Henry most kindly arranged for us that we should go to see Cap Eternité far down in the Saguenay, the greatest thing to see; but we were going away without seeing it, as the others had seen it. The G. G. very kindly allowed us to go, as it was only fifteen miles off. We left Captain P. and Mr. G. fishing at the Marguérite. The Saguenay is most grand, and the rock at Cap Eternité is 1700 feet high, and quite perpendicular; Cap Trinité opposite is 1300 feet. Not a sign of life, except a few shanties, in St. John's Bay, nothing but rocks and mountains. The river is *very* deep and very narrow, and it is thought that the whole thing was caused by an earthquake or some convulsion of nature, from the extreme depth of the river at the same time that it is so narrow. The rocks are *very* rugged on one side of Eternité Bay, and covered with wood on the other. We returned to the Marguérite, and picked up the fishers; they caught two dozen and a half more fish. We went on very quick to Tadousac, where we inquired for letters, and where flags were run up, and on to R. du Loup, where Dick and I took a walk on the sands, and picked up shells. Every one landed except her Ex., who was ill. Stanley slept on board that night. I gave L. some money to get me some Indian things as she went ashore, and she got me a bandbox made of birch bark, which is waterproof; it cost less than two shillings. We were all enchanted looking at the northern lights; the captain says they are supposed to be the reflection of the sun shining on the ice at the North Pole. One night at Tadousac they were like an arch of light across the sky. The sunset was quite Eastern, Dick said, the very reddest red and yellow over purple hills. Fancy! a black dog appeared on board the day we left Quebec, and never left the ship, except for a walk, till we arrived again at Quebec! The funny beast wanted change of air, we suppose, so it chose the Government steamer and the Governor-General's party for its trip. It belonged to no one, but joined any land party it thought would be pleasantest to it. It was a capital water dog, and swam very well. At R. du Loup it came ashore with Dick and me, and was so excited, barking at any one that came near us. We gave him a swim. We called him Spot, and he seemed to like his name very well. There was such a handsome man on board (the second mate) called Dominique Beaulieu, very Spanish-looking, and so civil and good-humoured; we all loved him! The captain had his little boy on board, and he told Miss Frend he brought him because he might never see a *Lord* again, and that he said to his boy that he ought to be proud to be in the company of so many titled people! He brought him also on board when the Princes were there, because he thought he would never see a prince again! We started on Wednesday morning (August 3rd) from R. du Loup for Quebec, which we reached at six p.m. Most of our party were glad to be on shore again (except, of course, the gentlemen), in large bedrooms, with space to turn round, instead of little cramped-up cabins and rockey beds, where you could not move without hitting yourself. Gordon the Good was *very* sorry to be home again, and so were Fan, Miss F., and her Ex.

Thursday, 4th.—Very early arrived Colonel Hawley, 60th, Sir Fenwick Williams, and the De Wintons. Sir F. is really most kind, and so handsome. He was much pleased because I told him the only two days I was free from headache were the days at his island. He asked us to go to him again. Mrs. De W. is very delicate, and so young. The whole day was wet—the only really wet day since I have been here. I wrote, and talked, and walked in the verandah, and in the evening there was a dinner-party according to enclosed list. I sat between Gordon the Good and Lord A. Russell, who is so amusing. Mrs. ——— was beautifully dressed last night, but her dress was so low at the back that Mr. G. said, "You could draw the map of Europe on her back!" She is like a hawk, but handsome. Mrs. De W. looked "La Dame Blanche" in her bridal dress. There is to be a great cricket-match to-day (Friday, 5th), between the Montreal and Quebec garrisons, and the band of the 25th is to play at four.

August 5th. — Cricket-match, Montreal against Quebec. The lovely band of the K.O.B.'s played under the trees at Spencer Wood. Dinner-party of cricketers.

Saturday, 6th.—Cricket-match continued;

Quebec garrison beaten, I am sorry to say. Sir F., etc., left. The Bishop of Quebec dined and slept.

Monday, 6*th*. — Cricket-match — Public Schools against "The World."

Tuesday, 9*th*.—Went to the Hotel Dieu with F.

Wednesday, 10*th*.—Two Thunder-storms!! very terrible to me; but the cellar is such a comfort.

Thursday, 11*th*.—Three events—a review on the plains of Abraham, a cricket-match here, and last but not least a Thunder-storm. The cricket-match was Captains and Ensigns against "The World."

Friday, 12*th*. — Match finished. "The World" won.

Saturday, 13*th*.—Lord Brabazon arrived from home, and was asked to stay here. *Very* hot. Thunder, wind, and rain-storm.

Sunday, 14*th*.—Hot. Mr. Stopford (Ld. B.'s friend) arrived.

Monday, 15*th*.—*Very* hot. We all drove to Montmorençi. Gordon the Good drove me with two bad-mouthed horses. We had an accident; in some way we got entangled in the wheels of a cart, and to my joy we had to get out of Col. G.'s open waggon, and to go in a hired one with a head to it. I was enchanted with the Falls; they are enormously high and magnificent, and one feels awed by their grandeur. We walked to see "The natural steps"—a set of rocky steps by the side of the rapids, very curious, and the scenery round so pretty—green fields and trees. We picked some pretty wild flowers. The drive to and from Montmorençi is so pretty. We found Ld. and Lady Alexander Russell had arrived here when we returned.

Tuesday, 16th.—Old Mr. Price and Capt. Hope, K.O.B., dined. The dear old Mr. P. admires Lady A. R. very much, and devoted himself to her. I sat next Ld. A. at dinner, and he made me laugh the whole time.

Wednesday, 17th.—Very hot afternoon. Ld. and Lady A. R. left.

Thursday, 18th.—Gen. Lindsay and staff arrived. We are always glad when they come. Review on the plains of Abraham. Very hot. The 17th band played in the Governor's garden in the afternoon, and we went to it. In the evening there was a very large dinner-party here — all the colonels of regiments, also Col. Neville and Col. Peel. Captain Eliot took me in to dinner; he is so pleasant and amusing. After dinner the 25th string-band played outside the verandah. It was all like a scene in a play—the moon made a silver path on the river, a ship standing out so clearly on the water that the rigging could be seen quite plain, and the "band discoursing sweet music" the while. The K.O.B.'s play so exquisitely. The red coats of the officers formed a very good foreground to the picture. The servants had dancing at one end of the verandah. Adieu.

Friday, August 19*th.*—After I had dispatched your letters, F. and I drove to town, and looked at Dick, Henry, etc., playing racquets at the racquet-court. We dined at seven, and the Gen. and staff left for Montreal per train after dinner.

Saturday, 20*th.* — Dull and foggy day. After lunch her Ex., F., and I drove to town, to see some coloured prints of Jerusalem at old Mr. Forsyth's house. He gave me a copy of his book of travels in the Holy Land. We then went to Col. Gordon's house (next door) to tea. The soldier servant, with his black moustaches and large white-gloved hands spread out very wide, made us laugh, he looked so odd and consequential. It is a very nice house, and Gordon the Good gave us "quite a feast"— tea, melon, cake, and peaches. When we got home, Dick and I walked to old Mr. Price's place (next to this).

Sunday, 21st. — Dull and foggy again. The evening turned out wet.

Monday, 22nd.—A very wet day; so unusual here! There was to have been a school feast here to-day, but it is too wet. After all, we are not going to P. Edward's Island; I *dread* the sea too much, though I long to go. Gen. Lindsay does not know whether he will go home at all. The R. Brigade come down to Montreal from Kingston, also the 63rd. The R.B. have been promised Quebec if they send another regiment here. Gen. L. is also anxious to get to Quebec. This is such a stupid letter; I have no news. P.S.—This moment three carriages full of, I suppose, Yankees, have driven up to the house. The Yanks stared well at the house, and *into* my room on the ground-floor, and drove off again.

August 22nd, Monday.—Oh, the wet of Monday I never shall forget! The rain stopped in the afternoon for a short time, and F., M. F., and I drove out. I went to see Mrs. —— (the bride). She told me they went lately on a fishing-expedition to St. Jean, where they found only a log hut to sleep in, and no food to eat, so they (four in number) slept on the ground, and had only a loaf of sour black bread to eat. We drove also to Mrs. —— —— house, where I went in and paid her a visit. The people out here are all hearty and kind. I was much amused at this visit. Mrs. N., sister to Mrs. F. T., was with her. After some talk, I asked to see Mrs. F. T.'s boy of two years old, and her *sister* said, "Bring him down, if he is awake *and* good. I think it wise to say this." In he came, sucking his thumb, and Mrs. T. informed me, by way of an excuse for him, that she had sucked her own thumb till she was five, that Miss —— had done so till she was seven, Col. —— till he was nine, and a lady who had visited her told her that her son was "a good big boy of thirty-two," and still sucks his thumb. When he is annoyed at anything, he says, "I will try a taste of my thumb." We had an awful rain-storm, and some Thunder and lightning after dinner, and the violent rain-storm went on at intervals all night.

Tuesday, 23*rd*.—A very wet day, but it cleared after lunch, and we drove. We had torrents of rain after our return home, and distant Thunder—at least, what I call distant *here*, but *near* at home.

Wednesday, 24*th*.—Very fine day, hot sun,

cool air. After lunch, Capt. and Mrs. ——
called by appointment. She was so well
dressed in her trousseau clothes. He wore
his wedding clothes, and his hair was curled.
Her boots creaked from shyness, and when
I asked her how many sisters she had she
answered, "Six or seven." Later her Ex.
gave a feast here to the orphan children of
the Church Home. The schoolmistress
(Miss Winter) was a great amusement to
me—a fat old woman with a short dress and
no crinoline, one fat grey shell curl rested on
each cheek. She wore comfortable grey
thread gloves and a bonnet instead of a hat,
which is the usual head-gear out here! The
"man-matron" is a retired policeman, well
able to keep the boys in order. Mr. Fother-
gill (the clergyman) came, also Mr. H. and
wife. They had been detained by a funeral,
which they seemed rather proud of. The
children were all so happy, and they ended
by singing a hymn, intended to be "The
Evening Hymn," but no one could have
recognized it as such; it was led by the
matron with her chin *en l'air*, followed by
the ex-policeman in quite another key! The
matron's fat hand was spread out on one of
the girl's shoulders during the hymn. Then
they all went away in an open van, the man

on the box and the matron on the *step*, as she slipped off the leather seats of the van. I had a letter from Miss Rose asking us to a "farewell" ball they are giving to the Guards on the 31st; we hope to go. That night dined Mr. and Miss Archbald; they have come out for the winter, and brought a letter from Lord de Grey. It makes home *sound* nearer their saying they came out for a pleasure trip for the winter. The father is like pictures of Abraham with a white beard; the girl is pleasant. Mr. Price also dined; dear old man! He and Mr. A. found out that they were old friends. We sang glees and Canadian choruses after dinner.

Thursday, 25th.—Mr. Price sent me a beautiful bouquet this morning. The house flies here would drive a saint mad; they are in black swarms, and get into one's mouth, and ears, and eyes, and prevent one from sleeping in the morning; they begin their raids at daybreak. I had a most pressing invitation from dear Mrs. Dundas to-day, but I fear the sea too much to accept it. Mr. Rose lunched, and told us that Miss Rose is having a ballroom built outside the house for the Guards' ball. The gentlemen dined with the 25th. We all played "Old Maid" at home. Mr. Wilkie's fuss for fear he should be "Old Bachelor" was good fun, pretending he hated it all the time, and saying *sternly* to Henry, "You should not let it be seen when you have the old maid."

Friday morning, 26*th.*—Mr. and Mrs. Rawson come for one night to-day. We had Thunder, lightning, and a terrible rain-storm last night.

Friday evening.—The Rawsons arrived, also Lord Mahon, Mr. Stanhope, and Captain Hayter. These men had missed the train from the Saguenay, and came here instead. There was a very large dinner-party; several of the Ministers dined and some officers. The flies were dreadful; old Sir E. Taché remarked, "Flies are very impertinent; they love handsome women's blood." In the evening I talked to Mrs. McD. She told me that one of the storms here went on to the States twelve hours later, and killed "Quite a number of soldiers, about thirty of them." Talked also (among others) to Mr. Galt, who begged of me to go with the Ministers to P. Edward's Island. It is only sixty hours by water. Had I known it was so short a passage, I might have settled to go, but now it is too late. What *am* I come to when sixty hours sounds short? Talking of passages, Mr. Rawson told me that Sir Samuel Cunard said that one thing that made his line so safe was that the ships are "Well prayed over."

Saturday, 27th.—Very wet morning till twelve. The Rawsons left after an early dinner. The T. G.'s (travelling gents) left after three.

Sunday.—Wet most of the day.

Monday, 29th.—We tried on winter clothes, fur caps, etc., in L.'s room. Dick looked very nice in fur cap. I went with F. and M. F. to see some of the poor in the village. One very disagreeable Englishwoman told me that she knew a lady who left her baby in England when she came out here, and it died—this was *à propos* to my having left B. B. at home. Mrs. Godley told me she always says the wrong thing; she saw some of them with goloshes one day, and pleasantly remarked that her mother once wore them, and slipped and died! Another (an Irishwoman) was very pleasant, her grandchild presented the P. of Wales with a bouquet when he was here, and he took her in his arms and kissed her, and sent her a locket and his picture; she is a pretty child.

Tuesday, 30th.—The G. G. and staff have

gone to the Volunteer Rifle Match ; the G. G. is to fire the first shot.

Friday, September 2nd.—We went to Montreal on Tuesday last. Mr. and Miss Archbald were on board the boat. No one could conceive the size of these boats unless they saw them, so enormous, like three-storied wooden houses, painted white. We had a *room*, not a cabin. The moment we arrived at the St. Lawrence Hall, we heard there was going to be a very grand review at Logan's Farm, so we got a waggon and went off to it. We found a great crowd on the field. Capt. King soon espied us, and made me get into Sir Fenwick's carriage with Mrs. de Winton. The review was beautiful—I send a paper with an account of it; swarms of Yankees were there, and their remarks, which were roared out at the top of their voices, amused me much. They said the Rifles were "very ugly," and the Guards' caps were the ugliest things they had ever seen, and the most disfiguring. They called each regiment "an army!" "Here's Stephenson's army," etc., etc. It was the prettiest review I have ever seen anywhere; the Guards looked beautiful ; the 60th also looked very pretty; and the R.A. grand, rushing down a ravine and up the other side, with their enormous cannons. The cannons frightened our horses dreadfully, and Dick and Capt. King had to hold them down; they kicked and stood upright. The horses of the next carriage were even worse; and one of them put its head into our carriage, and nearly on Mrs. de W.; at last we had to get out—we were terrified. Sir Fenwick looked very handsome, and was so kind to me. He said his carriage was at my disposal for the day, but of course I would not take it. This review was on Wednesday, August 31st. In the afternoon Captain Seymour took us out to drive. We went to see Lady Sarah, and found a "tea" going on to hear a girl of twelve read Shakespeare for charity. Lady Sarah made her read "The Quality of Mercy" for me; she really read very well. The *Jura won't* come in, and we want our letters so much.

Spencer Wood, September 3rd, Saturday.— This dreadful day I shan't forget in a hurry. We got up at 7.15 in terrible wind, with rain beating against the windows, and everything looking the picture of desolation and despair. We went on board the *Peruvian* with the travellers, and, having inspected the cabins, we all sat together in the saloon for the short time before the ship started. At last the bell rang, and we took leave. Captain Ballantine took care of me from the ship to the carriage. We then stayed in the wind and rain to see the ship move off into the river. How terrible it is to see a ship move off for so long a voyage! I thought so of "Gone," when I saw the ropes undone, and she moved slowly off. Then we drove home; the house is so sad and deserted; it is bitterly cold, to add to everything else. I must go back now and tell you more about Montreal; I left off so suddenly. After our "tea" at Lady Sarah's, we drove to the joint house of Captains Eliot and Seymour, and paid Captain E. a visit. They were so pleasant and funny. I told them they were like two old maids trying to let the house. Captain S. anxiously inquired, "Charles, has any one been here to look at the house to-day?" We then went to a shop where Dick bought winter furs, and then home. We joined dinners with Sir Fenwick, and had a pleasant party, which consisted of Sir F. and staff and ourselves. Sir F. knew about the odd Yankees at the review, as they went to his house, and called him "Mr. Williams." After dinner we went to the ball at Mrs. Rose's. It was a pretty sight, and very well done; the whole croquet-ground and

FAREWELL BALL TO THE GUARDS.

verandah were covered in with an enormous tent, which reached to the top of the house, so that from the upstairs balconies you could look down to the ballroom. The tent was done up with flags and lights, and there were lights among the trees and shrubs of the croquet-ground; the vine-leaved pillars of the verandah came in so well and naturally. There was a very handsome Southern girl at the ball, a Miss Preston. A black beetle appeared hopping and running through the ballroom. I tried to catch it in my handkerchief, I was so afraid it would be killed. A R.A. officer most civilly knelt on the ground to try to rescue it, but he failed, and at last it was captured by a R.E. officer. Conway came up to see the ball. One American elderly lady had about forty curls on each side of her head; she looked like a tree with branches. We got home at three. Outside the ballroom was like a Cremorne of coloured lamps and arbours.

On September 1st, went at one to the Guards' auction, and was much amused—horses, harness, sleighs, and carriages were sold. After dinner we left Montreal in the *Europa*, with our nice little captain, who again gave us our supper in the pantry, as the place of honour. The wind got up very much in the night, and by morning I could not keep my feet on deck. Dick had his new horse on board, "Bill Seward" by name, bought from Col. Bramston.

Friday, September 2nd.—I repeat about Friday, 2nd. A wretched day, very windy and dark, and every one sad. Saturday I have told you of. Gordon the Good came. Fires blazed in every room, and every one was shivering with cold! The small table at dinner was by no means a cheering sight, and the misery of the animals was sad to see. Sunday was very very wet and windy. Drove to church in the afternoon in the waggon with the new horse.

Monday, 5th.—To-day is very fine, thank God. Heard of the *Peruvian.*

Tuesday, 6th.—Very windy and fine, cold with hot sun. I went with all the gentlemen, and F. B. and Col. Gordon, on board the *Himalaya.* The captain sent his ten-oared boat for us. Dick, Captain Pem., and Gordon the Good were in uniform. I saw that the river was *very* rough. I wanted to stay behind, but they said "Go on," so I was *in* the boat before I realized it, the officer saying, "If you sit there, you will escape the spray." Oh, misery! We went up and down so high and so low, it was dreadful. Captain Lacy was very civil, and excused himself to the G. G. for not firing a salute as he had no guns! We went all over the ship, and saw where every one was to sleep. F. Burrowes told us that on Saturday the storm was so great the fires of the *Island of Orleans* steamer were put out by the water, and they had to put back. Before dinner three "shipwrecked mariners," viz. Colonel Warde, 60th Rifles, Mr. Turner (ditto), and Mr. Wilson Patten (Rifle Brigade), arrived. They had just turned up in the *Urgent*, after twenty-one days' passage from England, and all sorts of misfortunes. They told us at dinner all about their passage. The ship ran on a sand-bank, and nearly went over; the cabins were full of water, the boats were ready, and the women and children assembled, when she righted herself, but every one was terrified. They lost an anchor, were short of coals, and beginning to want provisions. Mr. Turner pleasantly remarked, "The *Peruvian* must have met with very bad weather."

Wednesday, 7th.—Dick and Captain Pem. went off at 7 a.m. to see the Guards off, and brought Captain Seymour here to breakfast. There was great mourning at Montreal after the Guards. In the afternoon we got letters from Father Point. The Godleys and a tribe of dogs came here during tea, and we had a violent dog fight.

Thursday, 8th.—After lunch Fräulein D. and I took a pretty drive all over the coves by the riverside. The day was so lovely and calm, one could almost see one's face in the river. Captain Pem. went to Montreal for a cricket-match. After tea Dick and I walked over to Mr. Price's, to thank him for a beautiful bouquet he brought me. He took Dick the famous walk to see where Wolfe landed, and I walked with the young ladies. Dr. Adamson and a few officers dined.

September 9th, Friday.—Very wet.

Saturday, 10th.—Fräulein Denny and I drove into town, and made F. B. take us to the racquet-court to see Dick play. Denny was so afraid going, and said the court was like "a bear-pit at the Jardin des Plantes" at Paris. The evening was so lovely. We saw people trying horses on the Plains of Abraham for the garrison races on Friday next.

Sunday.—Wet, as every Sunday is, and very cold. There were seven people at the eight-o'clock service. Mr. Scarth, of Lennoxville, is doing duty here now. Dick had a letter from Captain Pem. saying that Quebec had well beaten Montreal, of which we are very proud. We walked back part of the way from the afternoon service with the J. Burstals, who told us of the burning down of the Quebec Custom House the day before! Alas! the only fine building at Quebec is gone.

Monday, 12*th*.—*Such* a storm blowing from the east. We have been out looking at the river, which is *very* rough. I had a visit last Saturday, I forgot to say, from Mrs. Adamson and Mrs. Macdonald, the Dr.'s wife at Montreal. Mrs. A. was so amusing; she said she had just come from Ottawa, with which she was disgusted. She said, "What can you expect from a place where there is no water? You have to pay fifteenpence to a boy to bring you water; there are no waterworks." Mrs. M. asked me if I had ever been there; I said no. "*Keep* out of it," said Mrs. A., "*as long* as *you* can." On the 20th, I hope, Lord Lyons and Messrs. Malet and Sheffield come here, and General Doyle a few days later. Captain Seymour hopes to go with Dick and me to Niagara in October. Once the winter begins, I shall feel the time for going home is coming nearer. The leaves are beginning to turn. Conway told me that on board the *Asia* a steward told her that on a fine day when they passed an iceberg, the ship stopped, and they played the fiddle, and all the bears came out on the iceberg and danced! I wonder if she believed him? It is so cold and windy to-day. Dick and I are much amused to find that Sergeant Wingfield has set up "a visitors'-book" for us, and he has quite a long list of officers' names in it already.

Tuesday, 13th.—The great wind-storm of yesterday is going on to-day. We have been sitting round blazing wood fires all the morning. Captain Pem. appeared suddenly to-day; the weather being so wet, they could play no more. After lunch the rain ceased. The gentlemen dine with the 17th to-night.

Wednesday, 14*th*.—I sang a great deal for Denny last night. The gentlemen had rather a pleasant dinner, and whist all the evening. Sir E. Taché was there; he says the delegates from the Maritime Provinces are to meet here on the 10th—that will be fun. *Every day they bring us home news of a fire at Quebec.* No mail in. Denny and I have been picking some lovely autumn leaves. The Godleys come to stay to-day. It is quite warm weather again.

Thursday, 15*th*.—Captain Pem. is gone to Rivière du Loup, from whence to cross to

Tadousac, in an open boat, to see his friends the C.'s, who are detained there by Major C. having broken his back; they are both ill and helpless, so Captain P. is gone to see about getting them home. Every one has left Tadousac except them, so the kind Captain Pem. is bringing them provisions to keep them alive till they can get away. After lunch to-day we had Thunder and awful rain, and during the storm we could quite well hear the muffled drums of the funeral of a poor 25th officer, also the firing over his grave. All this was very sad and depressing.

Friday, 16th.—Another wet and windy day —cheerful and cheering weather! I do not know what I should do without books now. No races to-day because of the poor officer's death. No mail in, so no news of any one. "When things come to the worst, they mend." I trust it will be so. Adieu; mail going.

September 16th, Friday.—After my letters were finished last Monday, Mrs. G. asked me to go out with her in her waggon. I was so thankful to get out a little. In the covered waggon; the coachman is also under cover, so no one is wet. We went to the See House to visit the bishop's wife. The bishop was ill with toothache. Mrs. Williams said to me in a mournful voice, "You must be very dreary, and you are without your husband too." I soon undeceived her; but the papers had announced that Dick was going home, and set every one wondering about it. The bishop told us (in speaking of the window in the cathedral which was put up in memory of the late bishop) that there is a picture of the Ascension in the centre part, and some one said that they did not like it, it was too *Popish;* that they expected a full-length portrait of the bishop instead of the Ascension. The weather improved, and we drove in to town. We felt quite in spirits at seeing the sun once more, but the roads were in a most deplorable state; we were nearly bumped to pieces. I never lived in the country before. Oh, it is dull in wet weather! A soldier of the 25th fell out of the window at the barracks in this place, in a fit of D.T., and died in a few days, and we heard his funeral too.

Saturday, 17th.—Lord Newry and Mr. Campbell of Islay came for about an hour. They came out for the winter; I believe Mr. C.'s wish is to sit upon an iceberg. I fear he won't be able to manage it. I went in the afternoon with Dick to see a poor old soldier in the village. I brought him a pair of over-gloves I had made for him; at first he put them on with the hole for the thumb at the back! I had to root at him till I got them on, he saying the while, "I dare say, ma'am, *in a day or two* I'll find the thumb." Encouraging! For a wonder the day was fine. The river is lovelier every day; such a deep blue. We dined at six, and then went in to Madame Anna Bishop's concert. Gordon the Good, Col. Irvine, and Sergeant Lambkin met us at the door of the music-hall. Our party had a blue sofa, and blue chairs in front, with a clear breathing space before us. No one stood up when the G. G. came in. Madame A. B. is very old, but looks about forty; she has been beautifully taught, but her voice is now rather coarse. Her daughter is a stick, and moreover sang that dreadful song, "I love the Merry Sunshine." Mr. Lascelles was like a caricature of Charles II. of England. The buffo singer, Mr. Sedgwick, was funny, but a little vulgar. No news of Captain Pem. or of the Canadian ship *Damascus*.

Sunday, 18*th*.—Very fine day. Had a beautiful sermon from Mr. Hatch. After tea we were cheered by the sight of the Cunard letters. Thank God for the post.

Monday, 19th.—A fine day now, but wet early; it is blowing a hurricane. No ship, and no " Pem."

Tuesday, 20th.—Captain Pem. turned up yesterday, after my letter was gone. This morning was dull as usual, and very cold. Before breakfast Lord Lyons and Messrs. Malet and Sheffield arrived. It was very pleasant meeting Mr. M. again; we seemed to take up our conversation from where we left off at Brussels years ago. After luncheon I went to town with Captain Pem. to see Denny off *en route* to the United States. Later in the day came Lord Airlie. After tea the three lords went out to walk!! and Mr. M. and I took a walk also. Lord A. looks like a German professor, and amuses me much. At last we got our Canadian mail letters, but still nothing is heard of the *Damascus*, out nearly three weeks. A large dinner-party Tuesday night. At dinner I sat between Lord Lyons and Mr. Hatch, the clergyman. Lord L. detests ships and water as much as I do. When he was at Sir F.'s, he refused to go out in the yacht, and stayed at home alone, having arranged in his mind that if the servants offered him dinner in their master's absence he would not decline.

Wednesday, 21st.—Lord L. is ill with headache. News of an *émeute* about ships being burnt on Lake Erie; telegrams coming and going. After lunch Lord A., Mrs. G., the attachés, Dick, Captain Pem., and I drove to the Falls of Lorette. Some of us went in the open carriage and four, some in Captain Pem.'s waggon. The day was so bitterly cold that we were obliged to have the bear-skins. Lorette is supposed to be an Indian village still, though no longer such. There are no real Indians living there, except Paul, the chief, who looks like a Frenchman. The Falls are very pretty. We scrambled about, and enjoyed our afternoon much. We bought a few little Indian things from Paul. Mr. S. gave Mrs. G. and me some dried Indian hay, which has a nice smell, and scents one's wardrobe pleasantly. That night (Wednesday) there was another big dinner. We had the first frost that night. I forgot to say that while we were at lunch, there arrived for me two beautiful bouquets from Mr. Price, of which Lord Airlie carried one, Mr. Malet the other, Captain Pem. following with vases from the table. In this order they proceeded to my door.

Thursday, 22nd.—After breakfast we set

off for the Chaudière Falls. Lord L. went with Mrs. G. in her waggon. Dick drove me in the G. G.'s waggon, having Mr. M. in the back seat. Lord A. was not ready, so we left him to follow with Mr. S. and Captain Pem. in Pem.'s waggon. I wore my sealskin, and yet felt quite ill with the cold air, and felt the pain across my brow, which necessitates the use of a fur cap in this climate. At Quebec we met Gordon the Good, and then we went on board the ferry-boat, and steered for Point Lévis. Arrived at Point Lévis, we took up Lord A., and made Col. G. and Mr. M. go in a hired waggon. We had a charming drive; the day was lovely, and the air became quite warm with the sun. No sky so blue as the Canadian sky, and no leaves like the Canadian autumn leaves! Such rich red tints everywhere. Part of the road was so very rough and uneven, no vehicle but a waggon could have survived the incessant thumping and bumping. My umbrella had got itself broken the day before, to Lord A.'s great satisfaction, and he declared he might now enjoy the scenery only for my parasol, but he was in constant dread of having his eye poked out with its spike. The Chaudière Falls are broader than Montmorençi, but not nearly so high.

They are most beautiful. We had to clamber over gates, and were much sprinkled by the spray from the Falls. Lunch was laid on the green grass, and we lit a fire with sticks, and were soon warm and dry. Planks of wood were laid on the grass, and Mr. M. brought cushions from the waggons, so that we were most comfortably seated. Lord A. sat next me, eating pork-pie with his fingers, and humming tunes as he ate—he could not wait for a plate. Lord L. roamed away by himself, and would eat no luncheon. Mrs. G. and Captain Pem. set out after lunch on a voyage of discovery—fern-hunting; I followed them. We then walked to the waggons, expecting to find Lord L., but no Lord L. could we find, so Dick, Lord A., Col. G., Mr. M., and I drove to Point Lévis, leaving the others to follow. We arrived just in time to catch the ferry. Lord L. and Mrs. G. arrived home twenty minutes after we did. All had enjoyed their day extremely. Another large dinner-party. This night, for the first time since my arrival in Canada, I had no headache. Whilst we were at the Chaudière, Tom, the cat, had three kittens in my wardrobe! Oh, I was *so* angry! This was the great joke at dinner. Tom was extremely cross that night, and when we were all walking into the drawing-room in solemn procession after the G. G., who was bowing to his guests, Tom sprang out from some recess on Miss M.'s dog (she always brings her dog to dinner); they had a most terrific fight. The guests flew in all directions, Miss M. tried to separate the combatants, and in short the whole scene baffles description. With difficulty the animals were quieted, and we went in to dinner. Lord L.'s amusement was great; he went on all the evening alluding to the battle. I should like to have been able to draw the whole scene. Miss M. told Mr. C. in confidence that the cat had scratched her knees and made them bleed, upon which he replied that it was not quite so bad as Miss S.'s squirrel, which jumped from bar to bar of her crinoline.

Friday, 23rd.—Long after dinner last night arrived the delightful General Doyle from Halifax. He was in excellent force —looked as if he had just come out of a bandbox, kid gloves and all. At breakfast Lord Lyons asked after my little family! *à propos* to that beast Tom, etc. Miss M. played sweetly last night, and then we all sang the Christy Minstrels in chorus. Lord L. made us sing " Kiss me quick," etc. After breakfast got your delightful letters by

Cunard steamer, as well as other home letters by the disabled *Damascus*. Such a wet day! It cleared later, and we went out to walk. The party consisting of Dick, Gen. D., Mr. S., and self, Lord A. joining us *chemin faisant*. Gen. D. pretended to hate going out of the house, protesting that the wind was terrific, and that he should walk on the heels of his boots to keep the soles dry. This he proceeded to do, declaiming desperately, "Blow, blow, thou wintry wind." I made them come to Mr. Price's, where we found Mr. C. (25th) and his brother playing croquet with the Price girls in the wet grass. Gen. D. was an old friend of the Price family. Old Mr. P. had a bad cough, so we went in to condole with him. Mr. P. and I are great friends; he has given me five bouquets, or "bunched" me five times, as the Yankees say. On our way home we talked of Miss M. and her dog, and Gen. D. said she had no business to take him to church with her, and that no dog could stand a thirty-minutes' "buster" from the pulpit. We came home in time for five-o'clock tea, where we were joined by Lord L. and Mr. M. Lord L. regretted having missed our meeting at the Prices, and all our fun. Large dinner-party. In the evening we sang choruses, "Since first I saw your Face," etc.

Saturday, 24th.—Another wet day, worse than ever. A review was to take place, to which Lord L., Lord Airlie, Mr. S., and I set off in the open carriage, the others riding. Lord L. does not love reviews, having had too many in the States, where thousands upon thousands are being continually reviewed. I condoled with him, and he said, "We are very fortunate to be with you in this cozy carriage, from whence we need see no more than we choose of the soldiers." His voice has a gravely accented tone, which makes even the commonest remarks sound amusing; he never laughs at his own remarks. The rain soon descended in torrents, necessitating the hood, which Lord L. duly appreciated. A great many spectators were on the Plains of Abraham. Soon Lord A. and Mr. S. got out because our hood interfered with their umbrellas; no sooner were they gone than Lord L. pulled down the covers, and buttoned us up as snugly as possible. Presently the French Admiral Reynaud drove up with M. de Geoffroi (Chargé d'Affaires from France to Washington). They are here only for a few days. Lord L. bowed to the Admiral, and spoke a few words, then, turning to me, said, "The consequence of speaking to these gentlemen is that I have wetted my hat." They are great friends! The rain grew worse and worse, so we were ordered home, but I believe General Doyle went on inspecting. Lord L. said he cared not how much it rained, so long as we were dry. When we stopped at the door of Government House, he said, "If we can run through these rivers, we shall escape without a single speck!" and so we did. After lunch most of the gentlemen, with the addition of F. Burrowes, played battledore and shuttlecock under the verandah until they were tired, when they called out for "beer." I paced the verandah between Lord A. and General D. like people on board ship. Lord L. said, "Sheffield, get your top." This is a Yankee flying-top, which, when wound up, flew to the top of the verandah, and then spun on the ground. "The Russian Minister at New York," said Lord L., "one day met us in the street when he had been buying a top for his baby, and then he went and bought one for mine," turning to Mr. S. The flying-top is a pleasant toy. Gordon the Good arrived for tea. Lord A. read me part of his letter to his wife, in which he gave a vivid description of the fight between Quiz the dog and Tom the cat. They all want to read my journals. Lord L. says he knows that every one is so well abused in them that I don't like to show them. A large dinner-party; M. Cartier sat on one side of me. After dinner M. de Geoffroi, the French Chargé d'Affaires, asked Lord Lyons to introduce him to me. The French admiral is like an enormous Bishop of Cashel; General Doyle and Mr. Godley were both struck by the likeness. M. de G. is very pleasant, and speaks such lovely French. I had stolen one or two most exquisite autumn leaves from one of the dessert dishes at dinner, and felt truly vexed when this agreeable man asked me to give him my *feuille morte;* he chose the prettiest, the one I longed to keep; but, of course, I could not refuse to give it to him. His dress was so French—grey "pants," and a tail coat, and of course decorations of all sorts. In this bitter weather the grey "pants" quite made me shiver. Colonel Jervoise, R.E., dined also; he is here on some special mission about the defences, fortifications, etc.

Sunday, 25th.—Mr. —— told me such a delicious story about Mr. Lyulph Stanley when he was a boy of five; he was one day naughty, and scolded by his mother; when she had done scolding him he said, "Proceed; you interest me." Mr. —— also told us when a Yankee sees any one going out to shoot with his gun and his dog, he says, "Stranger, whither away with your burning irons and your smell dog?" I do not tell these stories *à propos* of Sunday! There was a sermon in the morning on "the burden of riches." After tea Colonel G., F. B., Dick, and I went shivering to the river walk.

Monday, 26th.—We are going to the garrison races to-day. It is now blowing a hurricane from the north; how cold the plains will be! To-morrow we hope to go on an expedition up the river in the Government steamer to a place called "Shawenigan." After several essays, I told Lord L. I had discovered we pronounced it wrong; he reassured me by saying, "Better leave it as it is; we shall only puzzle ourselves if we change our way of saying the word, and we only want to speak of it among ourselves." Lord L. has invited us to Washington, where he promises to give a party in my honour.

Monday, September 26th, Evening.—We went to the races on the Plains of Abraham. Captain Pem. and I went in the carriage,

and were met by Lord A. and Mr. Malet,
who had been to Montmorençi with Dick;
he rode, also Mrs. Godley and General
Doyle; and all the rest were busy writing
business letters at the office. Such a pity!
The wind was bitter, but the day lovely, and
it was great fun. Colonel Gordon brought
me to lunch in a tent, and there introduced
me to Madame Duval, who introduced her
daughter—Mrs. Serecold—to me. The 17th
supplied the food, and the 25th the wine.
The races were rather bad, but amusing, and
to *me* exciting, as I had never seen a race
before. Colonel G.'s horse came in a good
last; he did not care one pin! There was
no betting. The French Chargé d'Affaires
was there, also the Admiral. There were
three tumbles. The view from the plains is
so very pretty—the river beneath you and
the mountains beyond, and everything looked
very gay and bright. I was so perished
that Lord A. and Mr. Malet tucked me up
in the bear-skin robe and only my head
peeped out. The business people got home
at 6.30. In the evening dined Col. G. and
Mr. Marryatt (17th), Col. Jervoise and Mr.
Harrison, R.E., Col. and pretty Miss Kate
Irvine, and "Adamson," the librarian.
McGee also dined. These people were as

good as a play at dinner. "Adamson" began saying he knew General Doyle thirty years ago (he burrs the *r* of thirty so). " I beg your pardon," said General Doyle, " That was my elder brother," whispering to me that he never had one. "Adamson," in his grave voice, took up the joke, and said more about "your elder brother," ditto Col. Irvine. General Doyle said it would never do to make him out old at Halifax, "where I play the kitten." McGee was not in force, but told a few good stories. After dinner "Adamson" told Lord Lyons and me about his wife's grave at Montreal, where his boys were buried. Then I proposed our playing "Old Maid." Lord L. said he delighted in it. Some of the gentlemen played whist, but Lord L. preferred our game. We ended by playing "grab," and we all got rather wild and excited.

Tuesday, 27th.—Up to 8.30 breakfast, and off at nine for our steamer, the *Queen Victoria*. We had a most lovely day on the river, very hot and bright. I read the paper, talked and slept on deck; the gentlemen played "ship quoits" (see my journal of the *Asia*). We read in a Quebec paper that Lord A. was come out as ambassador to the Confederate States; this caused much fun. That night we had an alarm that the enormous fat stewardess was intending to sleep in *our* cabin (I mean Mrs. G.'s and mine). She had a great big boy whom she said *must* sleep with her; we said we would not stand it, and we made a row about it. The gentlemen were very kind. Lord A. proposed that Mr. M. should sleep in his cabin, and that the woman should have Mr. M.'s cabin. It ended by Mr. Malet settling to sleep in Captain Pem.'s cabin, and giving his up to "Fatima," as I called her. Mrs. G. and I were in small cabins out of a large one, where slept the two maids. Lord A. and General Doyle took such an interest in the stewardess' row, calling down through the top window to know about it. Lord A. said, "Once you get her into Mr. Malet's cabin, lock her in, and don't let her out.". General Doyle said, "Shall I come at her, ma'am?" in Irish. I forgot to say that poor Mr. Sheffield was ill, and was left in bed at Spencer Wood. We arrived at "Three Rivers" that night before dinner, and Dick instantly received a most quaint letter from a Mr. Lanigan, respectfully asking the G. G. and party to patronize some games on the 29th at the town of "Three Rivers." We parted with dear Gen. Doyle that night;

he went on to Montreal by the boat from "Three Rivers," to visit "our Fenwick," as he said. He was most amusing all day till he *would* write letters in the cabin. When Dick played the "ship quoits" badly, he said to me, "Oh, *me* husband!" with a rich brogue.

Wednesday, 28th.—Up ever so early, to very early breakfast, after which several waggons arrived at the wharf, and off we set! The first one had three horses (one small one in front and two fat big ones behind); in it went the G. G., Lord A., and Mrs. Godley, with Captain Pem. on the box. Then came the bridal one with two fat white steeds, in which went Lord Lyons, Mr. Malet, and I. In the third, Col. Gordon (who I forgot to say came with us), and Mr. Godley, with Dick on the box; and lastly came Lord L.'s Italian valet, and the Board of Works servant. Oh, can I ever express the roads! The horses had no blinkers, and we had a little boy to drive us, but he drove *so* well. Sometimes one wheel was on a bank, and the other very low down in sand, the roads were so narrow over corduroy bridges (made of trees laid together), with no rail on either side, through streams, up two awful hills, and down two dittos, through woods and what are called *dirt* roads, which means *no* roads! Altogether I need not try to describe it—it is useless. Of course I was much afraid. Sometimes we had to cling to the sides of the waggons to keep our seats. Lord Lyons was most delightfully agreeable, and the twenty-five miles passed over in very quick time. I asked him if he objected to my squealing out every minute, and he said, "No; it is much better to cry out when you are afraid, than to keep it to yourself, and I don't mind being pinched moderately." But I said I would not pinch him. He was in bliss at getting out of the ship. We saw a circus advertised in the town, and he proposed our going to it. He told me he loved a circus better than any- thing—that he went twenty-five days running to a circus in Italy, and always to see the same things done. We talked a great deal about books. Lord L. loves children's books. He and Mr. Malet both love "Cranford" so much that they always travel about with a copy of it. Mr. Seward asked Lord L. to go out to *market* with him one day, and he said, "I certainly should have gone, only I feared to show my ignorance!" He told me a great deal about the American Epis- copal Church, which is very much like ours.

Well! to return to our journey—at last we came through some exquisite woods, all bright red and yellow with the autumn tints, till, at the foot of a very steep hill, the lovely blue river St. Maurice burst upon our view, surrounded by these exquisite red and yellow woods, and with some curious yellow sands in the middle of the river. It was all like fairyland. No one can imagine the *red* woods who has not seen them; but you can judge a little by the leaves I send you. It was like what would be called in a pantomime, "The fairy forest glade, and the river with the golden sands." We all arranged beforehand what exclamation we were to make, when we saw the Falls. Lord L. proposed that one should say "Jee-rusalem," and Mr. Malet was to say "Golly." I think I was to say "Oh, *my!*" A Board of Works man met us, and conducted us to an enormous barge, so big that chairs were put into the bottom of it for us all. It was like pictures of real flat-bottomed barges painted dull reddy-brown, and rowed by men standing up, with gigantic oars. It held all our party, and several boatmen, and we had room for many more; so you can fancy the size. We rowed across this heavenly river, with the coloured trees down to the water's edge, to a bank, where we disembarked, and our barge was tied to a tree. So lonely was it that we left our wraps in the boat with no one to look after them. The boatmen all landed also. We then scrambled through this primeval forest till the Falls of Shawenigan suddenly came in sight, to our intense admiration and astonishment. Oh, they are most beautiful, immensely broad, and such a body of water coming down from the two blue rivers above. No words of mine can describe it all. Lord L. and Dick took off their boots and stockings, and scrambled bare-footed to a rock crossing part of the water, and were even more surprised than at first seeing it. Lord L. has travelled much, but he says he never saw a more exquisite view than that day. In this wild lonely place the Mayor of "Three Rivers" built an enormous three-storied and verandahed hotel, but it proved a bad speculation, for it is abandoned and looks most ghostlike, uninhabited and unfinished in the midst of this wild place. When we had feasted our eyes on the Falls, and picked leaves, we went to our grand lunch laid on a table made with boards by the servants and boatmen. The sun was burning hot, and the day perfection, though it began with rain; indeed, it was so hot that Lord L.'s Italian servant kindly held an umbrella over my head at lunch, and then made a tent with sticks and Mr. M.'s railway-rug to protect me from the sun. This Italian Joseph was a most gallant gentleman! After lunch Dick, Col. Gordon, and I strayed to the hotel, and had a grand view from the top storey, very weird and giddy it was. There were no window-panes in the windows, and the stairs were only planks. By going to the hotel we missed our party, and I did not see the "wood slides," which made me very cross. Dick left us, and Col. G. and I returned to the boat together, where we waited half an hour for our party, sitting on a bank. We then re-embarked in our barge, and had a lovely row down the river to "The Greys," a village where the carriages met us. It is called "The Greys" from the bits of grey rock seen everywhere about. We saw some very pretty Falls there, small ones, and we also saw some saw-mills worked by water, and some wood slides, very interesting, but I have not time to explain the process. The slides are used to slide down the great pieces of wood into the water, which carried them to a place called a *boom*. We shot a rapid on the St. Maurice, at the end of our six-miles' row, but our barge was so big, and the rapid so small, we scarcely felt it. We were amused by all the people of the village flocking out, open-mouthed and open-eyed, to see our party. They all bowed to the G. G. We got into the carriages again, and drove to the ship. It was horrible, worse than going, because it was dark. Once we were nearly upset over a precipice, because carts were in the way. I was terrified, and squeaked out lustily, but would not pinch Lord L. He told them afterwards that I was quite angry with Mr. Malet, because he did not ask the boy more than once every minute how many miles it was, if he could see, and if he had ever driven there before. Mr. M. was so good about asking. We talked and sang, and Lord L. repeated poetry. The stars were most exquisite, and the sunset eastern. One funny story Lord L. told me I must tell. Mr. ―― (a queen's messenger) is very pompous and grand in his way of talking. When he got to Niagara the noise drove him so wild he said to the waiter at the hotel, "Will this *daam'd* thing never stop?" evidently wishing it to be *turned off* for him. Lord L. told me the roads are so bad at Washington that driving in the streets there, he has been bonneted in his own brougham with the bumping! When we arrived at the ship, Doménique had a display of fireworks which he was letting off. They were very pretty, but rather dangerous. Lord A. left us per Montreal steamer that night. It always touches at " Three Rivers."

Next morning, 29th (Thursday), we returned to Quebec. It was very rough and cold, and the ship bumped about a good deal. The river was very rough, and the waves dashed up several times on the ship. Lord L. says when he is an Emperor he will only travel in a beautiful boat, pulled on by horses on a smooth canal. Had we stayed below we should have been sick. We all sat together in a sheltered part of the deck. We carried away a bit of the pier in getting up to the wharf. We found Mr. Sheffield quite well again. If you could hear Lord L.'s odd, grave, inquiring way of saying these things you would laugh as much as I am now laughing because I said, "A new animal has bitten my throat," and as I scoffed at the idea of its being a mosquito, Lord L. said, " Oh, dear! was it a tiger?" in the gravest way possible.

Friday, 30*th*.—The G. G. wished us and Capt. Pem. to go with Lord L., etc., to

St. Anne's, a very beautiful place near here. Neither he nor Mr. G. could come, and Mrs. G. would not leave Mr. G. We were on board the *Queen Victoria* at ten a.m. The day was lovely and calm after a hurricane and rain-storm all night. A sailor had been drowned just after we left the ship on Thursday, by falling off our ship and being sucked under before help could reach him. How dreadful! We went three hours down the river till we came opposite the great high hill of St. Anne, covered with red and yellow woods. The banks of the river were beautiful with tints, and Montmorençi Falls were fuller of water than Capt. Pem. had ever seen them. After lunch we landed in boats with some difficulty from the swamps, and the mud was so terrible on the road to the hotel that one of my goloshes—"gums" as the Yankees say— stuck in it, and my boot was wet through, so I had to get into a gig, and drive to the hotel, where I dried my boot. This gig consisted of the roughest back seat of a carriage on high wheels — *remember* this description! Then we got into a calache, even a worse form of conveyance than the last-named; it is like pictures of noddies in woodcuts; it has leather springs, so that

ST. ANNE'S FALLS.

it shakes horribly and dances up and down. The other gentlemen walked by a short cut to the Falls, whilst Dick and I drove; he held me round the waist with one arm, and with the other hand held my hand. I was more afraid even than at Shawenigan, and in my fear forgot all my French, and could not scold the man for going so quick. He said he did not know the way, so he got a boy to show him along. A four-wheeled conveyance could not have gone on such roads — hills like the side of a house, down the middle of which had been a torrent of rain and a slip, a tree trunk laid in the middle of the road, holes, ruts, and horrors of every sort. I sprang squealing out and walked as far as I could. Every time we came to a great jerk the springs gave, so that we were often nearly on the road, and were sometimes thrown off our seats. The horse at last happily could go no further, and was tied to a tree in the wood. We were met by a very fine-looking Irish 17th soldier, who was on outpost duty, and had been sent by the gentlemen to show us the way. Then came the scramble—the soldier preceding me to tear up little trees and break branches for me. The usual pathway was covered with water, as the Falls were fuller than they ever had been of water, so I had to scramble where no one goes, much to the soldier's grief. He evidently thought me a sort of wonder, and Mr. S. said the man did not care what any one liked, except what was nicest and easiest for me. I got on beautifully. They were suprised at me, sinking through rotten trees, slipping, catching and swinging *à la singe* by trees and branches. I got down at last, and was well rewarded by the grand Falls, the highest, except Montmorençi, we have seen yet, but not nearly so broad as the Chaudière or Shawenigan. We gazed at them for some time, the boy and the driver forming part of the party, and we were all truly delighted with them. The rocks are very fine and high. You must roar to make yourself heard, the noise of the rushing water is so great. Having feasted our eyes, we set about our return journey, which was even more difficult than our journey there. The soldier helped to pull me up the bank of trees and leaves and loose stones, etc. The last bit was done in a peculiar way : Lord L. sat upon a bank holding Mr. Malet's coat-tails, he held Captain Pem., who gave me his hand, and dragged me up with a run; Lord L. was the engine to this long train! Dick, Mr. S., and the soldier stayed at the bottom to catch me if I fell. The downhill calèche drive was miserable work, and I was truly thankful when we got to a ridgy field, for that was the best part of our most wretched and horrible road. The row boat seemed a haven of rest, and the steamer a paradise. She looked very nice with all her lights as we rowed up; the sunset and starlight were wonderful, and the aurora behind the high hill was fine. There seem to be hundreds more stars here than at home, and they seem much brighter. We had a merry dinner talking over our day, and after dinner we sat on the servants' deck and looked at the sailors, firemen, and men-servants dancing to a fiddle and an accordion, so well played, the fiddle played by a fireman. The sailors also sang choruses, "John Brown," etc. They sang one lovely chorus about "Ma barque est fragile." They had fine voices, and sang in unison, which always sounds well with many voices. The Board of Works' waiter (a French-Canadian) danced beautifully as a woman, and an Indian sailor danced a native dance, which appeared to consist in whipping himself, kicking, and screaming. Lord Lyons and

I then paced the deck while the nasty others had brandy and water in the cabin.

Saturday, October 1st.—The gentlemen (excepting Mr. Sheffield) were off before seven a.m. to see the Falls of St. Fêriole. I had gone through such misery the day before I would not go, and Mr. S. stayed with me. He was lazy, and I was very glad not to be left alone. He and the captain and I arranged a little trip for ourselves, which turned out to be terrifying fun to me. Conway was so ill. I let her come, also, for a change. We rowed very well for two miles in the boat, till we came to, oh, such mud, and we could not get near enough to the land, as the tide was *basse*, so the captain sent a sailor running through the water to the land to get us a conveyance to drive through the water in, as the boat was already aground. At last there appeared a "habitants" sleigh, on which one must stand upright. I said nothing would make me get on it, so I made Conway and the captain go on it together. Mr. S. had already jumped upon a man's back, and was rushing through the swamps to the dry land on his two legged steed. I then made a sailor carry me in his arms to a rock, and the captain then persuaded me to get into a sort of gig with him, like the one I told you of before; and he drove me through the swamps, whilst Conway got wearily along on her sleigh! Our horse was wicked, and had no mouth, and my terror was extreme. I could only hold on *by the reins*, and roar and shout! The captain had on a tall black hat for this "mud lark," and we must have looked a comedy sitting in this gig tearing along at the rate of a fire-engine, unable to stop ourselves, or rather our horse—sometimes the horse quite *sank* in the swamps— the captain cheering my frightened spirit with continual "ei, ei, ei," and "chuck, chuck," to the wild horse. When at last we were safely landed, I was so covered with wet mud that I had to take off my dress, and walk to the church in my petticoats! leaving my dress to be dried in a shanty, the girls in the shanty rushing to look through my eye-glass as if it was a wonder. We then walked to the Church, which is very old, and celebrated for a relic of St. Anne, which is honoured and prayed to, and the lame are cured. The Church is full of crutches hung up to show the results of the cure; but Mr. S. and I looked well at them, and they are quite clean and unused. Some of the "Ex-voto" pictures would make you die of laughing; in one a ship is represented sinking in what are supposed to be *waves*, but look exactly like a *flock of sheep*. Another is a rescue from shipwreck, the rescuers dressed in red coats and cocked hats, and the rescued in mob caps. Our return journey was better. We got a haycart, and in it I sat on a chair, the captain standing beside me, arm-in-arm with me, to keep me from falling; but sometimes, if the horse stuck in the swamps, he fell on me! Mr. S. and Conway followed in a gig. We all drove into the river to the boat, and so we at last got back safely to the ship. The rest of our party soon after returned, having been obliged to get to the row boat by means of a smaller boat in which they *shot* down the mud banks one by one! They all entered the ship in their stockings, carrying their boots in their hands! The sight they presented was too funny. We then had a grand lunch and much laughing. Something in our boiler burst, so we steamed half speed, and got back to Quebec only in time for tea. Sunday was wet in the morning. Went to church in afternoon.

Monday, October 3rd.—We are off to Montmorençi, so good-bye. We have great work arranging our long journey. Lord L.

leaves it most kindly to Mr. Sheffield and me to do as we like, and we change our plans every two minutes. After lunch we drove to Montmorençi Falls in the carriage and four—Mrs. Godley, Lord Lyons, Mr. Malet, and I. Mr. Sheffield and Dick up behind. The Falls were very fine; some of us went the unusual side, and had a beautiful view of all the country round; Quebec in the distance. Dinner-party according to enclosed list. The two English T. G.'s (travelling gents), Mr. Ashbury and Mr. Chadwick, brought letters from Lord Granville; both say they are going to have seats in the new Parliament. Ballantine dined and was great fun. He says I do everything for effect, and that he wondered I didn't go off without saying anything, in the *Peruvian*, that morning, September 3rd. I like Madame Tessier, and she amuses me. The people here have swarms of children. Mr. Rose, at Montreal, wants to know Lord L.'s movements, that he may give him a dinner, so he telegraphed to say we were with him. Col. Conolly is going to lend Lord L. his carriage at Montreal, and I am to drive in it with him. Mr. John A. Macdonald (or J. A. M., as we call him for short) told me last night that they are going to give a grand ball here to the delegates from the Maritime Provinces on Friday, so, having made all our plans, Lord L. offered to undo them so as to let me get back for the ball, which will be an interesting occasion here. Is he not kind? and although Mr. S. had telegraphed all the plans to the Legation about letters, now all is undone, and we do not go to Ottawa as we intended. The G. G. is going to have a Drawing-room, which, to my great annoyance, I shall miss. Lord L. says we are to be photoed in a group at the Falls of Niagara.

Tuesday, 4th.—We are off to Montreal per four-o'clock boat to-day. In answer to a question in one of your letters, a Rink is an enclosed place where they skate, roofed in and warmed with fires, and at night lighted up. We are to go to the Cataract House at Niagara on the American side, as the Confederate people are met at the Clifton House, and Lord L. does not wish to seem to watch them.

St. Lawrence Hall, Montreal, Oct. 5th, Wednesday.—We left Quebec yesterday. Capt. King, Sir. Fenwick's A.D.C., came with us. We had great work having our food to ourselves, but at last we managed it, Lord L. sending Mr. S. on before to see that no one was just getting into bed when I came down, for the eating takes place in the bottom of the ship, where some of the men sleep! I saw some men in bed! We got our *Asia* letters just as we were leaving Quebec; great joy. To-day we came on here, and had breakfast in a private room; we also have a private sitting-room. Mr. Rose came and took Lord L. and me out to drive, also Mr. Goldwin Smith, who is now staying at this hotel; he is very clever and agreeable to talk to. I am glad to have met him. I told him before I crossed the Atlantic, I agreed with him about giving up the Colonies, and wished then that I knew him. He is a democrat! We went to see Lady A. Russell, and then took a pretty drive to the cemetery, which looks lovely with the autumn tints. Mr. G. S. did not like this bright-looking churchyard. He said death was so gloomy that only cypress and yews were suitable for a churchyard, not bright flowers. We drove back to lunch here, and Mr. G. S. went off to Boston. He feared to stay here, as he was near being pelted in the streets. After lunch we unsettled our whole journey, and did it up again. I believe, after all, we do go to Ottawa. Dick was playing racquets all the afternoon with Capt. King. We then drove out in Mr. Rose's carriage again—Mr. Rose, Lord L., Mr. Malet, and I. I went to see Mrs. Carter (vide *Asia* journal), and then we went to see some military games, and hear the 30th and Rifle Brigade bands play. It was very pretty seeing the tilting at rings on horseback. Sir Fenwick joined us later ; it was a heavenly day, and the sight was gay — swarms of people and uniforms. Captain Seymour is at Ottawa with Mrs. and Miss Rose and a party, where we have telegraphed to him to meet us. We are to have a "special car." I am dressing for Mr. Rose's dinner, so excuse haste.

Cataract House, Niagara Falls, State of New York, U.S., Saturday Night, Oct. 8th, '64.—Mr. Malet made me put this long address ! We arrived here a few hours ago, after a most long and tedious journey. We have been "on the go" ever since Tuesday, and I am not a bit tired or sleepy. We have arrived in bitter cold wintry weather, and there is snow on the ground. I received your most welcome letters here to-night, sent on from Quebec. Now I must try to tell you of our very very long journey, and of Mr. Rose's dinner-party at Montreal. I am writing like a servant on paper with lines with a picture on the top; but I meant you to see where we are, and I have green ink, If you could *hear* the incessant *roar* of the marvellous rapids of *the* Falls of the world, you would be quite bewildered, and not wonder that my letter is full of mistakes and blunders. I must tell you about Mr. Rose's party now. It consisted of ourselves (five in all), Sir F. Williams and A.D.C., Lord and Lady Alexander Russell, Captain Northey (60th Rifles), Commodore M., and Miss E., Mr. Rose and his two eldest boys, the head of the Grand Trunk Railway, and Major W., 60th. I went in with Lord Lyons, and had Lord A. Russell on my other side. I laughed all dinner-time. Sir F. asked us most kindly to stay with him on our way back (he has taken General Lindsay's house), but we can't go, as we are in such a hurry. I entered the carriage with my hood over my head, Lord L. carrying my wreath! Next morning (Wednesday) we were up at five, had breakfast at six, and were off *in* the train to La Chine at seven. La Chine is near Montreal, and there we embarked in the *Prince of Wales* steamer for Ottawa. The boat is so nice and clean. We passed St. Anne's, where "they sang at St. Anne's their evening hymn." After being a few hours in the boat, we had to get out, and go in a train. At the wharf we met Mrs. Rose and party, and heard from Captain Seymour that, alas! he could not come with us, as he goes home next week. We went a short way in the train. We passed through little woods; the autumn tints made them look so pretty. Then we got into another ship, even nicer, larger, and, if possible, more clean than the last. It is called the *Queen Victoria*. The captains of both steamers were civil and nice. We were so hungry, and we had a most excellent English dinner —roast beef and plum-pudding! The captains remembered Lord Lyons with the Prince of Wales, and treated him with homage. I sat next to the captain at dinner, and Lord L. next to me; then a gap, and then the servants! The river Ottawa is a most curious, wild, and very pretty river, quite deserted-looking, with red and yellow tinted trees coming down to the water's edge; there are also many little islands in the river, covered with red and yellow bushes and rockwork. The day was cold, wet, and dreary. We stopped at quantities of places on the way, some of them just like the wildest pictures; one in particular we remarked was exactly like Eden, in " Martin

Chuzzlewit"—a wild lonely pathway or road, one house that looked like a forge, wild red and yellow trees and rocks, and wood piled up, two white horses waiting near a cart, and one old woman and child walking up to the forge; one or two men completed the desolate picture. The rain made everything twice as lonely. I dare say it looks quite different in summer. We passed the old French château, where lives the ex-rebel Papineau, now become quite loyal. He has lovely gardens to this château and a small chapel close to him. I believe he sent a bouquet to the Prince of Wales when he was travelling here. We read and talked by turns all day, till late, when a Thunder-storm came on—terrific rain and great lightning and some Thunder, and the ship was wooden! I was so terrified, and walked up and down the saloon till I was tired, pinching Dick all the time. You know I never can sit down when I am afraid. Lord L. laughed at me so, and the captain tried to quiet me with religious words, but I was in despair till it was over. We stopped at about fifty small places on our way, sometimes *one* passenger got out and sometimes *one* got in, and there was a great deal of pig-iron thrown on shore, with a terrific noise, and when there were any inhabitants they all flocked down as if no boat had ever been there before, and there was shouting and screaming. The men about here are a very fine, stalwart, handsome set. These boats, I believe, are rarely known to reach Ottawa or Montreal in time ; I can't make out why ! We reached Ottawa in torrents of rain at seven p.m., but the storm was over. I, on the arm of Captain Bowie, entered the 'bus ! and we drove to the Russell House (Hotel). There we were treated with great homage. We were much disgusted with the squalid look of Ottawa, though we only saw it by lamplight, which was scarcely any light, such *wretched* gas. The streets were so rough, like dirt roads. I went on wondering how we ever could live * there, when the seat of Government is moved there. The enormous signs over the shops amused us; just opposite to our room at the hotel hung an enormous boot. Lord L. begged Mr. Sheffield to go out and buy it, as he said he wanted boots. We had an early supper, and went to bed about nine, and were up at 5.30 next day.

Thursday, October 6th.—I was too tired to sleep that night till towards morning ; besides, there was a hurricane, and torrents of rain.

* I little knew how very very happy I should be there, after all.

OTTAWA CITY.

Lord L. got up at four! After eating a mouthful of breakfast, Dick, Mr. S., and I walked out to see the Houses of Parliament, which are building. Lord L. and Mr. M. were out long before. We went over part of the Houses, but they are in the most unfinished state conceivable, and in front of them nothing but mud and dirt. They will be very magnificent, built of grey stone, with a good deal of pink mixed; the architecture a sort of French Gothic. We saw the sun rise on them, making them all pink. We saw the Chaudière Falls in the distance. They do not look so pretty as our Quebec Chaudière. We then returned to the Hotel. We found a flag flying in front of it in honour of Lord Lyons, and the mayor and corporation wanted to come and pay their respects; but we all left by 7.30 a.m. train, which had been delayed half an hour for us. We had a "special car" for our party and the servants, and were very snug. They put about our arrival in the Ottawa paper, and said that "*this distinguished party*" were staying at the Russell House, and were going to inspect the Houses early and then leave. We were a few hours in the train till we came to the steamer *Grecian*. It was larger than any steamer we had yet been in;

it also had been detained half an hour for us. The scenery in the train was not pretty after starting from Ottawa. Rideau Hall, the future Government House, is some way from the town. We all groaned over Ottawa; it looks as if it was at "t'other end of nowhere," and we felt so out of the way. The Hotel was clean but third-rate, and the food looked and tasted uncivilized. When we got out of the "cars" to get into the ship, the people were all looking out for Lord Lyons; and I heard them wondering which he was. I think I was rather a puzzle, as I leant on his arm, and they knew he had no wife. He was so funny on board the ship. There is one large cabin in all these boats, which Lord L. says is called "the nuptial cabin." Mr. Sheffield took it for himself, and locked himself in to take a quiet sleep. It was blowing a gale when we got into the steamer at Prescott, the clouds looked most awfully wild and lurid. The river St. Lawrence was very rough, but it got smoother when we came to the Lake of the Thousand Islands. It is very pretty, in some places extremely pretty, when you come to a large number of these rocky and wooded islands together, and have to steer between them; but in general they are not so pretty as the

Ottawa river islands. The autumn tints made everything look its best. We went to Kingston, which we reached about 5.30 p.m., too late to catch the train for Toronto. I vowed I would not stay in the steamer which crosses Lake Ontario, and is more than twelve hours crossing to Toronto, out of sight of land. This gives one some idea of the size of the lakes here! People are often sea-sick on these lakes. There is "a nasty chopping sea" generally, like the Channel. Lord L. also determined to leave the ship. We saw that there was some idea of making us go on in the ship, so he gave me his arm, and we ran off out of the ship, and got into a cab without waiting for any of them. I saw a man looking like a mayor on the wharf. Mayors and corporations and addresses were great dreads to Lord L. all through the journey. We drove off to the Hotel in one cab, and the others walked. We were ashamed to go into the Hotel till the others came, so we waited at a corner of the street. When I asked the "carter" where they were, he said, "I guess they are gone astray." At last they came, and then, after seeing our rooms, we sallied out to walk about the town. It was nearly six p.m. The town is prim and desolate-looking;

it is remarkable for a fine Lake Ontario view, *and* the number of panes of glass in every window. We walked on in the cold wind and gathering darkness to the lake point. You could never imagine the Lake to be anything but a sea—so rough and stormy and enormous. I jumped with joy to think we were not in the ship! On our way back to the Hotel we all, including Lord L., climbed up on a railing to see the *Grecian* pass, and were more thankful than ever to be on land, when we saw how she pitched. We stood there clinging to the railing till we saw a policeman coming, and were so afraid of being scolded that we jumped down and ran away! At the hotel we had a capital hot supper in a long, low room. At these meals Lord L. and I always fought about the dry toast, which we both liked so much, and which in trans-Atlantic hotels is always so excellent. Lord L. always said before going into meals, " Now, let us go in state," giving me his arm all through the house. After supper I went to bed about eight. Lord L. told me if he did not get one night's rest, he would be ill, so he and Mr. Sheffield slept that night at Kingston, while Mr. M., and Dick, and I went on at 3.30 a.m.!! to Toronto and

Niagara. We got up in the dead of night, dressed, and drove two miles to the train in torrents of rain. I could not sleep much with fuss and excitement. I felt like "the Wandering Jew," or the "steam leg." They wanted us to get into a sleeping-car, where Conway and I, "two ladies," as the conductor said, were to sleep in one bed! Dick and Mr. M. were to sleep in a second bed; but the smell of coal-oil and suffocation was so stifling, and the heat so great, we preferred the day car, except Mr. Malet, who can sleep in a furnace, and ventured into this "hot bed." We slept very tolerably with our feet up on the bench opposite to us, and I felt quite fresh when we stopped at Coburg for breakfast. We got cold mutton-chops, tasting of *sheep and wool*, and delicious poached eggs, and bad coffee. We then went on to Toronto, which we reached at eleven, and had to wait an hour there. It was a wet day, and we could not walk about the town, which seems to be a large one. We contented ourselves with looking at the titles of books on the stand—all of the most sensational kind—blood, murder, bigamy, etc. We got into another train then, and went on to Hamilton, where we had to wait one hour and a half; but there we had dinner. I was so ravenous, I eat first roast beef, then hot boiled mutton, because there was no more beef! The dinners you get at railway stations in Canada are so much better than what you get when you are travelling at home. The station-house is a nice English-looking one, and you see cultivation about Toronto and Hamilton that you see nowhere else in Canada. The soil is good, and the meat excellent; quite different from what you get in Lower Canada. Conway sat next me at dinner; and, so dirty were the men opposite to me, that I could not look at them. They were third-class passengers, and their hands were perfectly black with dirt. After dinner the rain had stopped, so Dick and I walked as far as we could about the deserted, clean, airy town. We looked into the large, fine-looking R.C. Cathedral. We then took up another train, and went on to the Suspension Bridge, Niagara Falls. From the bridge you get a splendid view of the Falls, at least it is *said* to be a first-rate view, but, I must own, the bridge view disappointed me a little; but I will tell of my second view further on. Then we had to wait three-quarters of an hour for the train to take us only five minutes' distance, to the hotel on the American side.

Trying state of things, and very un-English! Our luggage passed through the Custom House without being examined. At last we found ourselves in the 'bus, on our way to the Hotel, shivering in snow and wind. This Hotel is enormous, and I often lose my way in it. It is very comfortable, except for the horrible stoves, which are a great *except*, my head suffers so from them. After our arrival, we went out in the snow to look at the Niagara curiosities, but all are so dear I don't think I shall buy anything. We then had supper, and were amused looking at the Yankee ladies in their many-coloured head-gear and shawls, and quantities of false hair in such structures. After supper I began my letter, and then, oh, the bliss of a good night's rest from 11.30 till near nine! But I find the excitement of travelling does me much good, and cures my head for the time. To-day I have suffered terribly, but on the journey I had no headache.

Sunday.—Lord Lyons meant to come on here to-night, but has not turned up; there are no steamers or trains on any part of Sunday. We expect him to-morrow. The servants asked Conway when "the lord" was coming. There is only an American Episcopal Church here. We were at breakfast when it began, and only found out about it when too late. Dick and Mr. Malet are gone to it to-night. After tea (at eight) my head aches too much to go. Conway was so ill to-day, she was quite miserable about herself. I thought yesterday she had the jaundice, which is going here. I made her send for the Yankee doctor of the hotel to-day. He says she has the jaundice. He is giving her a strong bitter, and says that she will be well in a few days. She is happier. She is better to-night, and I think the arrival of Lord L.'s "Thomas" will make her still better to-morrow. After breakfast to-day we walked out all round Goat Island, and we saw the Falls and rapids to perfection. I do not think I can attempt to describe them, but I suppose I must try to give you some idea of them. The best idea I can give you is, to say that when we returned and read the service, I could a thousand times better realize the goodness of that powerful God who made Niagara, and yet listens to our prayers. I almost felt as if I *must* say in the Litany, "Oh, Thou who madst Niagara, have mercy upon us." I say this in all reverence. It was better than any sermon, seeing what we saw to-day. The Falls are so magnificent, when you are close to them, and the rapids really too wonderful. The little bits of red colouring made everything look twice as beautiful. We dined to-day at the *table-d'hôte* at three, and were much amused with the Yankees. There are two or three pretty women, and one or two nice-looking men. There are several bridal couples; they look very loving. I looked into "the ladies' parlour" once or twice, and found the bridal couples walking up and down the room arm-in-arm, as hard as they could go, and talking confidingly to each other. In all Yankee and Canadian hotels there is a "ladies' parlour," with chairs all round the room—no table, a stove, a bad piano, a large jug full of iced water, and some tumblers. It is the same everywhere, I hear, from comparing notes and observation. The men are supposed to smoke and "liquor up" at the bar. We were waited on at dinner by niggers in white jackets and aprons. They are pleasant, funny creatures. Our rooms were *on* the rapids. When the windows were open, we could not hear ourselves speak, and when shut we were stifled from the stoves, and I felt as if my head was bound round with a band of iron. After dinner we went out to walk, and crossed in the horrid ferry to the Canadian side. The sunset was fine beyond expression: bright orange, crimson, yellow, pale blue, pink, grey, and purple were the colours of it, changing every moment; and, now the moon is shining over the rapids, it looks so beautiful. The moon is twice as bright out here as it is at home. We did all this side this morning, except the whirlpool and more rapids. I would not drive on Sunday, so we could not go to them. Oh, the giddiness of crossing bridges over the rapids! I rushed over with my hand over my eyes, and *would not* go to the tower in the midst of the Falls where Dick went. I felt as if I *must* rush after the rapids; it is a sort of feeling difficult to describe. The cold is too intense. One of the niggers came to us at dinner, and whispered that he had a prairie hen for our table—no one else was to have it. It was very good, and tasted, Dick said, like black cock. The Austrian Minister to Washington, Count Georgi, is here. He will, I fear, join our party when Lord L. arrives. I have waited for Dick to help me to make you imagine the Falls as to immensity. Imagine the water of the Channel half-way between Boulogne and Folkestone rushing over rugged rocks, and then falling over a height twice as high as Nelson's pillar in Dublin, and as broad as the width of Sackville Street, Dublin, twenty times multiplied! then boiling up from the bottom, the spray reaching as high above the top of the Falls as the water has fallen beneath. This is only a faint and quaint description of what no pen (especially a steel one) could describe. The body of water falling down is a mile in breadth.

Begun Cataract House, Niagara Falls, October 10th.—I over-walked myself to-day. Dick, Mr. M., and I walked to the whirlpool, hoping to drive back, but we could get no vehicle, and I nearly dropped from exhaustion. It is a very long walk, and the sun was very hot. Dick left me with Mr. M., leaning against a tree, and at last found a carriage. The whirlpool is well worth seeing, and very wonderful. All the waters from the Falls gather there, and make their way out to Lake Ontario. There is a handsome college for orphan boys near there. A lady died in this hotel this morning of a sort of jaundice, I believe. Conway is better and happier. This day is lovely and fine. Dick and Mr. M. were so amused with their sermon yesterday, which was interesting and good, but too familiar. The preacher spoke of God and Ahab as the "opposite parties," and stopped to spit in the sermon! There was a large red cross with I.H.S. on it. The service is very like ours, and they sang rather well. The housemaid here is Irish, but has been fifteen years in the States, and speaks like a Yankee; but she *loathes* the North, and told Conway how they deceive the wretched Irish, and get them into their armies. She said she wished she were a man, and she would fight for the South. This hotel has been kept up this season by the "shoddy" aristocracy, which means people who have made their money in bad ways by the war, selling bad cloth; and the housemaid complained that you see people now with watches and chains who, before the war, did not know how to sit on a chair! She also complained to Conway that the Duchess of Athol was very proud, she did not "converse" at all with her when staying at the hotel! I must tell you a story of Conway and a nigger, which Lord L. says is like the Christy Minstrels. He came to tell her tea was ready, and she said she would not be ready for a quarter of an hour —he was to come and fetch her. He said, "I advise you not to be so late as a quarter of an hour, you had better come in ten or fifteen minutes." Dick and Mr. M. went to the Cave of the Winds this morning. Very awful it is, and they went without a guide, as the man was away, which I am glad I did not know till after. You know it is a cave under part of the Falls, caused by a rock shelving out, and the water falling over it. " The currents of wind there are terrific, the noise deafening, and the spray blinding," says Dick. That morning Dick took a " current bath " in the hotel ; it is made by letting the rapids run through the bath by means of an open grating at each end. After lunch I walked a little way to see the sun on the Falls, and found Lord L. and Mr. Sheffield had arrived on my return. We were charmed to meet again. Count Georgi joined us at dinner. He asked Mr. M. why I wore the Order of the Medjidie, which was my Coldstream star brooch. He is going on to Quebec. After dinner all except myself went to see the Falls by moonlight. It was too cold, and my chest ached from over-walking, so I stayed at home.

Tuesday, 11*th.*—A lovely day. Lord L., Mr. M., and I got an open carriage very soon after breakfast, and drove over to the Canadian side, where we were joined by Dick and Mr. S., who went by ferry-boat. The carriages are so grand, and have a furskin in them to keep you warm. I would not let Lord L. go in the ferry-boat, because I should have been afraid, and you have to get to it in a sort of little tramway, running down a very steep inclined plane; but Lord L. said he had looked forward to going up and down in this all day long! I walked down by steps on Sunday. The path of the rapid where the boat crosses looked so rough and horrible to me. Lord L. had been at Niagara with the Prince of Wales, and had seen Blondin cross the rapids on the tight-rope. He never crossed the Falls; but the rapids were quite awful enough. When we got to the Canadian side, we were photoed in a group on the Table Rock about eighteen times. I will send you some when they are finished. It was very amusing being photoed. We are sitting on this Table Rock, with the Falls in the background. They will make you giddy when you see how near a precipice we were! When I thought of it after, it made me feel sick. Two different men did us—one an English Jew, the other a Yankee, and the jealousy of the men was funny. The Yankee said, "Now then, Mr. Lyons;" he also said to Dick, "Have you got your women together?" Dick's *women* being *myself*. Oh, how free they are! these Yankees. I bought some blue birds for you; they are

so cheap, only half a dollar apiece. After
the photoing was over, we drove to Mr.
Street's lovely place, and nice English house.
Lord L. sent in his card, and Mrs. Street
asked us all in. Mr. Street was in England.
She is his mother, and a sweet, kind old
lady, so pretty and ladylike. Two old maids
were with her on a visit—one a very meek,
cat-like old lady, the other (Miss White)
merry and bouncing. Lord L. had been
there with the Prince of Wales, and was
supposed to know the way to the Island Walk
(to which he had not gone that time with
the prince, however), so he was entreated to
show us the way, as the old ladies feared
wetting their feet. We all sallied out to see
the Island, where the rapids *rush* past you
in the walk, and make you giddy under
shaking bridges. It is very beautiful and
peculiar. Lord L. did *not* know the way,
and told me he feared *setting out* wrong
before Mrs. Street. Mr. Sheffield and I
were famished with hunger, and longed for
food, so I told Lord L. if he was offered
lunch he was *not* to refuse, because we were
hungry; he never eats lunch. I think Mr.
Street has not shown good taste in putting
fantastic seats about near the curious rapids
and among the wonderful underwood and

trees at the water's edge; it looks too like a tea-garden business. To our joy, on our return to the house, we found ginger cordial, wine, cakes, and fruit. We were so very cold, besides being hungry. I drank two glasses of ginger cordial, which, they afterwards said, ought to have made me tipsy; but I had no idea it was strong, and it did me no harm. We looked at the stuffed birds. In one case there is an enormous eagle, and a tiny humming bird shot close here. Miss White gave me some lovely autumn leaves, and, when they were questioning me about how I pressed them, Lord L. overheard me saying, "There is a *person* who does them for me" (meaning Captain Pem.), and Lord L. laughed well at this afterwards. I did not know he was listening to me. We took leave of the old ladies, and drove away to the "Burning Springs," a curious spring of sulphur water, which takes fire when a lighted match is put to it, and burns like gas. Dick and Mr. M. put their pocket-handkerchiefs on it, and they did not burn, so it is a harmless flame. It was discovered by some Indians, who were so afraid they ran away from it. Lord L. said we had better go and see it, or we should be worried afterwards by people saying, "You missed seeing the best thing." We had another look at the Falls from the Canadian side; they are more and more beautiful and grand every time you look at them. The water in parts of them was of the deepest green!. The driver wanted us to be photoed for the third time at another photographer's, "where you can be taken with a splendid view of the hotels in the background." We drove back as we came, over the Suspension Bridge, one of the wonders of the world! It is over the rapids; but I must wait till I ask Dick about its length, and how many hundred wires it took to fasten it to the rocks. They made us pay duty on our photos done on the Canadian side. The man was so afraid when he heard from the driver just too late that it was Lord Lyons. Conway and Lord Lyons's servants had themselves photoed in a group also. The sunset was so lovely. After late dinner, which Lord L. insisted on having instead of at two, we all, except Mr. S., went out to see the lunar rainbows over the Falls—very curious and grand; but I felt so *eerie* on Goat Island, among the Falls and rapids in the dark, that I ran away from the rainbows. How Lord L. laughed when I said I have an aunt who would not stay alone in a room with the moon for anything.

I meant moonlight; but, of course, my words were not ever forgotten, Lord L. getting into fits of laughing often, speaking of "a tête-à-tête with the moon." Some of the photos came that night, and we had great work choosing. I was given the first choice. Lord L. said, "Of course we think them all bad — everybody thinks themselves better looking than they are."

Montreal, Thursday, October 13*th.*—Here we are, rather tired, having left Niagara yesterday at 9.30 a.m. We were so very sorry to say "good-bye" to each other. Lord L. said he hoped we should be late for the train. We travelled for twenty-four hours in the train from Niagara to Montreal. The scenery is mostly flat, and not pretty, and it rained on and off. The Customs officer was so civil when he found out Dick's name, and made *me* come and rest in his room. None of the trains this side the Atlantic *connect*, so we had to wait every now and then an hour or more, and they are all always after their time. I know nothing more irritating than travelling in this country—what with the trains missing "connection," and the spitting. We had a very good dinner at Hamilton—roast beef, potatoes and butter, cabbage, apple pie, beer, and cheese. I give you our bill of fare to show how much more civilized the food is than what you get in civilized England, where you rush in at stations to get old and cold soup, and very horrid sandwiches. At Toronto we "embarked aboard the sleeping cars," where they can't spit much because there is matting, and they are not allowed. We were more comfortable than the others, as no one was allowed to sleep over us. I must tell you of the vulgar people who got in there and amused us so. This is what I made out about them by likenesses and conversations. Two canny Scots (men) had evidently married two Irish girls; all had made their fortunes out here, and one couple were just married, and were going to Scotland. The men looked like bricklayers in their Sunday best, the ladies wore feathers in small hats, and talked with stingy fine brogues, which sounded delicious after the Yankee twang. "Maggie" was the bride, and "Sally" was the sister come to see her off. There were promises of writing from Montreal and Quebec, and talks of photos. Sally's husband said, "Remember me to all inquiring friends in the old country, and tell me if there is room for me there." The newly married were to go first to Liverpool in the *Peruvian,* and then to Ardrossan. At last, after a hundred vulgar jokes, the sisters fell on each other and kissed, and the bride cried. "None of your *gum-sucking,*" said Sally's husband. Then they parted, Maggie's husband telling them not to pay their cab back, as he had paid it. Then they talked out of the window to each other, and then Sally was called "Sarah" in a more stingy and fine brogue than before, and Sally said to the bridegroom, "Won't you make Maggie laugh?" and he vowed he would make her "roar." Then she was made to look out to show she had done crying, and she sighed, and wiped her eyes under her small hat like a kitchen-maid. It was all so natural it interested me, and I felt for them. When we were off, Maggie said it was hot, and the man said, "It's better than to have you getting cold," and he put his red hand and arm round her *neck,* and sat petting her for some time, and got quite sentimental! She was rather well-looking; he was red and hideous. At last, seeing my eye-glass levelled at her, she undid herself from the man's embrace, and said, "I am tired of this position;" she seemed, however, to like him much. They talked over their family, etc., till it was late or dark, and then they went to bed, and, oh, that was a horrid sight! Off went the man's coat, waistcoat, braces, and boots, and then they tucked themselves into bed. We had no curtains, and only cloaks for bed-clothes, so we were lucky; but these wretches tucked the curtains all round them. Ugh! Trying to sleep was not easy; the shaking was something I could not describe, and we seemed to go on for five minutes and then stop; it seemed as if we were shunted off on to another line every few moments, and every time we stopped I awoke. We stopped in the night for supper, and had fish, chicken, and potatoes. We were not sorry to arrive at Montreal. We breakfasted at the St. L. Hall. Then Dick went to see Captain Seymour, and we were invited to dine at Col. Conolly's, where Captain Seymour is now living. We drove out in pours of rain to see Miss Rose. We also went to see Sir Fenwick, who is settled in General Lindsay's house. He showed us all over the house. We finished our day by dining with Colonel C. and Captain S. After dinner, in the twilight and cold, we two and Captain Seymour drove off to the wharf, and embarked in the *Europa* for Quebec.

Spencer Wood, October 14*th*.—We arrived

here all right to-day. We were late in arriving, because of the fog, but I slept tolerably well on board. Crowds of people were on board going to the delegates' ball to-night. My friend Maggie and her bridegroom I found in the ship. We all had much laughing here over our different stories. The dresses at the Drawing-room were much improved; some wore feathers. George Augustus Sala dines here to-night. We dine at seven, and then go to the ball. Captain Seymour goes home in the *Peruvian* to-morrow.

Saturday, October 15*th.*—My room feels so snug after the stovey hotel rooms. I have double windows, warm red curtains, and an enormous fire all day long. There dined last night Mr. Chandler, who is a Minister from New Brunswick, Mr. Johnson, Attorney General of (I believe) the same place, Mr. G. A. Sala, Mr. Livesay (I believe a writer for *Punch*), Gordon the Good, and Major Brice. I went in with Mr. Chandler, who amused me much. Sala was rather amusing. His bows to us were worthy of a courtier. He speaks like a book, and says "garments" and "nay, nay," instead of "no, no." I showed our Niagara groups. He said to me, "Your *pose* is most graceful, madam." I said I thought I looked very cross, whereupon he answered, " Nay, nay, madam." Mr. Chandler got quite excited over it, wanting to see Lord Lyons's portrait. He observed that " I did not look myself in it; I looked serious." He had never seen me before, so I don't think he was much of a judge. In wind and rain we set off for the ball. We were received by the Ministry in the speaker's room. Some were in grand official uniforms. The G. G. and Mr. Godley looked very nice in theirs. This ball, you know, was given in the Parliament House by the Ministry to the delegates from the Maritime Provinces, who are come here to arrange about a United Kingdom of Canada. The Maritime Provinces mean Nova Scotia, New Brunswick, Newfoundland, and Prince Edward's Island. It was arranged that I was to follow the G. G. with the Prime Minister, Sir E. Taché, and to dance the first quadrille with him, but Sir E. is so very old that he can't dance, and he would not take me in for fear of having to dance with me, so he walked in first alone; then came the G. G., then John A. with me, and then Cartier and Mrs. Godley. " God save the Queen " was played, and we marched up to the throne in procession. Sir R. M. and wife (Gov.

of ——) came very late. Between their being late, and old Sir E. hiding behind a screen to escape from me, the first quadrille was upset. The G. G. danced with Madame Cartier, and I with a New Brunswick Minister, Colonel Grey by name. The Ministers were very angry about my being left without my proper partner, and made apologies; but poor Sir E. is about seventy, so I think he was right to hide! I made acquaintance between the dances with Lady M. and with Mrs. Jervoise, who came out here for ten weeks with her husband, and they were nearly lost at sea! She is very pleasing and handsome. Lady M. is also pretty. The G. G. then introduced me to Sir R. M. He asked me to walk about with him and have some refreshments, so off we went. He wore a red riband and order. Well, this old king and I wandered on and on for a long time. A vulgar waiter ran after us and said, " Do you want to go upstairs, sir ? " meaning the servants' gallery, upon which my friend waved him off and went on. With difficulty I at last got an ice, and then we lost ourselves quite, and found at last that we were seated under the wrong throne, in the wrong room! This all took up some time, and when we at last found the right

THE DELEGATES' BALL.   177

room, I danced with Dr. Tupper, Prime Minister of Nova Scotia. The 25th string-band played in one of the rooms; it is a lovely band. When supper was announced, Sir R. M. wanted me again; but it was decreed that Sir E. Taché was to take me. We walked in procession. Sir E. proposed the Queen's health. After supper I danced a quadrille with Sir R. He talked a good deal about "the French element," which, looking at Madame Duval dancing, he said it was delightful to see. He and his wife had been out moose hunting; he said unfortunately he had not shot one animal the ten days he was out. We call Lady M. "La reine Blanche." Captain Seymour came to the ball with us; he was almost the only young man I danced with. Sala was not seen at the ball, though he was said to be there. Sir E. Taché is the only non-dancing old man here—wigs, spectacles, and grey hairs don't hinder people from dancing. We came home early. That Mr. Chandler who took me in to dinner told me a great deal about the happiness of slaves, and how miserable they are when emancipated. He says slaves are treated like servants, and well cared for, and they adore their masters. After dinner, I forgot to say, I asked Sala to write his autograph in my book. He just wrote his name—"only this, and nothing more." He said he could not write anything else! To-day Captain Seymour left early per *Peruvian*. We are so sorry he is gone. The Godleys left also for their own home. I went out to drive, covered by a buffalo robe, it is so very very cold. I paid visits, and brought Dick and F. B. home with me.

Sunday, 16*th*.—A wet day. Went to afternoon service in waggon. There are waterproof curtains to the waggon, which can be put down, and one is kept quite dry.

Monday, 17*th*.—Dick and I, and Captain Pem. are going, I hope, to-night to a "drum" at Judge Meredith's.

Tuesday, 18*th*.—After lunch yesterday, Dick and I tried to walk to the village; but the wind was so great I could not face it; the day was dark and damp. The G. G. dined with the Godleys, and Captain Pem. with the 17th, so we dined alone, and went to the "drum" at Judge Meredith's. There was a very large party, and the house is large. I was much amused, and talked to many people, among others to M. Duvergier d'Hauraune, a young Frenchman, who is come over here to travel, and has brought a letter to the G. G. from Lord Clarendon. His father was a well-known man in France under Louis Philippe. My friend, Sir R. M., rushed to me, and asked me to *walk about* with him, and invited us to Government House at H., which he told me was much finer and larger than "Spencer's Wood." Lady M. and Dick flirted together for a long time; she is so pretty and pleasant. A Miss Tilstone sang—a handsome girl, with a pretty voice. Then a Madame Tachereau sang—good voice; and then *the* man sang, Mr. Harwood, an M.P.P., half French. He has a very fine voice, and is a pupil of Garcia's. He was offered an engagement at the Italian Opera, London. The large rooms were too small for his voice, which wants modulation. I got quite giddy with the loudness of it! He sang from operas; he wants expression and more teaching. Judge Meredith introduced him to me, and he sang again for me. My friend Madame Tessier (the Speaker's wife), asked us to a party she is giving on Wednesday night for us and the delegates. We did not stay very long at the party. We were in an open waggon, and the cold was intense. The home letters came very quick this time by the old *Damascus;* they were written the day after we went to Niagara, and we received them to-day. To-day is showery, and dark, and cold. Dinner-party according to enclosed list. Count Georgi took me in. He is a great aristocrat; is said by Mr. M. to wear a red shirt at dinner, and always; he wore a white one this time, but buttoned his coat over it, as if ashamed of it. He talked German, French, and English with me— English the most hard to me to understand. Some of his stories I pretended to understand, and made remarks according to his own faces, not having an idea what he was saying. He spoke fluently, but shut his mouth. He put down his knife and fork every time I spoke, so I feared he would never finish. He admires English women more than any other nation. He is from Sclavonia himself. He told me some rambling story about his staying with an archbishop somewhere, and shooting birds with a pistol, and he showed me the way he did it, shooting in the air, and saying, " Ei-ei-ei," to show each shot. This is a coherent (?) story, but more so than some that I caught. He says Mrs. Lincoln knows nothing about society, often keeping her company waiting while she finishes her toilette. He wants us to go to New York in spring; write him a line, and he is to receive us at the train, and give us a grand dinner, where the best people of New York are to be got to meet us. He told me the difficulty he has in getting a room at the hotels where he is not known. I think his embassy is at Washington; but he has so little to do that he generally lives at New York. After dinner we sang choruses. Count G. wanted to walk into the drawing-room after dinner with me on his arm—and I had to try to get away from him; he persisted, however, till he was stopped by the French Consul, and made to stay where he was. M. Duvergier d'Hauraune told Dick he would not go to the armies, because he could not then write to his family. He always writes twice a week, and his mother would be disappointed without a letter. Colonel G. is gone to stay with Sir Fenwick.

Wednesday, October 19*th*.—Fine day at last, but cold. I am reading "Prescott's Life," by Ticknor, doubly interesting to me from having been at Boston, and knowing something about the country. I forgot to tell you of a tomb at the Montreal Cemetery; it is a pretty white Grecian cross with a little garden round it; it is where poor young Mr. Disbrowe is buried; he died out here—the last brother. I got some flowers from it, and Mr. Goldwin Smith settled them for me in an envelope, and I sent them to L., to send to his poor sisters.

Thursday, 20th.—We drove after lunch yesterday to hear the 25th band play on the esplanade. After dinner, Dick, Captain Pem. and I drove to Madame Tessier's ball in the open waggon. M. Tessier is the *orateur* of the Upper House. I opened the ball with him, opposite to Madame and Dick. At French parties there are no fast dances, all quadrilles and lancers; it seems so odd. The R.C. Bishop won't allow "round" dances. Six of the 25th stringband played so well. So many old people I don't think I ever saw, and the older they were the more they danced. No officers but Captain Webber, 17th, and Colonel Hassard, R.E.—they were in uniform, because this is considered an official week. Amongst others I danced with Dr. Tupper, Premier of Nova Scotia, and with Honourable Mr. Coles, leader of the Opposition in the Parliament of Prince Edward's Island. Colonel Grey is gentlemanly. I like Dr. Tupper. Mr. Coles asked to be introduced to me, and, when I said we were going away, he got introduced to Dick, and said to me, "Silence means assent, so come and dance." He does steps, and gives you his hand with a bow of the head and a shake of the body. He said to me, "I'm a sort of fellow who talks away and forgets to dance. He said, "*We gentlemen* don't know *how* to decide between Mrs. Dundas and Lady M., they are both so pretty and nice." The G. G. has had a telegram that has fussed him, and he is gone on now the moment after breakfast to Quebec; it is about Confederates and Yankees, I believe. The K.O.B. soldiers' theatricals come off to-night for the Canadian Mil. Asylum (for widows or orphans of soldiers out here). To-morrow night is the Bachelors' ball, given by six rich bachelors in the Parliament House—they are lumberers and merchants. It is to be "select." The invitation has on it "Quadrilles nine," which does *not* mean only quadrilles.

Friday, 21st.—Had an early visit yesterday from old Mr. Archibald (Abraham, I call him). He made me quite angry about Lord L. He said, "I hope he is going back soon to Washington; there is a great deal of important business awaiting him there," just as if he was neglecting it. His brother is Consul at New York. The day was fine, cold, and dry. We dined at 6.30, and after dinner we drove to the 25th plays; Mrs. Godley and Capt. Pem. came with us. They took place at the music-hall, as you know there is no theatre at Quebec. They never replaced the burnt-down one. I send programme. The actors were soldiers of the K.O.B.'s, and acted so very well, with such nice voices; the women's parts were done by men. The house was *crowded*, and very demonstrative. Our seats were quite in front, so we had a good view. Some of the delegate people were there. There was the cleverest Irish soldier I ever saw at the plays. He was inimitable.

Saturday, October 22nd, '64, Spencer Wood.—Yesterday evening after dinner we went to the bachelors' ball at the Parliament House. At the door there was a guard of honour of volunteers. We were received by ladies in the ballroom, mothers of the bachelors, who themselves never came near any one the whole night. The G. G. opened the ball with Madame Duval. There were forty bachelors, not six, as I was told. The attractions of the two rooms were supposed to be equally divided. "One room had the G. G. and party, and the other the 25th string-band." I only danced quadrilles, as I feared to tear my lace. Amongst others

I danced with Mr. Cartier (Attorney-General East), and with Mr. John A. Macdonald (Attorney-General West). I went to supper with Judge Caron (or Caw-ron, as they say here), father of a bachelor. Dick's conduct was atrocious; he flirted with two married ladies all night. Madame Duval says she is going to give a ball for Colonel Monck. John A. is very agreeable. I asked John A. what the kingdom of Canada is to be called—some say "Canadia." He said that in some speech he had said that, to please the Nova Scotians, it should be called "Acadia," Ottawa should be called "Evangeline," and Mr. Brown shall be "our Longfellow"—he is very big and tall. There were several pretty people at the ball, and the dresses were some of them very good. There is no more to tell of the ball.

Monday, 24*th*.—The thing that made the G. G. go early into Quebec is a raid made by some Confederates into Vermont in the States, but it is all right now; they have been caught, and the Yankee papers praise him much for his prompt conduct. On Sunday we had a very fine sermon in the morning from Mr. Hatch. Mr. C. (25th), our Commandant of the Guard at Spencer Wood, walked home with us. He says he hates balls because he can't dance, and that when he goes to them people who like him at other times, and talk sensibly to him, don't care for him there, and that he talks nonsense, and so do they.

Wednesday, October 26*th.*—I have very little to tell this week. After a storm comes a lull, so this is one of the much-ado-about-nothing letters. On Monday we drove in the phaeton, and paid visits. Dick drove his new horse " Bill Seward." I had a visit from a Mrs. ——. She is rather cracked. She sat on an uncomfortable chair close to me, staring at me. She hesitated when I asked her how many children she had (I really did not know what to say to her), and she answered, " I have ten ; but I believe it is considered very vulgar to have many." To please her, I said I did not think it could be " vulgar," as the Queen had so many. She said at the beginning of the summer she had two in arms, but now she had one ; she thought two a great trouble; one died, and she did not regret it ! Captain Pem. went to Montreal to try and prevent his friend from marrying some girl. As I said before, we paid some visits in town. There was an extraordinary light from the setting sun on Point Lévis and the Isle of Orleans ;

it made them look perfectly pink, and the tin roofs looked like burnished gold. I never saw anything more beautiful and curious, as the sky was quite grey at the time. It looked like lights in a panorama. Tuesday was wet as usual, but not very cold. Got home letters. Your story of my pet Cecil saying "Day-day," to make Major M. go away, reminds me of a story Lord Lyons told me of some one that paid a very long visit to his father, who got up and shook hands, saying, "I'm sorry you are obliged to go." Lord L. envied his father's pluck, and said he couldn't do it. It is said that this winter will begin late, and they know this from the Indians observing the beavers who are not beginning yet to build their winter houses. Lord Airlie told us such curious things about the dams the beavers make; he saw them. Dick drove me out after lunch, when the rain stopped. The day was very dark and damp. We were asked to the delegate ball at Montreal, but I fear we shall not go to it.

Thursday, 27th.—Dick has just dressed himself up in his winter clothes (Astrakan furs), and is saying he thinks they are very becoming—so they are. I am to go and choose my fur cap to-day, and the G. G. proposes to go to the shop and help me to choose one. Mr. Godley says choosing a fur cap is a momentous question here! Yesterday Dick drove me to Cap Rouge to see Mrs. J. Forsyth. The drive is lovely, and from a summer-house in the place you have a beautiful and curious view of the river, and of much lumber in all directions. The sunset was as usual now quite Eastern, such deep yellow and red. My box arrived last night from home, a great event! Colonel Gordon dines here to-night.

Friday, 28th.—A *bitter* cold day, blowing a gale of east wind. My head is always better in east wind; the rain comes from that quarter here. We have hard frosts every night and icicles. Dick drove me out after lunch; it was terribly cold. I paid some visits, and I did not really feel cold, as I wore my velvet bonnet for the first time, and two veils, a warm knitted cape, a velvet coat, and my Astrakan-trimmed cloak; besides, we had our bear-skin robe and an apron in the phaeton! We drove to the racquet-court to meet the G. G., who, with Mr. G., followed us to Henderson's, the furrier's. I there chose a beautiful velvet and seal-skin cap which costs ten dollars (about two sovereigns English). The G. G. is very kindly giving me a present of it. Dick ordered a handsome buffalo sleigh robe, which is to be trimmed with a rim of brigade colours. You must have two robes to cover you in a sleigh. I mean to get a white cloud — "a cloud" is a long knitted scarf, which goes all over your cap and round and round your throat, and ties in long ends, and hangs over your back. My cap is to be very high—the fashion this year, for we have our cap fashions here! Captain Pem. went for two reasons to Montreal, first to prevent his friend from marrying, second to try and make his friends, the C.'s, settle to go to England. He has failed about both errands, for —— is on the *eve* of marriage, and the C.'s sent their baggage to go by the *Jura* (Allans' line), and set off to go themselves, but have not been heard of, and no one knows anything about them. Col. G. was full of Montreal stories. He and F. B. dined and slept. The Delegates' ball will be very mixed. Many Quebecers are gone up for it. The leaves are nearly all off the trees. They were *so* beautiful. I have been reading Bryant's poems. In speaking of the autumn woods, he says—

> "But 'neath yon crimson tree,
>   Lover to listening maid might breathe his flame,
> Nor mark within its roseate canopy,
>   Her blush of maiden shame."

If we have fine weather now for two weeks, it is said the winter will not appear so long.

Saturday, October 29*th.* — We had the most awful hurricane yesterday, and it was so cold that the rain froze, and the verandah was slippery with ice! I walked up and down a little, and was nearly blown away and frozen. That night the thermometer was ten degrees below freezing. Saturday was fine, and I drove myself to town, and Dick came with me to the 25th band on the esplanade. Sunday was lovely, hot sun, but very cold. The smell and suffocation in church is great. We had a beautiful sermon this morning from Mr. Hatch. In the afternoon Mr. Pleese preached a very good sermon.

Monday, 31*st.*—To-morrow I mean to drink tea at four with Gordon the Good, and go to church at five at St. Matthias. Captain Pem. still away; he thinks he is succeeding in his mission. I must tell you a story Gen. Doyle told us when he was here; it only struck me yesterday, and it is so funny. There was an officer who "drew the long bow" very much when telling stories, and he told his servant every time he told these "bangers" to pull his coat-tails. One day he told some people that at Gibraltar the monkeys' tails were six feet long. The servant gave him a pull. He then said, "I'm making a little mistake, they were only five feet long;" another pull. He went on then, and said, "I'm wrong again, they were only four feet long;" another pull. He then turned angrily on his servant, and said, "D—n it, do you want to give them no tails at all?" It is nothing to hear Gen. D.'s stories second-hand; his telling them is half the battle. No mail in yet!

Tuesday, November 1st.—Yesterday, after lunch, I drove to town, and went with Dick to see the window to Bishop Mountain in the cathedral. The colours are very brilliant; it was done in England. We then went to Gringas, the sleigh-maker, and Dick ordered me such a beautiful sleigh painted in brigade colours, and the robes of buffalo and bear are to be trimmed to match. It is to be so comfortable and slanting that one nearly lies down in it. To-day is very cold and dull—a regular "dun November day." The day before, though cold, had been fine and bright. All Saints' Day is a statute holiday. Dick played a match of racquets in the morning, and drove me afterwards to tea with Gordon the Good, and after that we went to church. After dinner, Mrs. G. and I sang together; my voice is miserable, the bitter winds hurt my chest so.

Wednesday, 2nd.—Dull dark day, but fine.

Thursday, 3rd.—Lovely and bright, but very cold. I have nothing to tell you, so I must go back to "old yarns" about our journey with Lord L. He told me a funny story about Mr. Lincoln—he is always running off with the umbrellas of other people, and one day he wanted one, and said to his boy, aged about seven, "Go and get my umbrella from the hall." The boy returned without one, saying, "Father, I guess the owner's been round." The day we went to look at the bishop's window at the cathedral, we came in for a soldier's marriage. The man would say "Yes," or "yea," instead of "I will," and the clergyman had such work with him.

November 4th.—I drove yesterday to the Hotel Dieu. We went off in the open waggon that bitter cold night to dine at Mr. Price's. I wore three cloaks and a hood! We had rather a nice party: four daughters and two sons of Mr. Price, captain and Mr.

E. (25th), Mr. Sitwell, R.E., and Mr. Coulson (25th), and a Mrs. Stayner, from Upper Canada. Having given me so many bouquets in the warm weather, I was curious to know what Mr. Price would give me now; and you will laugh when I tell you his gift is to be a saddle of very small brown Saguenay mutton (!!) from his estate; he says it is like Welsh mutton! He is such an old courtier. The stars were so marvellously bright coming home. The sunsets now are wonderful, so orange and red; and sometimes they throw a soft pink light over everything, which looks mauve on the mountains. Conway thought the sunset last evening was a fire! To-day we have snow, and it is blowing so hard. Fancy, I heard Mr. Coles, of Prince Edward Island, once went to Windsor and lunched with the Queen! and that her Majesty asked him if he was not afraid crossing the Atlantic. He answered in praise of the Cunard line, "No, your Majesty, I go in a line whose steamers never land fewer passengers than they take out."

Monday, November 7th.—I must go back to Friday, the most awful day I ever saw—snow and a hurricane. I was quite afraid that Dick and the G. G. had been blown away, they were so late coming home. I find that the night we dined at the Prices' was the coldest night we have had yet, fourteen degrees of frost, and I drove in an open waggon. Tozer, the coachman, went to Boston three weeks ago to-morrow, and no news has been received of him yet, so the G. G. is getting anxious, and is going to make Colonel Irvine telegraph to Ticknor (whose "Life of Prescott" I am now reading), to know something of him, as he is a friend of Tozer's. The G. G. fears he has been drugged, and carried off to the Federal army. On Friday night dined Colonel Rhodes (a naturalized Canadian), Mr. Coulson (25th), and two R.A. officers named Williams and Heberden. At the Prices' Mr. Colson showed me his photo-book. Among his photos were four of his father's old servants, "each with a device," as he said. The butler carried a silver bottle, the cook was cutting bread, the gardener carried a rake, and the coachman harness. They looked so unutterably quaint. Colonel Rhodes came in a sleigh to dine; the snow was so thick. On Saturday Colonel G. brought us the news that Captain ——'s father-in-law had failed; however, when merchants fail here they get up again very soon. Sunday was a very fine bitter day. Captain Pem. returned by breakfast-time, with so much Montreal news. I walked to church in the afternoon; such slipping and sliding, and the snow so hard it hurt one's feet. I never had such a horrid walk as down the avenue here; on the road it was much better. Mr. Petrie preached. I could not help laughing at one thing he said; it was on the parable of the sower, and he said, "All the little birds sat on the branches just ready to fly down." His voice was so odd, and the idea struck me of a row of little birds flying down to peck away. To-day, thank God, is warmer, and it is raining, so that there is a thaw. I am so glad; I don't want the snow yet. I heard from Mr. Malet, and the letter took seven days to come from Washington, a three days' journey! Captain Pem. drove the G. G. to town to-day in his sleigh. The bells sound so pretty, and it looks so nice. I have no news to tell you; there is no gaiety to chronicle. I hear Mr. L. is going to give a ball on the 16th. We are invited to dine at Mr. J. B.'s on Tuesday, but I fear the cold, so we have refused. Dinners out here last three hours, and the rooms are stifling. My white "cloud" came home to-day. I am getting scarlet over-stockings; you wear the stockings over your boots, and the mocassins over *them;* very warm and snug! On Monday the sleighs were out for the first time from this house, but there was a decided thaw, so Capt. Pem. had to send for his waggon to bring the G. G. and himself home. Dick, however, stuck to the cariole, and when he returned home I drove round to the stables in it, and was much pleased. You feel as if you were flying over the ground, and the bells sound so nice. A cariole is a very low sort of rounded sleigh, painted red. We walked in the verandah, and admired the sunset, which made everything look pink and mauve on the opposite shore; the contrast of the snow making it look more curious.

Tuesday was a fine, bright day, quite warm, such a nice change, the snow going fast, so that I was able to drive in the phaeton. I went to ask for Colonel Rhodes's sick baby; the maid told me in a merry voice it had "ingestion of the brain." To-day is very wet, and such a thaw; the snow is nearly all gone, thank God. Dick does not want the snow to come till his own new sleigh is ready. Mr. Godley is to go to Washington to-day to take some private papers to Lord Lyons, which can't be entrusted to the post. Mrs. G. comes here. On Monday I was to have driven with her in her sleigh, but it thawed so that we could not go. There is a fog to-day (Wednesday) —unusual here. The G. G. hopes that Abe Lincoln will be re-elected, instead of McClellan, as Lincoln would not wish for war with us, and "Little Mac" might. Tozer has been heard of, and is all right at Boston.

Thursday, 10th.—Last night dined Colonel Jervoise, Mr. Galt (Finance Minister), Gordon the Good, and Major Earle (17th). Old Mr. Price had sent me some Saguenay mutton, which was very good, not woolly. Felix called it "*agneau* à la Saguenay," it was so small; but I think mint-sauce spoiled it. This day is like summer, very warm and fine, but windy. Soon the 17th begin their small dances, I hear. *On dit* Parliament is to meet "quite early" this year. Thank God for our chance of getting home.

Monday, November 14th.—Of course I have very little to say this time. Friday last was windy and cold. I drove into town for Dick, and on my way went to see poor Mrs. W. Her child was made to sing one verse of "My Mary Anne," and one verse of "The Evening Hymn"! a broad grin being on its face all the time. Mrs. W. told me she was once in Jamaica, where it was so hot, and she lived so far from a church she did not go to church for three years; and she added, "I that was accustomed to my church twice a day and my Sunday school." Sunday was a very fine day, frosty, but not too cold. We heard of the death of poor Count Georgi at New York. I was much shocked. We do not know what he died of, but he looked dying when here. He had been so anxious about plans for entertaining us at New York. Sunday was a very fine, sunny day, cold and frosty. Walked twice to church and back. We had a sermon of eighteen minutes in the morning from Mr. Botwood, on "Fools make a mock at sin." It was a very practical sermon. Mr. Botwood is such a good man; he has lived among the snows of Labrador for some time, doing so much good; he was a sort of missionary, and there, away from every one, he lost two children; he is to come here for the winter. He read so nice and fast. In the afternoon he preached again for twenty-four minutes. Returning from church, we heard of the loss of the *Jura*, one of the best Canadian ships. The days seem to get longer here instead of shorter; it is light at five; but we are supposed to have no twilight here. The Bishop of Quebec told Mrs. Godley that Ernest Hawkins, the S.P.G. man, was once sent out here, and the clergy petted him so much, and gave him turkeys for dinner every day (which are very cheap here), and when he went back to England, he said the clergy were all so rich that the Canadian Church could want nothing, so they took away a quantity of money from Canada. I think it was very sly of this S.P.G. man; he ought to have found out how common and cheap turkeys are here. The 17th dance comes off next week. They do not dance here in Advent. My journals get duller and duller. To-day is a fine bright day, but so cold that I could scarcely bear driving home from Quebec in the open carriage. I went to see Mr. Price, who was so glad to see me. I was startled by seeing him in an immense fur cap, and with a fur respirator! Madame Gautier was there. She told me her husband heard from the Consul at New York that Count Georgi's death was the termination of a long illness which he had had for years. I went to fetch Dick from the racquet-court, where he had been winning all the games. The sunset was most exquisite, deep scarlet, red, and yellow, and pink.

Tuesday, 15*th*.—After lunch, Mrs. G. and I drove to see the Church Home, which I wanted to compare with our Guards' Home. It is very nice and clean, and such a useful institution. We went on to see Mrs. Malcolm Cameron, and found she is always a cripple, and can never leave her chair. She seemed so cheerful, and said she had such a beautiful view of the St. Charles Valley to look at from her window. Mr. M. C. is the queen's printer here. The snow began to fall again about six.

Wednesday, 16*th*.—This day is quite a picture, deep bright blue "American sky," quite cloudless, everything white with snow—even the trees all bent down with soft white snow—the sun shining brightly over all. The fir trees look so lovely. The snow is not deep enough for a sleigh, I am glad to say. The sun is so hot. Did you read Goldwin Smith's letters in the papers lately about Canada? Lord Lyons remembers him a little boy with a white frock and red shoes! I am so anxious about Lord Lyons, he continues so ill. After lunch, Mrs. G. and I drove to town to see if the mails were in, and were so disappointed to find they were not come. We then drove to the convent of the Ursulines. The snow was very slippery, and just as I got out of the carriage, my feet slipped, and down I fell on my back. I was so wet, and felt much shaken, and a little bruised on my arm and ankle. A lady passing by screamed; the footman picked me up. We drove home quick instead of going into the convent, as I feared to sit in my wet clothes. F. Burrowes came to dine and sleep, because of the L. ball. We went in the waggon, and oh, how I did wrap up! We were announced as "the Honourable Colonel and Mrs. Monck." Cataraqui is such a pretty little house. The dancing was in two large bedrooms, with part of the 25th string-band in what used to be the G. G.'s dressing-room. I enjoyed the dance extremely. I danced all night, and all my partners danced well. They were all officers in different regiments. Judge Caron asked me for my *beau petit garçon*. Oyster pies one cannot escape from here at winter balls —enormous ones, like meat pies, of nothing but oysters. They had such pretty flowers, and ornaments, and china about the house, and everything was very well done. Dick took Madame D. and Madame G. "to give them some drink," as he expressed it, and of course called each by the other's name. Major Earle invited me to go and see a racquet-match, and to lunch with the 17th afterwards. Major E. had one of his thumbs shot off, and somehow one of his eyes put out at racquets. He told me he desired his servant to cut the thumb off the glove of his thumbless hand; when he came to put it on at the ball he found that the wrong thumb had been cut off, and instead of the glove thumb there was only a hole!! The ball really enlivened me, I so seldom see a soul; people, when they call here, rarely come in. The stars were so exquisite coming home, it was almost like day. Dick says there *is* twilight here, but I don't see it.

Thursday, 17*th*.—Mr. Botwood, the new clergyman from Labrador, called, and the G. G. made me come in and see him. He was so intelligent and so interesting, and like a book to talk to. He was five years there, and never saw any one to speak to but fishermen and their families. We heard (but not from him) that he was educated at Oxford, and he asked some bishop to give him the most difficult cure he could find, one that required the hardest work. The parish extended two hundred miles along the wildest sea-coast. He married during the time; but, having lost two children there, his wife came to her father's near here, and they were separated for eleven months. When he used to go out visiting his parish, he said his wife was so nervous about him, as the sea rushes up in such a curious way, people are often suddenly drowned. The snow-storms are so violent that he had seen a sleigh of the country (which are very low, and are called "Kometiques"), with a team of twelve strong dogs, and with four men on it, overturned by the violence of the hurricane. There is only *one* horse in all this place, and it is at the lighthouse; dogs (half wolf and half dog) are used instead, and are so wild and ferocious that they bite people sometimes to death. Some of these dogs once set on a woman, and bit her in eighty-six places; a man came to her rescue, and threw himself on her. These brutes lifted him in their mouths and carried him away, and laid him down, not touching him, and returned to the woman, whose life was only spared by men with bludgeons that ran out of the woods on the dogs. They are driven in a team of twelve, without reins, guided by the voice. The G. G. asked if they ever ran away? "Frequently, my lord," answered meekly Mr. Botwood. There is snow at Labrador all the summer in the valleys, and he always had to wear a greatcoat there all the summer. He was once caught in one of the terrible snow-storms—the account of it is in one of the S.P.G. Reports. Once winter sets in, the people there are really dead to the world, for they never hear anything of any one till spring, and then only by chance. Letters are sometimes thrown on the shore from ships, and *if* any one picks them up they get them, if not, they don't ever get them. Mr. B.'s sister in London once wrote to him, and the letter did not reach him for sixteen months! He did not laud himself at all; our incessant questions found out all these facts. The G. G. said it would be pleasant to him to look back on his Labrador life. He said, "Oh yes, I liked it; the hard work was pleasant!" He said, alas! he had no schools, as the people were scattered over two hundred miles, but he had two churches; one he built himself. He said, as if it was a joke, that he had often in November to wade through streams, and take off all his clothes, and they were so wet and cold when he put them on again. He is very happy to be here, and so delighted with the church, singing, etc. I fancy it was because of his wife that he gave it up; it was so terrible for her, he said. I enjoyed listening to him, telling all these stories. He had two Labrador pups, which he is sorry he did not bring here. I drove to town after lunch, and nearly died of cold across my brow. I longed for my fur cap.

Friday, 18*th.*—A few mornings ago, at five a.m., a waggon drove up, and frightened poor Mrs. G. so (I did not hear it). It was a telegram to say that our Cunard letters were all late for the last ship; every Canada letter was late because something happened to a train. I drove myself after lunch to pay some visits. Tozer said I was much improved in driving. Cap. Pem. came with me to the Parliament Library, where, like all other libraries, I could get nothing I wanted but the *Cornhill*. The gentlemen dined with the 17th, and Mrs. Godley and I had a very pleasant evening together. The day was fine, dull, and not cold.

Saturday, 19*th.*—Fine day, but very cold. The thermometer went down as low as nineteen last night; and to-day it is twenty-six only. I think I will inaugurate my fur cap to-day. The G. G. had a satisfactory letter from Mr. Cardwell about his going home. Mr. Godley returned to-day, bringing a good account of Lord Lyons; he suffers much from neuralgia in his head, but it is nothing serious. He brought me a full-face photo of Mr. Lincoln, and a photo of Mr. Seward. Mr. Godley had an interview with Lincoln, who said he was glad Lord Lyons had not typhoid fever, as the papers said; " For," said he, " in this country typhoid fever is worse than small-pox, yellow fever, or any disease. I know only two things that are worse, viz. the last stage of consumption, and hydrophobia." We are invited with Capt. Pem. to dine on Monday with Madame Duval, and go after to the opera. I refused.

Monday, November 21*st.*—I drove to town, and did inaugurate my fur cap and "cloud." The cold was *intense*, but I was warm. Col. Gordon's hands were in agony when he came in from driving; he nearly roared with pain when he came in to tea. Dick's ears were in great pain, and he and Mr. Godley found a little bit of ice on their moustaches, which delighted me. The thermometer was twenty-two above zero; that night it went down to fifteen. There are three stoves in the passage here, so in the house one is quite warm; and, driving, you are quite warm also. The fur robes and "cloud" keep one really *hot.* My "cloud" is two and a half yards long, and it is wound round and round one's throat, and over one's face; it ties round the throat in front, and hangs in long ends behind. On Sunday we went to eight-o'clock service. The cold was very great; in the afternoon it was quite warm, not even freezing, and the walk to afternoon service was delicious. Mr. Botwood preached for twenty-five minutes. The G. G. is now covered with furs, be the day cold or warm. We are invited to dine, I believe, and dance, at Madame Duval's, on Tuesday, but we have refused. There is the 17th dance on Wednesday, and sleighing in the cold two nights running is no joke. It is snowing hard to-day and quite warm. This must be the "Indian summer." There was a good deal of snow yesterday evening, and good sleighing for the first time this winter. After lunch, Mrs. Godley took me out in her cariole; it made my head feel giddy, we were so very low on the ground, lower than a wheel-barrow, and every one walking looked so big. We met Mr. Coulson (25th), who could have jumped over us easily. I felt as if we should be run down and trampled on, and one felt so helpless. We met several sleighs and

carioles; the bells sounded so gay. Some
"Muffins" were out with their men friends,
and looked very bright and nice flying
along in sleighs. It rained nearly the whole
time, and was so hot and muggy that I
wore a bonnet and thin veil. We passed
Mr. Aylmer (17th), who laughed at us tearing along in our red, round wheel-barrow.
It looked so quaint, seeing carioles and
sleighs on the stand, instead of waggons.
Capt. Pem. dined with Madame Duval, but
would not go to the opera, which is said
to be very bad, only five singers, no chorus,
and no scenery.

Tuesday, 22nd.—It rained all night and
half the day, so most of the snow was gone.
I drove *on wheels* again with Dick to town,
where he bought an enormous pair of high
boots; every one wears them here, and they
look so nice. The roads are in a terrible
state.

Wednesday, 23rd.—Very fine day; rather
cool, I am glad to say. A most curious
tradeswoman came to-day to ask me to buy
from her; she came from " Up Canada " (as
they pronounce here). She amused me with
her Yankee voice and manners. She said
she would not fall on the snow as she
had " creepers " on—" creepers " are spikes

strapped on to the heel of the boot. Got letters per Canadian mail, they came in our new ship, the *Moravian*. Ships now go from and come to Portland, in the States, not Quebec. Drove part of the way into town on wheels—it was too slippery; every one in sleighs but ourselves; the ground is all ice. Had a visit from Mrs. L., who that night sent me an exquisite hot-house bouquet for the 17th ball. Dick and I drove to the ball in the open carriage with the hood up. Thermometer thirteen degrees above zero.

Thursday, 24*th.* — Last night was the coldest night we have had yet! The ball was very pleasant. A fire took place at the citadel; one of my partners came to me about it, just as I was going to dance with him. It turned out to be Capt. Hope's room that was burnt. There were several pretty girls at the ball. Major —— is supposed to be paying attention to a girl, and Major E. advised him to call on her. He said, " No, I never do those sort of things; they don't suit me, my dear fellow." He has a beer-barrel in his room, and a beer-tankard in which we found stuck (without water) a bouquet he had got evidently from some young lady. This we discovered when we were leaving. To-day is terribly cold. Ice appeared in lumps floating about in the river to-day, for the first time. Dick has a thermometer now in my room, and worries me so with it; if it gets above sixty-four degrees he opens the windows, and in five minutes brings it down ever so much. I have not yet begun a fire in my bedroom in the morning. When people have been here some winters, all the caloric of their English blood goes away, and they are such sufferers then from cold. At the ball Captain Hope was joking about the fire at the citadel, not knowing that his own room and all his clothes were burnt. It is said he does not care, as he will not have the bore of packing them up. He is quite a hero now, and people went to see his room. On Thursday I drove in the open carriage, only my head peeping out of the furs. It was *so* cold and so slippery. Both horses and carriages slipped so much, it was scarcely pleasant. Mrs. G. went out in her cariole.

Friday, 25th.—It is snowing to-day, the right thing for it to do, as St. Catherine's is always the snow day here; it lies after that day. Dear old Mr. Price sent me another saddle of mutton yesterday. Last night dined Mr. John A. Macdonald and Mr. Howland (the new Post-Master General), and some officers. "John A." was very amusing. He said I had come out here in time to found a new empire. My mutton was considered excellent. Mr. McGee has the cholera, and nearly died.

Saturday, Nov. 26th.—Yesterday got quite warm after lunch, and was only at freezing-point. Capt. Pem. dined with the K.O.B.'s; they have a dance at the citadel on Monday. I must tell you "John A.'s" stories. He told me that Sir E. Head had the greatest horror of sentencing a man to be hung—it used to depress him for weeks, and make him utterly wretched, so that "John A." used to *dread* having to announce to him when it was necessary. When Sir E. went home on leave, Sir Fenwick Williams administered the Government here, and during his reign came the necessity for a man being hung. "John A.," in dread of having to tell Sir F. of it, went to him and said, "This man has committed an atrocious murder, and I am afraid he *must* be hung." He was electrified by the cheery answer, "I *quite* agree with you; *of course* he must be hung; hang, hang, hang them all, when they deserve it." Sir R. M. is so against this confederation scheme, because he would be turned away. He said to John A., "You shall not make a mayor of *me*, I can tell you," meaning a deputy-governor of a province.

Monday, 28th.—When I left off on Saturday we were just going to the racquet-match at Quebec. The players were Dick and Major Earle on one side; Capt. King and Mr. Williams, R.A., on the other. I sat in the gallery covered by a buffalo skin, provided by Major Earle. Some ladies came to see the match, and of course several of the 17th officers were there. The ladies were Mrs. Serecold, Miss A. Bowen and her two nieces, the Misses Webster. Kirwan the horse-dealer was also there. After the match we went to the 17th mess and had lunch, and were very pleasant and merry. I grieve to say Dick's side lost the match; Major Earle blamed himself for it. There was much excitement about it. On Saturday there was a thaw all day. Sunday it was so slippery coming home from church. Some more snow had fallen in the night; it was not cold, and the snow was very good for sleighing. Dick and I drove to afternoon service in the cariole. In the afternoon the bishop preached for twenty-five minutes; we also had a baptism. The morning service had also been very long.

BALL AT THE CITADEL.

Tuesday, 29*th*.—Yesterday got quite warm, and I drove in the cariole, which is so rough that it gave me quite a headache. I went to see a poor woman in the village. Whilst I was there, the girl called out, "Oh, ma'am, there's a funeral!" I went to look out. There were many sleighs, and the bells jingled merrily as the *cortège* moved quickly on. All funerals go fast here; I suppose it is from the cold weather. I went to see a poor man, and the snow was so deep where he lives that I could scarcely struggle on. That night it rained so tremendously that we had to have the shut carriage instead of the sleigh to go to the 25th ball. When we with difficulty got up the very great Citadel hill, we found everything very nicely done, the soldiers had decorated the stairs and ante-room like a miniature Guards' ball, with two tall soldiers and two pipers on the landing, and flags and designs done with bayonets and stars, and theatre scenes painted by Col. Fane. The string-band was of course exquisite. There were many pretty faces at the ball. Great fat —— was introduced to me, and took me to supper; he is exactly like a fat boy in pantomimes, that brings in balls for clowns to play with. The shell-jacket made this thought come

into my mind. A few people danced "The
Reel of Tulloch." Capt. Hope's hats and
shirts were about the only things burned.
We slid all the way down the citadel hill in
coming home.

Wednesday, 30th, St. Andrew's Day.—We
had a fog like a London one all yesterday.
To-day is fine and warm, but not bright.

Thursday, December 1st.—It rained yesterday, so I could not go to church at Quebec.
There was very little snow on the roads.
Thermometer thirty-nine degrees. I had a
letter from Mr. Sheffield, giving a better
account of Lord L., and sending me an autograph of Mr. Seward, a great contrast to the
bold strong hand of Abraham Lincoln; it is
weak and shaky. Dick met Col. R., who had
just returned from the States; he and Major
W. had been to "The Armies," and had been
treated very civilly by Gen. Meade. Mrs. R.
had been to tea with Mrs. Lincoln, and she
asked a lady how she was to dress, and the
answer was, "Whatever way you like; she's
just the same as you and I." Mrs. Lincoln
offered to show Mrs. R. her "saloon," and
began lighting the candles herself. The
G. G. showed us the plans just received of
Rideau Hall, the horrid Ottawa Government
House! How I wish the Parliament Houses

were burnt down! To-day is a lovely warm spring day, nearly all the snow gone. Did you see the pictures of Cartier, Brown, and Galt in the *Illustrated News*, also of the Dundas house.

Friday, December 2nd.—No mails in, though both ships are due. Yesterday was rather colder in the evening, and went down to twenty-seven degrees at night. To-day the thermometer is thirty degrees; and it is very fine. I was caught in such a snow-storm yesterday that I could scarcely see to drive. I do not know whether Mr. Botwood is High or Low Church; he gave out that the Vigil of St. Andrew's Day was a fast, but called it the "preceding day." Capt. Pem. dined last night with Kirwan, the horse-dealer, *alias* the "Doctor," because he once lived as groom to a doctor. It was a fare-well feast to one of the 17th, who is "horsey." They talked of nothing but "M.D." and "Sunshine" (Kirwan's two horses), the whole evening. Mr. Godley says the "Doctor" is "in society" now.

December 3rd.—Snow-storm all day; did not go out at all.

December 4th.—Threatening snow all day. Drove in sleigh to afternoon church.

Wednesday, December 7th.—I must go back

to last Monday. I went out in the beautiful large sleigh her Ex. used to drive in, with bear, buffalo, and wolverine robes. It was a fine but dull day, and not very cold. One requires to be accustomed to a sleigh drive to like it; it gave me a headache, and the snow hurt my eyes, and I felt as if big dogs would jump on me, as I was so low. We met some officers' tandems; I got Dick at the office, and we took a drive; we met a funeral; the hearse on "runners," and all the people in sleighs, trotting along! It was so very sad, and the bells sounded so merry, and made everything worse. Really the bells on the horses bewilder one so much in town, one hears no sounds but "bells, bells, bells, bells," etc. Tuesday was dull and windy, said to be cold, but I did not feel it so. Soon after breakfast, got our two mails; one bag had gone astray to Montreal, and Cunard turned up with Canadian. Oh, the delight of letters! I will write no journal per Cunard, as we have to write on Saturday instead of Monday, because of the snow. I drove out in a sleigh, and met so many tandems; it was a fine but dull day. At luncheon the footman had left the room, and coming in again with a bow, said, "The cat is at the door, ma'am, will I let him in?"

I said, "Who?" and he repeated the question. I laughed so. The slide is up now for tobogganing, but no one has begun yet. The slide is a raised wooden platform with an inclined plane placed on the top of a hill upon which the snow falls, and when rolled and frozen over, you slide down on a toboggan, which is a flat piece of thin ash wood curled up at the end to receive one's feet; two or three people can go down on one toboggan, one behind the other, as close as one can pack, and one guides the toboggan with a bit of wood; terrible sport, I think, but I must try it once! You shoot down a hundred yards further than the slide, all across the cricket-ground.

Thursday, 8th.—The two Misses Irvine lunched with me. There are four of them, and the eldest is nineteen years younger than her father! The youngest is very pretty and very young. I left them at home in *such* a snow-storm of *wet* snow, and as the day was warm we were all white and wet. I was astonished to see the Quebec girls sauntering along without umbrellas in the snow-storm! Mr. G. laughed at me with my umbrella. He says they are unknown here in winter; but I stuck to it, as the snow really was very wet. To-day is a statute holiday (the Immaculate Conception). We had rain and hurricane all night. To-day there was fine fun at the slide; Dick, Capt. Pem., and F. Burrowes all went down once together and got a nice upset. It is a most singular amusement, but great fun to a looker-on. I laughed so at them. One time Capt. Pem. was going to take Dick down, but before " Pem." was on the toboggan behind Dick, Dick, thinking he was on all right, had flown down alone, and flew from side to side unable to stop, not having the bit of wood to guide it. It froze last night, and is blowing a storm to-day with occasional showers of dry frozen snow. There is a man dinner to night, plain clothes.

Friday, 9th.—Dick and Capt. Pem. went to town yesterday to play racquets, and F. Burrowes and I tried to drive, but we met Dick, and soon turned back. It was blowing a hurricane and snowing hard, and all the snow was also blown up from the ground. We then went to the slide. Mr. Godley and his swarm of dogs came also, and he *made* me go down with him once. Oh, I was so afraid! It was a dreadful feeling flying down the height, and made me feel sick for hours after. Dick's beard was thick with ice; the thermometer was twenty degrees, and it was snowing hard all the time we were out; I had no warm stockings, and yet I was not very cold. Tobogganing is the funniest sight conceivable! Last night the thermometer went down to six degrees above zero, and to-day it is ten degrees above; the atmosphere so beautifully clear, you can see miles with the greatest distinctness, and you can hear, with the window shut, the snow crackling under the toboggan as Dick flies down some fifty yards off from the house. A few officers dined last night. I expect this evening we shall have one of the marvellous pink sunsets which are really like the transformation scene in a good pantomime; first everything is pink, then mauve, then grey. The sun is lovely and warm to-day, but the cold of the air intense. I have not yet begun a fire in my room in the morning. My room was fifty degrees this morning, which is cold for a room here; but few rooms at home are much warmer with a good fire. Double windows are such a comfort. The moon last night was so bright and clear one could almost read by it. The opposite bank of the river has a *bordure* of ice to-day. There is that foolish Dick, in his summer clothes, paddling down the slide; he is guiding himself along with two little bits of wood that they light fires with; he looks so funny! He is just come in burning hot, with his beard a mass of ice and his pockets full of snow, having been upset many times.

Saturday, 10th.—A very cold day. Thermometer twelve above zero. Dick as usual went "a sliding," as Conway calls it, both morning and evening. Col. Gordon came from town a mass of snow. It was blowing and snowing hard all day.

Sunday, 11th.—Not nearly so cold, but dull. Went *en* sleigh to afternoon service. It is quite martyrdom, in a very small way, going to church now; the intense cold of getting there, and then the intense heat of church with hot air, and horrid smells of leather big boots, and fur coats, and the weight of one's own fur cap on one's brow, all these miseries have to be contended with. Neither door nor window are ever open.

Monday, December 12th.—This will be a long and stupid journal. I must return to Friday last, 9th, *very* cold, thermometer ten degrees above zero in the daytime, and went down to five below that night at Quebec. I never could describe the intensity of the cold; it was the worst day we had had, and when you sat down long, even indoors, you felt pains in your legs like rheumatism. The day was glorious: sun and bright blue sky. I drove to town to fetch the G. G. and Dick. The mountains were first deep blue and then purple, the snow was sometimes pink, and the sky faded from blue into light green, then to yellow, and then to orange, like pictures of desert scenes in Africa; but still I had not my favourite transformation scene, sunset. It sounds almost irreverent to compare nature with such a thing, but I have such an admiration for the scenery of a London pantomime that I consider it great praise. The G. G. constantly felt his nose for fear it was frost-bitten; my veil, or rather "cloud," was a mass of ice, so that I could not see, all the holes being full of ice. When we came home, Dick rushed off to slide. I wore my scarlet worsted stockings over my boots, and nothing over them, so I looked like a shoeless cardinal! I had on a worsted cape, crossed over my chest, also another worsted thing over my chest, a seal-skin, two veils, and a cloud, and still I was dead with cold. The wind crossing the Plains of Abraham was dreadful that evening. Dick found my room seventy degrees, so he cruelly opened the window, and in less than five minutes brought it down to fifty-six degrees. Cruel man! I have begun a fire in the morning.

Tuesday, 13*th*.—I walked in the verandah; for a wonder was not cold, though the verandah was deep in snow, and the thermometer was six degrees above zero; it blew a hurricane, and snowed hard all the time. Capt. Pem. dined in town, and went with some ladies to see the volunteers drilled at the drill-shed. The thermometer here in the verandah went down to ten degrees below zero, and fancy the misery of the drill shed! If there were any balls now, I don't think I *could* go to them. Most people here go at night in open sleighs, but I dread even a sleigh with hood and curtains, and what must an open one be! My sleigh arrived to-day; Dick says it is very pretty; it has my monogram in red on it. No mails, but we have heard of the arrival of one ship at Halifax. The telegram says there were awful storms on the coast of England. The river is smoking to-day as if on fire; this is caused by the air being colder than the water. There are enormous blocks of ice on the river, which looks grand and desolate.

Wednesday, 14*th*.—Still no mails; it is very sad work waiting. The sunset was very fine yesterday evening, it made the opposite side of the river quite pink, and also tinged the citadel a lovely pink. Whenever the sunset is fine, we may be *sure* of a bad day on the morrow. To-day it is snowing hard, but is not nearly so cold. (Oh, these pens! The heat of the room makes them all split!) Last night we had a little excitement, for which I thank the gods. A loud ring came to the hall door, when dinner was nearly over, and soon the G. G. was mysteriously called out; as he hurried out of the room, he said in fun, "I suppose this is an invasion of the Yankees." I longed so to listen at the door of the next room. Soon the G. G. came back, saying that dinner must be prepared for Mr. Cartier; he was just setting off on a journey, when the news came that the stupid Judge at Montreal had on his own hook let out the raiders that were taken up and kept in prison, and they were again at liberty to scamper about the country and attack the Yankees. John A., Cartier, MacDougal, and Langevin were all obliged to come out here about it; the fuss was great fun. To-morrow night we are invited to a party at Mrs. D.'s. Mr. D. is the image of Lord Elgin, and was often taken for him by the sentries. They have asked us at nine, and the Godleys at 8.30!

Very odd. It is mild to-day, twenty degrees above zero. We have church to-day at 3.30 in the village, also on Friday and Saturday (ember-days).

Thursday, 15*th.*—No mails yet! Four are now expected. Dick drove me to church yesterday in my new sleigh; it is so comfortable. I had a hot bottle, and nearly lay down among the furs, so that only my face was cold, and *that* was terribly cold; my veils were a sheet of ice. We are not going to Mrs. D.'s rout; it is too cold to venture to town for a quadrille and music. I must tell you a funny story to enliven this dull letter a little. There was a family at Quebec who went to a ball in a covered sleigh, and were upset at the door of the house; the mamma and one girl were pulled out through the window by putting their arms round a gentleman's neck. When the other girl's turn came, nothing would induce her to move, and she remained sitting in a corner, saying, "*She could not* put her arm round any man's neck, as she was engaged to be married," and after all she was not married at all! Poor thing! My journal would be hopelessly dull without these old stories.

Friday, 16*th.*—I believe the old Cunard mails are at Quebec, but we shall not get them in time to answer them, as our post must go so early to-day, because of the difficulty of crossing the river to the train through the ice. I drove in my new sleigh yesterday with Dick. The snow-drifts were up to the top of the hedges in some places. It was a heavenly day, but two degrees above zero. The sky was so blue and cloudless, and the river was a deeper shade of very bright blue, covered with blocks of white sparkling ice. Facing the wind in driving was almost *unbearable*, and I lay down under the fur robes, so that nothing could be seen of me but the top of my fur cap. The insides of my eyes seem sometimes frozen, it hurts me to shut them. I send you General Dix's proclamation. We are, I find, only thirty miles from the frontier here across the river; but I should think the ice will keep us pretty safe. I believe the Canadians mostly sympathize with the raiders. It is snowing to-day.

PROCLAMATION OF GENERAL DIX.—Head-quarters, Department of the East, New York City, December 14. General Orders, 97.—Information having been received at these head-quarters that the Confederate marauders who were guilty of murder and robbery at St. Alban's have been discharged from arrest, and that other enterprises are actually in preparation in Canada, the Commanding General deems it due to the people of the frontier towns to adopt the most prompt and efficient measures for the security of their lives and property. All military commanders on the frontier are therefore instructed, in case further acts of depredation and murder are attempted, whether by marauders or persons acting under commissions from the Confederate authorities at Richmond, to shoot down the perpetrators, if possible, while in the commission of their crimes, or if it be necessary, with a view to their capture, to cross the boundary between the United States and Canada, and commanders are hereby directed to pursue them wherever they may take refuge. If captured, they are under no circumstances to be surrendered, but are to be sent to these head-quarters for trial and punishment by martial law. The Major-General commanding the departments will not hesitate to exercise to the fullest extent the authority he possesses under the rules of law, recognized by all civilized States, in regard to persons organizing hostile expeditions within neutral territory, and fleeing to it for an asylum after committing acts of depredations within our own, such an exercise of authority having become indispensable to protect our cities and towns from incendiarism, and our people from robbery and murder. It is earnestly hoped that the inhabitants of our frontier districts will abstain from all acts of retaliation on account of the outrages committed by Confederate marauders, and that the proper measures of redress will be left to the action of the public authorities.—By command of Major-General DIX. Signed, D. F. NANBURN, Colonel and Assistant Adjutant-General.

Saturday, 17th.—Yesterday after lunch I was so thankful to receive the old Cunard letters of the 26th November; it was a great comfort to get them, though they were full of allusions to the Canadian letters which we have not yet got. I must ask you to get a table of the ships, and only to write short letters by the *St. David's*, the *North American*, the *Damascus*, and the *Nova Scotian;* all these are the Canadian line, and we can never be *sure* of getting letters by them, so when they sail, write your long letters by Cunard. I went to church, and while waiting for my sleigh after church, I talked to Mrs. Botwood; she told me that at Labrador Mr. Botwood used to have all his services on the week days; he used to have three a day, and go from place to place to hold service where there were about six people together. They were always glad to go to his services. We took a lovely country drive after church. The thermometer was ten degrees above zero, much less cold than the day before; the day had cleared so beautifully, and was cloudless. The sunset was lovely, light green, yellow, and light orange; the tin spires and roofs looked so sparkling and curious. To-day is fine, and not very cold. Captain Pem. is so afraid of me now; he says that he makes it his business to collect news for me at Quebec, and he tries hard not to forget it. When he is paying visits, he thinks, "Now, Mrs. Monck will ask me about that." The G. G. had such a nice note from Lord Lyons (who was just starting for England from New York), hoping that the friendships so happily begun at Spencer Wood may continue, on whatever side of the Atlantic we may all meet again. Poor old Mr. Forsyth has lost a son in the 60th; he has not been home for ten years, and was on his way home from India, when the cyclone came, and he was drowned in one of the P. and O. steamers.

Monday, 19th.—It turned to snow on Saturday, and snowed all the afternoon. Went to church, and took Mrs. Botwood a short way in my sleigh. She told me her husband regrets Labrador so much; he always thinks he has not done enough. She stayed there from June of one year till July of the next year, and there was snow the whole time she was there! Her husband was away at his duties most of the time; she never stirred out, and had not one single friend! What desolation! I drove on to Quebec, and got Dick, who had been hard at work from eleven till 4.30. He and the G. G. had been calling out the Militia! General Dix has been made to alter his proclamation by the authorities at Washington, and they are *not* to follow raiders into Canada. The reason of calling out the Militia is to catch raiders on the frontier. It is an interesting year to be in Canada, between the Confederation business and seeing whether Canada is able and willing to defend herself, or rather to be *on the alert* in case of danger.

Sunday was a most exquisite real Canadian day, a cloudless deep blue sky and bright cold sun. At morning service I sat in the last seat in church, a dirty big boy sat next me; I was much amused at him helping Dick to wind my "cloud" round me! All the seats are free, but one or two are set apart for the G. G.'s party. I prefer the door, because of the heat. After our return from church, the G. G. came to Dick, and told him to write off to Mr. J. Burstall to come to the office about ten a.m. next day, with some Militia officers who have offered their services, and they are to be sent off to Windsor and Sarnia, Canada West, as John A. wrote off in a tremendous fright on Sunday to say that things must be hurried on; the G. G. had wished them to be sent five weeks ago! After tea, to my joy, came the letters of the 30th and December 1st Canadian mail. This is an awful day of snow and hurricane, and the gentlemen are gone in at ten about the Militia, so I must occupy myself as best I can with books and papers till evening, all alone. Writing is a great solace to me. We meant to go to the

K.O.B. theatricals to-night, but of course weather does not permit.

Wednesday, December 21*st.*—We must return to Monday, although I have nothing to tell you. The weather was horrible all day, and we could not go to the theatricals. Capt. Pem. went, and told me the room smelt worse than church of high leather boots. Tuesday, 20th, was a lovely day; thermometer five degrees above zero. When I went out to drive after lunch, my veil was a sheet of hard ice. I paid some visits; among other people, I went to see Mrs. D.; I was told she was at home. The servants here never announce one; it is so very unpleasant, they generally escape downstairs as soon as they open the door. The maid hustled me into what she called the "library," but *would not* announce me. I found myself in a very dark room, with three ladies dressed to go out walking, and a gentleman. I had to roar out my own name at the door. I knew no one in the room. One of the ladies, with great tact, said, pointing to one of the others, "Miss D." So I shook hands with Miss D., and felt grateful to the strange lady who introduced me; had she not done so, we should all have sat looking at each other to the end of time, as I had no idea who the ladies were, and the Miss D.'s had not very wonderful manners. Mrs. D. was out. We all sat at the door, which was open, as doors always are here, to let in the heat of the hall stove. I went to the office, and tried on some cloth mocassins; they are very snug; the man told me no one here minds their feet looking clumsy in winter. Sergeant Lambkin chose them for me. Heard, thank goodness, of the arrival of the old *St. David's.* She broke her screw from the violence of the storms, and had to *sail* for three days, when she met the old tub *Damascus*, which went back and towed her to Portland, so you will have your letters four days late by that. While I was waiting for the bootmaker, I amused myself reading Dick's notes of the Militia reports; one corps was spoken of thus: "Very fine young men; not at all efficient for service." Dick had copied them from Col. Lowry's (47th regiment) report. One would think there was going to be war to-morrow from the talk and fuss about the Militia; the papers are full of nothing else, and Capt. Pem. says they will want medals when they come back. It is amusing to see the great fuss; one heading in the paper is "Military Ardour in the City." They want to have a demonstration to the Militia who are going. The secretary of the racquet-court has run off with some money; Dick heard it as a secret from "Johnny Earle." To-day, of course, is snowy and windy; every other day is bad here now. I mean to try and go to the rink with Dick and Captain Pem. to hear the band, and see the skating, but I fear the wind is too strong to cross the plains. Mrs. Godley is making wreaths for the church; they are obliged to be made at the school-house, *close* to a hot stove; if air gets on the flowers, they will turn black, and must be carried in tin boxes shut up. Mrs. G. told me that once during the time that Mr. Botwood was at Labrador, he came here for six weeks, and said he *must* find a wife in that time to bring back with him. The girl he found had just come from school, and was a mere child when he married her, three years ago. She must be very delicate, for she can't walk at all. He says she has a fine "missionary spirit, and would go to the north pole with him."

Thursday, 22nd.—Yesterday turned out such a terrible day. I went to help at the school. It was snowing and blowing terribly. I was much amused helping. Mrs. Botwood was there; she told me there was no doctor at Labrador, and her baby died from having no doctor. Her mother once went to see her at Labrador, and could not get away for ten months! They lived in a wooden house, and the church was wooden, and they decorated it at Christmas with firs. She was also at Newfoundland with her husband, and hated it quite as much as Labrador. The secretary to the racquet-court has been seen at Montreal, so there is a chance of his being caught. There is to be a masonic ball on St. John the Evangelist's Day, "to celebrate the day," the papers say! I hope to go to it. The office-keeper at Quebec (a man of colour) is one of the masonic "swells." I believe it will be a very low ball. The K.O.B. officers act on the 5th; they have asked the G. G. to patronize them; he has promised to go if it is fine. The Godleys dined out last night; it was an *awful* night; I sat up in terror till one a.m.

Friday, 23*rd*.—The Cunard mails of the third are now at Quebec, but the stupid orderlies have not brought them out yet; very trying. We have just heard by telegram from Halifax of the death of dear Lord Carlisle. I am so very much grieved about it. He was always so kind to me. I drove yesterday to the school-house, and assisted in wreath-making. Miss Mountain and her dogs were there. There was growling going on every moment at the school-house. Mrs. Godley heard at her party that the 17th give a dance on the 4th. The K.O.B. plays are to be good; Col. R. is to speak the prologue. I helped for an hour, and then drove to meet Dick, and we visited Col. Irvine, who is ill. We have just got our Cunard letters, thank God. Mrs. R. dined where the Godleys dined two nights ago, and told such amusing stories about New York. She was staying with a Mr. and Mrs. ———, proprietors of the Fifth Avenue Hotel, very very rich people. Mr. ——— has five carriages, and horses for them all; Mrs. ——— has four carriages. The back of the R.'s bed was quilted satin, and gold fringe; the carpet was velvet, and the jugs and basins red Bohemian glass. They each had a dressing-room and a bath-room. With all this grandeur they had to ring five times for a maid, who would say, "Was you ringing?" Then the footman would make familiar jokes with Mrs. R., and say, on bringing her in cards, "I guess you'll have to return these visits." The butler roared with laughing at dinner, and when told to bring iced cream, said, "I will do it when I choose myself; I'm not ready yet."

The pillow covers were trimmed with Bruxelles lace. Conway had a letter from a friend in England, who asked her to answer some questions, among which were the following:—" Is there a church where you are?" and, " Do you get plum-pudding on Christmas Day?"

Christmas Day.—I am thinking so much of you all to-day, I must write a few lines. I am *so* tired. There was no early Communion to-day, so our service lasted from eleven till near two, and tramping back through the snow is most fatiguing. The others tramped off again to afternoon service as soon as lunch was over. We have a dull day to-day as to weather, but oh, such a blessed change as to temperature, twenty-four degrees above zero! No wind, and so nice and warm. We had a sermon of twenty-eight minutes long to-day, and a soldier snored out loud in the middle of it. The decorations were very pretty, the windows all wreathed with fir and mountain ash berries (meant to represent holly); the chancel arch and door ditto, and the font with a mitre of firs and a cross, and there were crosses and stars of firs about the church, and a cross on the altar of white camellias.

Monday, St. Stephen's Day.—I must return to Friday last. The bitter bitter cold of that day is beyond conception. Conway and I went to the church to help; we fastened the wreaths on wood which went round the doors and windows. On Saturday I offered my services again, but, happily, was not wanted, and so I went instead to see the G. G. inspect the volunteers at the drill-shed, before they leave for service in the West. I was much interested and amused. The G. G. addressed them in a few well-chosen words; they all looked so funny in their fur coats and caps. Captain Gingras (the man who made our sleigh) and his company of workmen all turned out so well that I did not know them. The thermometer was ten degrees above zero, so it was not so *very* cold. Dick then drove me into town, and on our return homewards we met the volunteers marching through the streets, and singing in chorus as they marched; very nice it sounded. On Christmas Day dined Captains Grant, R.E., and Glynn, Rifle Brigade, and Major Earle. Captain Glynn and Colonel Rhodes have been shooting in the woods; they have been a month away, and have shot twelve cariboo. They had most dreadful weather the whole time they were away. This morning I went out "a sliding" with Dick; the day is nice and warm, so my breath did not leave me so much as the last time. I don't think it a pleasant amusement; but as others do it, why should not I? sea-sick as I feel afterwards. The G. G. had a very pleasant letter from Mr. Cardwell by last mail, saying that everything about confederation was so satisfactory, and that it would be a page in history.

Tuesday.—Yesterday was a nice warm day, not quite freezing, and it was delicious driving. I got Dick, and we went to the skating-rink. A marvellous boy was skating there, to the astonishment of every one; such wonderful skating it was; his legs seemed as if they did not belong to him, but as if they were wound up and set going. A girl skated very well. It looks delightful to skate; Dick is going to learn. They won't let me go to the Masonic ball; it is considered too low; I am so sorry. People are skating across the St. Lawrence, above and below Spencer Wood.

Wednesday, 28th.—Yesterday was so warm, and scarcely freezing. Drove to town, and to ask for poor Dr. Adamson, who fainted in church on Sunday. I saw Mrs. A., who was as amusing as usual, though very sad about "Adamson." Her nephew was in the old *St. David's* (twenty-eight days out), and she told me she was not afraid about him till one Sunday, when she found her stool not in its usual place at church, and nothing comfortable; then she thought something bad had happened, because her stool had never been wrongly placed before. I found at the office that all the Cunard and Canadian letters had arrived 7th and 9th of December; great joy! I hope to drink tea with Gordon the Good to-day, and go to his church. We have quite English weather now; damp and not cold, barely freezing.

Thursday, 29th.—It rained all yesterday; most unusual here in winter. I could not go to church or to tea with Colonel G. We are invited to the Stadacona ball to-night; it is a subscription ball. I never now can do anything I want to do, so I dare say the weather will prevent our going. Stadacona was the old name for Quebec, and Hochelaga for Montreal; much prettier than the present names. It is snowing to-day, but *hot*. The *Peruvian* is telegraphed from Portland, but can't get in because of the fog. Whenever it gets colder than *even* it was, Mr. Godley says to me, "I should not be surprised now if we had some cold weather and *snow.*" The thermometer below zero, and hetacombs of snow everywhere.

Friday, 30th.—Yesterday was wet and unpleasant, thermometer nearly forty degrees all day. After dinner we drove in to the ball. I shall not easily forget my drive, and I wanted to turn back as soon as we had set off. The "cahots" (or *holes* from the thaw) were terrible, and with the curtains of the sleigh down, I felt quite sea-sick; no air could get in, and I felt as if we were sticking in the snow, and unable to get on. The "cahots" make many people sea-sick; they feel exactly like a ship on a rough sea. We went very late, and only stayed a short time; the floor was nothing but dust, though perfect to dance on. The best couple in the room was an old greyish man dressed like a clergyman, with buttoned-up coat flying and *knocking* round, with a great big woman with one of these false backs to her head, who in her enormity looked like Mrs. Major O'Dowd in "Vanity Fair." I must stop now, and finish the ball by next mail.

Saturday, December 31st.—The account of the ball must be finished now, though I have only a few more little remarks to make about it. Capt. W. told me that at the Masonic-hall he saw a young boy with his arm round a girl's waist, for fifteen minutes (?) trying to begin, and fearing to be knocked out of time, and jigging up and down all the time to keep time in his own mind; at last he set off, and was instantly knocked wrong. Capt. Pem. saw the very same thing at the Stadacona ball. I made acquaintance with Mrs. K. (25th), and liked her because she said she was a coward, and was in terrible misery crossing the Atlantic. I asked M. Cartier (when I was dancing with him) if he was very proud at seeing his portrait in the *Illustrated London News;* he said he was, but that he was prouder still at seeing his speech quoted and spoken of in the *Times.* It was blowing terribly coming home, and I was so frightened. Sergeant Lambkin said to Dick, when we arrived at the ball, "Will you lift out Mrs. Monck, sir, or shall I?" Yesterday, happily, it got colder, and was perfection, and to-day it is just the same, twenty degrees above zero. The sky is the deepest, most cloudless blue, and the snow-covered fir trees look lovely glistening in the sun, and the river is like a sheet of silver. I went to see Mrs. ―― ; she invited us to a party at the barracks on the last night of the year. We are not going; Dick said it is ridiculous for a woman to ask people to a barracks party. I then went to pay the G. G. a visit in his room at the office, and he gave me ess. bouquet, which, with other delicious scents and eau-de-Cologne, are provided by the Province. I also went to see a Mrs. S., whose husband is head of the Indian department. There has been a terrible tragedy here : three young men, well-known here, went into a chemist's shop (or " drug store," as they call it here) the day after the Masonic ball ; feeling tired, they asked for a " pick-me-up." The shop-boy gave them poison in mistake, and one of them died in agonies in about four hours ; the others were only saved by their good constitutions, but they suffered tortures. Mrs. S. knew the one who died very well ; he had been with her last Monday ; she told me he was the only son of a widow, who has nine daughters, only two of whom are married ; another is a cripple ; he was the idol of his family, and so good, so clever, so promising. Less than three years ago his father was brought home dead to his mother ; he died of apoplexy. Is it not dreadful ? When Mrs. S. first heard it, she was told they were drunk and out " on the spree." She said, " Then it can't be true, for Edmond Murney would never be out on the spree." This quaint expression, used in such a sad tone of voice, amused me much; but oh, how sad and awful the whole story is. I drove myself to the office; my first trial in driving a sleigh. This morning I have been tobogganing with Dick; I am getting to like it. Ask for *London Society* for February, 1863; page 177 gives a capital picture of tobogganing.

Monday, January 2nd.—On Saturday I got "quite a number" of letters per Cunard mail. I drove myself, to the groom's terror! Bill Seward is such a pet; he rubs his head against me, and eats bread from my hand. Dick came with me to Henderson's shop, and he chose some snow-shoes. Captain King and Major Brice, and "Paul" (the latter's dog) were there. Captain K. says ours is the prettiest sleigh he has seen. On Sunday the cold was great, only five people at the early service. To-day is very cold, eight degrees above zero, and last night it was two degrees below. The 17th give a dance on Wednesday, and the 25th theatricals on Thursday, under the patronage of the G. G. They are to have "Macbeth Travestie," and "A Charming Pair." Dick walked all round the place on snow-shoes yesterday.

Tuesday, January 3rd.—Yesterday I drove to Quebec; the streets were unpleasantly full of sleighs, every one driving to pay visits. My veil was *covered* with ice, thermometer ten degrees above zero. Before I went out I had a visit from dear old Mr. Price, who came to wish me a happy new year, and to ask us to dine some day soon, to taste some canvas-back ducks. Capt. Pem. was to dine that night; but Mr. Price said, " I said to our daughter Mary, 'We will not ask Mrs. Monck to-night, as it is to be a rollicking party.'" To-day I am to lunch at *one*, because of the levée. I went out sliding this morning, and flew all across the cricket-field. I took off my crinoline, and tied myself up in a sheet to keep the snow from my petticoats. I begin to think it very exciting.

Wednesday, 4*th*.—The levée was great fun. I stayed behind a door with glass windows to it, and saw without being seen. The officers all looked very nice in uniforms, with furs. There was a very good lunch laid out for them. The G. G. had to shake hands with *every one* of the people. Col. Hassard drove four white steeds in his sleigh. I got Col. Gordon to look with me. He sat on a coal-box in uniform. Two dogs came of course to the levée. Nothing can happen here without dogs; Dick says one pointer walked into the room with its master, and then went to lunch. Tom (the cat) sat in the hall, looking very dignified, and taking no notice of the dogs; but Fuss and Beauty (the two dogs here) were fighting together upstairs. Some of the shopmen were volunteers in uniform. The new R.A. colonel was there. There were about four hundred people. They settled their hair before they went in, but some had one foot in the room before they took off their fur caps. The "French element" was largely represented, also the Church — Anglican and Roman; the Bishops of both denominations were present. The priests looked too funny with their furs and succession of coats on. Old Judge Caron *y était;* he and many others sent me their "respects and good wishes." Col. R. (25th) was full of bringing his regiment up here to-morrow on snow-shoes, and making them sing a song when they come! Many of the people came in yellow Indian slippers. Mr. S. shook hands warmly with Dick, whom he had never seen before. Dick says most of the men yesterday shook hands with him.

Thursday, 5th. — After lunch yesterday Dick and I went to the rink; he met me in town; we saw some most exquisite skating.

Miss M.'s skating is just what Captain W. said of it—"the poetry of motion." I believe he borrowed this expression from Captain Parker, in speaking of a *horse*. She wore red petticoat and stockings, and had a brown dress and pretty fur cap—no cloak, and she looked like one of Leech's pictures; she has lovely fair golden hair. She flies through the rink, and does figures on skates, and bends on one side like a swallow, and she is so perfectly graceful all the time. The sunset was eastern, and finished by throwing a pink hue over everything. After dinner we went to the 17th ball. I had two lovely camellias in the front of my dress, but I forgot about the frost, and when I looked at them during the ball they were both turned black! The ball was very pleasant, but I danced too much, and I am so dreadfully tired. I was asked to dance eighteen times. Miss Archibald was there with no chaperone but a friend's brother, so as she came to me rather in a fuss, I offered to take charge of her; but I never saw her till I was leaving, and she came out of the room with me. There were "quite a number" of pretty girls. Madame D. at the ball began telling me how she was refused Absolution and the Holy Sacrament because she had fast dances at her house. I missed Dick from the ball for an hour, and found that he and some elderly men were playing whist off in some room far away. Mr. W., R.A., dances just as he plays cricket, with such *force*. He spends his days skating, and now skates beautifully; if you could see him trying over and over again to learn figures at the rink, and never giving up, although almost falling in the attempt. The funny sight at the rink was black Captain —— struggling between two other officers, looking in agony, but still working on; he looked so helpless. It is not worth while for me to learn to skate, and I fear I may break my arms and legs. This morning the 25th marched up here on snow-shoes; a very fine sight! The snow-shoes are like enormous racquets, and are fastened on over yellow mocassins. Some of the men were left behind, and tumbled about sadly. They gave three cheers, and one cheer more for the G. G.

Friday, 6th, Epiphany. — I drove into town yesterday after lunch, and found they were waiting for the Canadian mail to arrive at the office, and I went to ask for "Adamson" *en attendant*, and found Mrs. A. at home; he is much better. She told me she had a hundred and twenty gentlemen to see her on New Year's Day, or rather Monday. She said she could not go to live at Ottawa, "because there is no water in the houses, and no earth for my mignonette." When I returned to the office, I got my welcome letters. After a six-o'clock dinner, we all went off to the music-hall. I went in the hooded sleigh with the G. G. I walked into the room on the G. G.'s arm, preceded and followed by officers; they played "God save," etc. I felt rather grand. You never saw a better or a more enthusiastic house. I enclose programme. The play was "Macbeth Travestie." The prologue was very well spoken by Col. Robertson, and the acting of the first piece was capital. Dr. Lawler (25th) acted very well, but did not know his part. Capt. E. was very good, and looked so hideous in a yellow coat covered with red hearts. Mr. Stoney made a most lovely woman. Every one was in uniform, and the room looked gay. I have just been to Church here, and walked back; it snowed all the time, and I am so hot with tramping through the snow. Col. R., who makes a fuss about everything, came and apologized to us for Mr. C.'s bad legs! In one scene they all had a ballet in night-gowns. The band was lovely. In the witch scene, where they made apparitions, was Mr. Collis, in a night-gown, followed by his enormous Maltese dog, also in a night-dress and night-cap; it ran in on its hind legs. Such a sight I never saw; the house almost came down with applause. The "gods" were very quiet this time. Lady Macbeth, in a pink sun-bonnet and watering-pot, was delicious. F. Burrowes is come out to-day, but I fear the snow has spoilt the slide for to-day. Mr. Brown, President of the Executive Council, has been staying with Lord Palmerston in England. Conway has been invited to the grand ball next Monday, given by the 25th sergeants to the 17th sergeants. I am letting her go with Sergeant Lambkin (orderly) and wife. Mrs. Lambkin is to wear a black silk, with low body and short sleeves, and is taking dancing-lessons. Happily Conway won't wear a low dress.

January 9th.—Last Friday, F. Burrowes and Dick and I tobogganed for a long time; the slide was not spoilt. We went down all three together on the same toboggan, which must have had a funny effect. Saturday was very fine and cold. I drove to town after lunch. "Bill Seward" was frisky, and frightened me two or three times. I sat at the office with Dick while the sleigh went to have its back robes fitted on; it looks so lovely with them; they are black bear trimmed with Brigade colours. We took a drive. Ice is covering the river; they expect an "ice-bridge" to be formed very soon. It is not a real bridge, as I fancied; it is only that the ice on the river *connects*, and people can walk, skate, or drive over the river. I remember once in London showing Thackeray a photograph of the ice-bridge at Quebec. He asked me where the *bridge* was, and I, very much abashed, had to say I supposed the *bridge* part was left out by mistake, though we were sent the photo as an "ice-bridge." The sunset was gorgeous, brightest scarlet and yellow; the sun a ball of fire, and the moon came out so clear one could almost read by it. It looked like a cold sun, it was so bright.

Sunday was *too* cold. Thermometer ten degrees below zero on Saturday night, and on Sunday morning it was two degrees above zero; in the afternoon two degrees below. I did not go to church till the afternoon, from sheer dread of the cold out, and the heat of the church. I drove there and back, and thought my nose would drop off, so I hid my face under the robes. To-day is snowing, and sixteen degrees above zero. Dick has been snow-shoeing all over the place; he does it very well. I got my Cunard letters, thank God, on Saturday, written on Christmas Eve.

Tuesday, 10th.—I drove with Dick after lunch to see the ice-bridge. From Durham Terrace (platform over the river) it has taken beautifully; the paper says it is the best one for years. It looked most curious to see people walking and driving across the river, and skating upon it. Dick had already walked across. You know he is at the office most of the morning, and in the afternoon is generally free now, when there is so little to do. I was amused watching the new R.A. colonel and wife and niece, who were also looking at the bridge. He is celebrated for his love of a pet cat. He once lost a passage by going back to fetch his cat, and he had to pay his own passage instead of Government paying it for him. We then went to the rink, where the R.A. band was playing, and we saw some exquisite dancing on skates. Captain H. would adore his "muffin" if he could see her on skates. Poor Captain E. was struggling alone on skates, working his arms like a wind-mill, and

AN ALARM OF FIRE.

looking broken-hearted. Conway went to the 25th soldiers' ball. We had a fine fright in the night. About four a.m. the G. G. came to our door with a thundering knock, and told Dick to get up, saying, "There is a fire in the house." I jumped up too, but could do nothing to help, so I tried to pacify Beauty, who was in a state of terror. Dick soon came, and said it would be nothing. This is the way it was found out: the G. G. was awake, and smelt some smoke in his room. He got up, and found the smell much worse in his sitting-room, and then thought of looking into the drawing-room, which was full of smoke, and flames were issuing from the ground. It is supposed to have been a spark that flew out, and set fire to the carpet and rug, and it burnt all through the floor, and a large beam which goes under all the rooms on that side of the house was quite charred in the drawing-room. The men-servants were roused, and with buckets and jugs of water it was after some time put out. I was terrified at the dreadful smoke, and the running about and calling. When they came to tell me it was going out, I went and stood where I was on the levée day, and was much amused at seeing the page (who, by the way, has the same face as every other page), coming up when everything was over, dressed in his best, with his hair well brushed! We might all have been burnt to death if the G. G. had not awoke. Thank God we are all safe. If you could see the hole in the drawing-room floor you would be shocked. Dick's first act was to call the sentry; but no sentry could he find, so he went off this morning and spoke to our "commander-in-chief" in the little barracks here about it. Conway enjoyed the ball very much. There was a Maltese woman there, a sergeant's wife, who had had a baby five weeks before, and she had the baby with her at the ball, and gave it to some one to keep while she danced! The officers' wives were there, and danced with the sergeants. A few days before the ball I instilled into Conway's mind how terrible was the life of a soldier's wife. There were twenty-four dances and two extra ones, and they had engagement cards. We dine to-night at the Prices', and to-morrow there is to be a tremendous "drum" at the Bishop's. To-day is not cold, and snowing and blowing.

Wednesday, 11*th*.—Yesterday we had the worst snow-hurricane known for years. I enclose you what the papers say about it. I passed a most dreary day all alone. Dick walked home just before dark, wet and white with snow. We dined at Mr. Price's, and I was quite ill with terror as we plunged through the drifts of snow, and felt the hurricane. If it had not been close by I should not have gone. Two officers of the 17th were there, and beds were ready for them as the night was so terrific, but they could not stay. M. Cartier dined in full uniform! no one knows why. There were fourteen at dinner. We had canvas-back ducks, and found them very good. M. Cartier sang after dinner, and made every one he could find stand up, hold hands, and sing a chorus. The wretched servants brought in tea, and he pushed them away till after his song was over. Miss Price told me that at the 25th theatricals, when there was "The grand pas de night-gowns," one girl nearly cried, and said she could not look at such a sight, and only remained in the theatre by her brother saying the men had clothes underneath their night-gowns. Mrs. Gilmour (who dined) told me a great deal about the Protestant Home; it is for all destitute people of every sect, except Roman Catholics. The people are fed and clothed if very poor; there are fifty inmates now. They have a children's place and school there also, and "ministers" of every denomination visit it. If the wind rises again, I will not go to the bishop's.

Thursday, 12th.—I drove in to town yesterday. You cannot conceive what the drifts are since the hurricane! up to the top of the walls and gates—one in the shape of an iceberg; it is like pictures of the arctic regions. It was five degrees above zero, with a wind. My blue veil and "cloud" were lumps of hard ice, which kept me quite warm, as no air could get in. This mail will not reach you for ages, as the ship has to stop at Newfoundland to pick up passengers. There is to be a big dinner here on Saturday.

Friday, 13th.—Thermometer yesterday seven degrees above zero, and snowing dreadfully. I drove out in the snow. I see you have had it very cold at home; down to twenty-five degrees. We are invited tonight to a ball at the rink; it is a lovely and curious sight, I hear. The Skating Club have invited us. There will be immense Parliamentary dinners here every Saturday night. Thermometer to-day thirty degrees above zero—very changeable climate; to-day only two degrees of frost, and yesterday twenty-five degrees.

Saturday, January 14th.—This is even a more awful day than last Tuesday; a frightful hurricane and the worst snow-storm we have had yet. The gardener told Dick he had some difficulty in getting here to-day, even on snow-shoes. There is a drift nine feet high on the road. How the people will ever come to-night I can't say. After lunch yesterday I drove to town as usual; I paid Mère St. Charles a long visit at the Ursulines Convent. I could only see her through the grille, poor thing. She was so glad to see me, and told me so much about her life. She had a fancy for being a nun when only five years old, and instead of choosing to wear fine clothes on Sunday, she used to ask to have a nun's dress in which she used to sport about. She was left an orphan when young, and told me she was a "child of the convent." When twenty-one, she took two years to consider whether she would take the black veil, and she took it, and told me she is very happy. She had just parted with her brother, so she did not seem very happy. She told me that a young girl had come to the convent lately, very clever and accomplished, and had taken the white veil for two years, and then could not like the convent life, so she has left it; she said only some people have a calling for it. She hated teaching music when she was young, but now she teaches twenty-four pupils a day, and likes it because it is part of her duty. She told me that six nuns had died last year in the Ursulines; very sad. She interested me. The Romanists are not bigoted here, and she did not try any controversial talk. After the convent, I went for Dick, and we went to look at the ice-bridge again. They have five roads across it now, planted with little fir trees to mark the track. They make roads here in the snow in this way; they stick little fir trees in the snow to prevent your driving into deep snow, and to show you where the road has been ploughed and rolled. They plough it regularly like a field first, and then roll it. The day was nice and mild, twenty-four degrees. We call that rather mild here, though it rarely gets as low as that in England. After dinner I dressed for the rink ball, by putting on over-stockings and boots, many warm things under my seal-skin coat, and my fur cap instead of a wreath! Dick invited Captain Pem. to the ball; you know he had no right to do so, which amused me. When we arrived, I was struck with the very pretty and novel sight; the rink was lit with gas, and decorated with flags and ornaments; there were tables with refreshments on the ice, and the 25th band was playing. It looked like a fair in a Dutch picture; most of the girls wore *very short* red petticoats, and grey or black dresses; some wore scarlet, and some white feathers in their fur caps, and most of the officers wore their mess uniforms. I sat at the end of the rink till F. B. skated up to me, and told me there was a place meant for me on a sofa near the top of the rink; so up there I struggled. I found M. Cartier there, and Mrs. R. M. C. looked so odd in fur coat and cap, with spectacles on his nose! I cried with laughing looking at the skaters; some did it too beautifully. To see Miss Maxham and a Miss Eppy Ross waltzing together was prettier than any ballet. Captain E. I spied in his mess uniform with the saddest face, teeth set, and arms like a wind-mill, struggling on alone, heeding no one, and looking as if nothing but death could stop him. All the time the others were dancing quadrilles, lancers, or valses, there he was steadily tearing round the rink alone, sometimes knocked against, but always righting himself, and looking as awkward as possible. He looked like a person shuffling along with slippers too large for him; do you know what I mean? Then there was Mr. Wingfield with his head on one side, *arm-in-arm* with another beginner, both shuffling along against time, and ending by a good tumble; they looked like two helpless tipsy men. Then Colonel Hassard came up near me, and I remarked that he did not bow; at last he shuffled up holding on by Mr. Harding, R.E., saying, "I *daren't* bow to you." Mr. Sitwell skated about looking intensely composed. It was funny to see the gentlemen skating over with wine and water to the ladies. I never was more amused, and was very angry at leaving; we left so early—about eleven. Miss Archibald skated through some quadrilles wonderfully, having only been ten times on skates.

Monday, 16*th.*—I must tell you of Saturday. It got worse and worse every hour; the hurricane was terrific, and snow in clouds was blown from the ground. After lunch Dick went out snow-shoeing and sliding in this terrific weather! About four I saw a snow-covered and frozen figure come to the door on snow-shoes: his hair, whiskers, etc., so covered with *ice*, I could not discern his features; a belt was round his waist and a capuchin on his head. This, to my utter surprise, turned out to be "Gordon the Good." In the hall, even, I did not know him. He begged for a towel, which I got him, and he scrubbed the ice off his face, and soon came and sat over the fire with me. Presently another figure entered the house, *much more* ice-covered than Gordon the Good, and with a capuchin also, face quite undistinguishable from ice—ice hanging from his eyelids, eyebrows, and beard and moustaches; this iceman, who looked like old Time without his scythe, turned out to be Dick! He had to sit at the fire over a basin thawing! Soon Captain P. and F. B. arrived. F. B. had waded in big boots through snow-drifts up above his knees. Some refusals to the dinner came on account of the weather, and the party ended in *thirteen*, only one lady had courage to come. *Twelve* did not come, most of them neither came nor sent refusals. The Bishop of Quebec took me in, and was extremely agreeable; he says things so abruptly that he finishes off people in two words, when another man would take twenty to give the same opinion. M. Cartier sat on my other side. The Bishop told me he was very angry with Mrs. Botwood for making her husband leave Labrador, and that she said she would go to the north pole with him before her marriage. There is a clergyman near there now whose parish extends a hundred and twenty miles. He said he longed always to choose the clergymen's wives for them, that was a piece of preferment he coveted. Before he came out here, he says he knew nothing of Canadian geography, and fancied there were only three towns out here — Quebec, Montreal, and Toronto. He said, when the Bishop of Nassau (Bahamas) was to be consecrated, that the Bishop of Oxford took the bishop-elect aside, and said to him *confidentially*, " I think it would be well for you to have the Bishop of *Sydney* at your consecration," evidently implying that he would be a neighbour, and might be kind to him! After dinner I set M. Cartier and Judge D. fighting, and I helped on both parties. At last Judge D. got so excited he pushed me with one arm and Cartier with the other. Yesterday I did not go to Church till the afternoon; the cold was frightful, zero all day. We had another fire alarm last night. After dinner the drawing-room chimney went on fire, and made smoke go into Conway's room and press. There is so much snow on the roof, there was no danger, but I was startled. Dick dines with Sir E. Taché to-morrow, a man's dinner at the club. May Dundas writes that their little island is much against confederation (Prince Edward's Island).

Tuesday, January 17*th.*—Yesterday was so frightfully cold (six below zero). I did not take my everlasting drive to Quebec, but went in the sleigh for Dick. Poor Major Earle is very ill. Dick went to see him, and he is very cheery. To-day is a glorious day to *look* at, but a terrible day to feel. The sky is cloudless and the sun so bright, the thermometer four degrees above zero. "Adamson" went to see the G. G. one day, and said he was better, "but when a man falls *head over heels* twice in the cathedral, at least it is a warning." We are invited to a dinner and dance at Madame D.'s on Thursday. I shan't go if the weather is bad.

Wednesday, 18*th.*—What do you think happened to poor Tom the cat? On Saturday night she went out, and in some way was shut out, and remained frozen into the snow till Monday, when she was discovered! She could not move, and one of the maids, in rooting her out, got her own fingers frostbitten! We found Tom's feet and ears swollen and much hurt by the frost; she was in great pain, and lay fainting, unable to eat anything. We warmed her and gave her warm milk; by degrees she took a little, and was at last able to stand; she took meat yesterday, and is by degrees getting better. It was a piteous sight to see her. Dick, the footman, and I did our best for her. After lunch yesterday I had a visit from Madame Gautier (French Consul's wife) and her son. She is very pleasant. She told a funny story about a Baron who went to see one of the Rothschilds, who was very busy writing, and said only, "Take a chair, sir." The Baron got impatient from waiting some time, and said, "Do you know I am the Baron of ——?" Mr. de R. got angry, and called out, "Then take two chairs," and went on writing. I drove into town, thermometer zero, or below it. I was quite ill with cold, my head felt quite dull and dead; I don't mean to drive again in such weather. Dick dined with Sir E. Taché; sixteen people and a very good dinner at the club. Colonel G. and Colonel R. there in uniform, to please Sir E. Poor Major Earle continues very ill. Some of the invited of Saturday night were not to blame; Judge Stewart set out and got stuck in the snow, and the snow was up over his ears sitting in the sleigh. Mr. MacDougal was told by a sleigh man he would bring him here, but would not undertake to bring him home again. I asked the footman yesterday before I went out what the thermometer was; he answered in delight, "Twenty-eight degrees below zero, ma'am." It has never been so low in the daytime the whole winter; he did not know he was romancing. I believe it had been that the night before at Quebec. If you could have seen his joy in telling me this.

Thursday, 19th.—I only walked in the verandah yesterday, I was too cold to drive. Conway has a very bad throat, lumps inside and outside; the doctor says people here are very subject to these throats. There was a man official dinner here, and I was let to come in in the evening. Each of the gentlemen made me a low bow as they came in from the dining-room. Mr. Kimber (Usher of the Black Rod) is celebrated in public life for his bows, which are quite marvellous. An Honble. Mr. Alexander, of the Upper House, was introduced to me; he lived eight years in Germany, and is going to lend me German books; he begged of me to come to the library, and that I should be escorted over it. I did not say that I had been there before. Mr. Kimber also offered me German books which his son had just brought over. Mr. Kimber's great subject is Sir A. Clifford; I hear he is always writing to Sir A. about points of ceremony. Mr. Brown dined; he is just come from London, and looks quite happy; he says he was received with open arms in England, was asked about, and treated very grandly. He was invited to Broadlands, and Lord Pam. said, "Brown, will you take a walk? You don't mind snow, do you?" He says there is great excitement about confederation in London. He was enchanted with his visit. General Lindsay and Captain Eliot came back in the ship with him, so I shall soon, I hope, get my parcel. Dick skated for the first time yesterday, and found it very difficult. The new extra Provincial A.D.C., Major Bernard, dined last night; he is in the volunteers. To-day I hope to go and see Parliament opened. I must tell you the Bishop advised me to go and see the Protestant Home, and said though he did not approve of it so much as the Church Home, yet he believed it was well managed, and he thought it better to take in all sects without characters, than let them die of hunger in the streets. Here is a riddle for you. " If you saw a conundrum sitting on a rainbow, and wanted to shoot it, what chorus of a popular ditty would you sing?" I half guessed it. Here is the answer. "Ri-fol-de-riddle, de riddle on de ray.—*Rifle* the riddle, de riddle on de ray." Is it not a quaint riddle? Dick of course says it is a thing that no fellow could see, a conundrum on a ray!!

Friday, 20th. — Dick lunched with me early yesterday, and drove me in to see Parliament opened. The streets were lined with soldiers; it snowed much all the time. There was a guard of honour of the 25th at the Parliament House. I went in by a private door to the Speaker's room, and there took off my wraps. M. Tessier, Speaker of the Upper House, took me on his arm, and deposited me in an armchair in a very good place. I was the only lady without cap or bonnet. The House was immensely crowded with ladies and women. The G. G. and "a brilliant staff" arrived at three; he looked very well in his handsome dress, and he read his speech so well and distinctly, first in English, and then in French. The M.P.P.'s of the Lower House came to the Bar of the Upper House when the speech was to be read. The heat was stifling, and I thought I should have fainted. The speech was very long but very good. The G. G. came in a shut sleigh with four horses. As soon as the *cortège* left the room, "Adamson" whispered to me that I might go, so I crept back to the Speaker's room. It was much milder driving home, but still I had ice on my chin through all my veils and cloud. We had to go off to Chief Justice Duval's for 6.30 dinner! The old Chief took me in to dinner. I sat between him and Mr. Serecold, who is very agreeable. We had wild turkey, which I was curious to taste; it is excellent. It is great fun hearing Judge Duval and his son-in-law fighting about Canada; it seemed a fresh subject, but Captain Pem. told me it happens *every* night. The Chief speaks English with a *little* foreign accent. Mr. S. told me Mr. —— used to be called, "Look to Washington, ——," as he wanted union with America, and now he is in the Ministry. Mr. Serecold told me that Boston is a very literary town (the Athens of America). There is a public library there from which *every* citizen may borrow books, high and low just the same. After ages, the dancing began. Some of the 25th played. We had only very few fast dances because of Madame D.'s conscience! There was scarcely any one I knew there; I wonder why? two or three came in at the end. Dick played whist nearly the whole night. It was most amusing to see Mrs. E. dressing up before she left; she is appallingly thin, and nearly *dies* of cold, and is afraid of sleighing, so she walks. I saw her putting on a warm dark-red flannel cloak, and I said, "What a nice warm cloak." She answered, "Do you know this is my dressing-gown!" Over it she put a dark blue jacket lined with chamois, and over that her husband's military cloak! a fur cap, fur gloves, and a "cloud," completed her costume. I like Mrs. K. (25th) because she is a coward. To-day the thermometer is twenty-two degrees above zero. No mail, or news of one.

Monday, January 23*rd.*—We must return to Friday last, which was a fine day, thermometer twenty-two degrees above zero in morning, and fourteen above in afternoon. I drove to Quebec, where I got Dick, and he drove me down on the iced river nearly to Point Lévis on the other side. It was a most curious feeling to be *driving* where we had gone in a steamer a few months ago. I felt as if I was in the Arctic regions, ice surrounding us on every side. There are several first-rate roads on the ice, marked out by trees, and covered with drifted snow; one can drive on the transparent ice, but

I should not like that. They were practising for a trotting-match between quick trotting horses and sleighs like spiders. It amused me to see them fly over the ice. The wind had got up, and it was so bitterly cold on the river I was glad to get home again. I had a visit on my return from Mr. and Mrs. S. I asked about poor Mr. Murney's family, and she said his mother was not the least surprised to hear of his death, and bore it very calmly; she always expected he would die suddenly. Mr. S. said, "You know his father died suddenly." Whereupon Mrs. S. said, "that had nothing to do with it," and they had a slight difference of opinion over the affair. They left an invite to dine on Tuesday. Mr. S. is head of the Indian department. Saturday was a most perfect day, thermometer twenty-eight degrees above zero—quite warm. I drove to town, and got F. Burrowes, and he drove me to see some Misses Pemberton—their house is hard to find, and down a horrid snow-hill, terribly steep. The house is a large grey building like a book-house, looking over the St. Charles valley, a wonderful view. I then got Dick at the office, and he drove me a long way on the river, first to Point Lévis and then home on another ice road. Dick had seen Major Earle; he found "the doctor," *alias* Kirwan the horse-dealer, sitting with him and amusing him. The view on the river was exquisite, the clear blue sky made the ice look quite green, and the sun made the blocks of ice sparkle like diamonds. Hundreds of skaters made the river look very lively, and sleighs were flying about in all directions with their tinkling bells. After a nice long drive, we returned home, and found Major W. and Gordon the Good. Major W. wore a pair of yellow mocassins instead of boots, which smelt horribly. Sunday was a very fine day and not at all cold. I drove to morning service and walked back. The heat in church was so unbearable that I thought I should have a fit. I never mean to go again in the morning. You cannot conceive what it is; two hot-air places, a gigantic stove, and swarms of people in a small church! Walking in snow is so tiring. To-day (Monday) we have wind and snow. We are invited to-morrow to a picnic to Montmorençi with the Prices. I can't make up my mind; I dread the long excursion in the cold; but one ought to do one picnic.

Tuesday, 24*th*.—Yesterday I drove to Miss Price and talked about the picnic;

they are bringing musicians and food, and mean to slide first on the Cone; she said I might leave it uncertain about going. The Cone is formed of frozen spray from the Falls. I toiled, or, rather, "Bill Seward" toiled through the deep snow to see Mrs. Botwood, who was absent. The avenue is quite unswept, and it is so hard to get on. The maid pressed me to go in and see Mr. B., but though I longed to go in, I thought it wiser to refuse. I met Dick on the road; the wind was too high to venture to Quebec across the plains. There is to be a dinner-party here on Thursday, and we are invited on Friday to a dinner and dance at Mr. Gilmour's, near this. No mail yet; very sad. To-day is warm and windy; I do not mean to attempt the picnic.

Wednesday, 25th.—The wind was so high yesterday with drifting snow that I did not think of driving out; but I hear they went to the picnic. There was a function at the Council-chamber of presenting addresses in answer to the speech from the throne—they do that here—and there was a guard of honour, and people were in uniform. The G. G. and Dick went in early. I got my parcel from Captain Eliot in the evening—great delight! It is great excitement opening a box from home. To-day is lovely, and being the festival of the Conversion of St. Paul, I have arranged to go and have tea with Colonel ——, and go to church after. The Botwoods are to dine here on Thursday; I am so glad. Some of the 17th ladies have just had babies, and Colonel G. is so angry about it, he says, " It's *disgraceful* in a marching regiment." No mail.

Thursday, 26th.—Two mails may come to-day; they are in. Yesterday I drove to town and went to see Madame Tessier (Speaker's wife), and the wife of the new R.A. colonel. Madame T. made me talk French; but her English is so pretty, and amuses me so. She says Madame —— thinks everything wrong, and says that every woman is blind when she marries, and that she was blind when she took her husband. Dick came then; they had had another function on presenting the address of the Upper House. We then drove down on the ice, which we found covered with snow and very heavy. There was a soft, pinky, mauve light on the ice from the setting sun. The tide was full in, which makes the ice rise so high that one has no descent to drive down to get to it. If you could see the enormous thickness of the blocks of ice taken from the St.

Charles you would fancy that no tide could affect it. I would not go to tea with Col. —— because of the function, as he had to be at it. I met him, and told him so. He was very sorry, and said his servant was so disappointed. I said, " I shall not have much time ; but if you like, I will come now ; " and he answered, " No, you can't come now, for *I have sent my cake back to the baker's ! !* " Old Mr. Alexander sent me a paper containing his speech in the House the other night!

Friday, 27th.—After lunch yesterday I drove to town and found, thank God, the Canadian mail letters of January 5th. At dinner Mr. Rose took me in, and I always find him very pleasant. Mrs. Rose was loud in lamenting the Guards, and says the green jackets will never come up to them. Mr. Botwood has beautiful hands with long taper fingers. He said to me, clasping his hands, " I'd give *all* I possess except the coat on my back to be back at Labrador." He said the people have no one now specially to look after them, only some one from another parish. He was so sorry to leave them, and they *so* sorry to lose him ; he felt he was doing them good. He said only for Mrs. B. he would go back to-morrow. How good he must be! He says he will show me the shoes they wear at Labrador, so high out of the snow, the Labrador people say they have so much "bear up" in them. Mrs. B. is so delicate that if she takes a walk she is sick for three days. I promised to take her a drive sometimes. Mrs. R. Ross invited us to go on Saturday at 8.30 to her house to hear the K.O.B. string-band. There is a man dinner here, so I shall not go.

Saturday, January 28*th.*—Yesterday I was rejoiced by Cunard letters of January 7th. I never can be thankful enough for letters. It was a cold and fine day. We dined at Mr. Gilmour's, near this. Our party consisted of Mr. and Miss Rose, Colonel and Mrs. M., and Miss R. (the girl cousin), Colonel Gordon, a Miss Gordon from Montreal, an old man, name unknown, and Mr. Allen, M.P.P., from Toronto. I sat between him and Mr. Gilmour. Mr. A. is very pleasant, and I learnt a good deal about the American war from a fight between him and Mr. Gilmour and Colonel Mc. all against Mrs. Rose, with her "northern proclivities." Some of Mr. A.'s talk I pretended to understand, but did not (you know I am rather hazy about the war). In the middle of the dinner Colonel Mc. said, "I can *bear* it *no longer,*" and got up and left the room saying his toothache was so fearfully painful he must leave the room, and so he did. Colonel Mc. soon reappeared, and said it was a bare nerve that he could not get rid of; he added, "I had one nerve *cut out* once, and it was such *agony* that I jumped out of the chair up to the ceiling." This he said in quite an angry tone of voice; Mrs. Rose and I laughed so. To see his determined face was charming. We were thirteen at dinner! Mr. Allen told me that in some of the houses in the Southern States you find old English pictures by Copley and such artists, and quite old things. We had a long moan over horrid Ottawa. Mrs. Mc. had been in Newfoundland for two years, and before she came out she was told that the wind there was so awful that people never could walk without being tied together. There is an exquisite long greenhouse at this house, there was one wild primrose in a pot which reminded one of home. They have a lovely ballroom at Mr. Gilmour's. Some 17th soldiers played infamously. I was very much the better for my ball. We had the usual oyster pies at supper; the very look of them makes me feel ill. This is a heavenly Canadian day—cloudless, deep blue sky, etc.

Monday, 30th.—After lunch on Saturday

I drove to town. I paid the Roses a visit, and heard an account of a fancy ball at Montreal, given at the rink, on skates, you know. One woman went as "Hooflands' Golden Bitters," in a jar! I went to see old Chief Justice B., to thank him for his photo. I went to his study to see him, and he was much pleased; he called me "My dear lady." He says he never goes out from the time the snow begins till it is gone. I asked him if his spirits suffered, and he answered, "Why, I am only eighty-five, and I feel younger and younger in spirits every day." I finished up with Mrs. MacD. She comes from Upper Canada. The street was full of boys playing, and she told me they were all hers; she has seven sons and three girls! In the evening there was an immense Parliamentary dinner of twenty-four. I went in to the drawing-room after dinner, and Colonel Irvine introduced the M.P.P.'s to me. I talked a long time to old Judge Day, who is very pleasant. He lives at Lake Memphramagog, and wants us to go down there again in the summer. He asked me to accept some photos of the lake, Owl's Head, etc., just what I wanted; but we could not succeed in getting them. He knows Bryant the poet very well. Bryant is seventy years old; he is different from Longfellow as a poet. Bryant seldom writes, and only when a good thought strikes him; but Longfellow is always writing. I also talked to Dr. Robitaille, the seconder of the address on the speech. Colonel I. introduced him as "one of our youngest members." He is M.D. at Gaspe, and I suppose all his patients die while he is attending Parliament. Whenever he does go to them, he has to walk seventy miles on snow-shoes. As soon as the session is over, he means to go through the military school, so his patients are to be pitied. I also talked to a Mr. de Beaujeu; his family the only remains of the old French families here. Do you know, seventy M.P.P.'s are going to learn their drill, and have begun already. I think they deserve credit. *Sunday* was fine. I only went to church in the afternoon. The heat was great; the sermon happily only eighteen minutes; the morning one had been thirty! This is a heavenly day, like July.

Tuesday, January 31*st.*—We may get more letters to-day, as I hear the *Peruvian* is in; she only left home on the 19th—a very quick passage, for she was in yesterday. Yesterday the weather was most lovely and cloudless; not cold. After dinner we went in to the 25th ball. The terrible cold of the citadel was almost past enduring; they have made snow walls to keep the wind off round the yard. The crowd was very great; it was impossible to dance. A reel was danced. Fancy M. Cartier dancing it; he had never tried it before; he did it wonderfully. I did not care for the ball, as it was too crowded to dance; but old Mrs. T., in spectacles and with grey hair, danced a quadrille with Mr. Bridges of the Grand Trunk Railway. With Mr. Alexander I had some conversation on the militia out here; Canada's duty, etc. He told me there had been a row in the House about the Militia Bill that day, and that Sir —— had insulted him! He is going to send me a paper with an account of it. It was snowing; I drove to town and got Dick, who drove me to Mr. Gilmour's, where I had arranged to go and see his underground farmyard. We found Mrs. G.'s mother in the drawing-room playing "solitaire," alone. We then trudged out in the snow (I on Mr. G.'s arm) to the farmyard. It is very nice and curious, all underground, and heated by a stove. He had sixty hens; one black hen has become quite white since the snow came; it was black "last fall;" another is becoming white. One hen was in a place alone with one little chicken, and the man who showed them said quite angrily, "She has only one chicken, and makes as much work with it as if she had thirty." Mr. G., when he goes to England, goes to Hull, Liverpool, Glasgow, and all those horrid seaport places; he is a ship-builder, and very rich. We then went to see the boys' snow house, a regular house with a table, etc., in it. At home I found an invite from the R.A. and R.E. to a ball next week. We are also invited next week to dine with the "Orateur du Conseil Legislatif, et Madame Tessier."

Thursday, 2nd.—Yesterday was a heavenly day. The G. G. says to me every day, "*Now*, what do you think of the Canadian climate?" Dick and I went to the rink, where the 17th band played. There were many spectators, but few skaters. Captain E., in uniform, was there, shuffling round and getting on better than before. After dinner we went to the Stadacona Ball. The crowd was very great, and at first I could not see any one I knew. At last my partners found me, and I danced a great deal. There were only quadrilles and galops, and but *one* valse, whilst I was there. One man wore a bright red cravat. Many wore black ties. You know these balls are very mixed; all the shopkeepers attend them. When I first came to the ball I remarked several paper bags flying about the room, and I verily believe that people brought refreshments in these bags, as you only get tea, ice, etc., there. Yesterday I drove to see Miss Mountain. From her house there is a grand view of the river, and the American hills beyond. Her house is situated at the top of a very high hill; inside it is more like an English house than any I know here. She has a nice organ in her dining-room. I met Dick at the gate here; he drove me to Durham Terrace to look over the ice. It looked lovely with an occasional pink and mauve shade thrown over the ice that had been cleared for skating in different places about the river. The day was perfect. To-night we are invited to a children's ball at the rink, and hope to go; it is a very pretty sight. This afternoon " John A." MacDonald is to make a great speech on confederation. Dick means to go to hear him. I could not bear the heat! This day is lovely.

Saturday, February 4th.—Yesterday after lunch I paid some visits, and then went to see if Dick had gone to hear J. A. M. speak; and found he had not gone, as J. A. M. was not to speak till 7.30. We drove to the

Parliament library to look at some illustrated books that Mr. Todd (under-librarian) wanted to show me. We looked at the marriage of the Prince and Princess of Wales, illustrated by Day in chromo-lithographs; it is wonderfully well done. The colours are marvellous. I poked about among the reading-books, and then went home. After dinner we went to the children's ball at the rink; it was given by the boys of the High school under Mr. Hatch, the clergyman. The boys issued six hundred invites! Mr. Hatch said it taught them how to manage, as they formed a committee and appointed a secretary for the occasion. There was a tremendous crowd. Mr. Hatch stayed with us most of the evening. He introduced the secretary boy to Dick. The boys were so civil, offering food and drink, and flying about on skates with cakes and wine and water. Poor Captain E. was almost an illustration of perpetual motion. There he was in red uniform (the only red man there), shuffling round, never stopping; he was like the brook, running on "*for ever.*" At last he shot himself up against the wall, which he *held* till he shuffled over to me. He said, " It is not that I *want* to go on so long, but the fact is, I *can't* stop, once I set off; the more I try to stop, the more I go on." He said, "I am taking care of a little girl to-night, but she skates so much better than I do that I need not think of trying to catch her." Mrs. E. was ill. The 25th band was most lovely. One man skated a polka mazurka alone so marvellously. Mr. S., R.E., came to talk to me, and shocked me by saying that the Yankees would certainly take Canada in a few years. I said I was sure they could not (not knowing anything about it). He says we never could resist their legions of men. Dick came back from looking for the sleigh in the middle of the argument, but I mean to finish it another time. Dick and the G. G. are on my side, and Captain Pem. is against me. Old Mr. Price thinks war will be immediately, and has arranged how many Yankees are to be in each Canadian town. To return to the rink! Captain E., after sitting with me said, "Now I think I must go, to look after my little *chaperone*," meaning his little charge! He managed at last to capture her. I felt so ill at the rink; I caught cold there, wet was dropping from the roof, and damp ascending from the ice, and a broken window behind me. Every one catches cold there. I have a chill all over me and headache. There was a terrible "Yahoo" skating in grey clothes and yellow boots. The "muffins" looked lovely. Mr. Alexander sent me the newspaper he promised me about his fight with Sir ——. The G. G. was very glad I had it, and asked me to lend it to him.

Monday, 6th.—I left off on Saturday, so I have not much to tell. That afternoon it was snowing, and I felt inclined to stay at home, but I made myself drive to town for Dick, and felt better for the exertion. You can't think how sick it makes me going over "cahots" on the road. "Cahots" are enormous ruts worked out in the snow; you go down and then up, and feel just as if you were in a ship on a rough sea. When the "break up" begins, they are quite awful. I will try and make Dick go to New York then. Every one gets ill at the "break-up" time, and takes tonics to keep up the strength. Saturday night there was a large Parliamentary dinner. Colonel G. came to tea. M. Cartier talked to me nearly all the evening after dinner. I also talked to Mr. Street, of Niagara, and to an old Hon. Mr. Moore, an M.P.P. Cartier gave me an account of his staying at Windsor with the Queen, and how he *would* go to the Anglican service, much to Sir H. Bulwer's annoyance, who wanted to make Cartier an excuse for not going at all! Cartier offended the people out here by going to church. He says the English ladies are both "pretty and handsome." He said the Queen dined with her household to do him honour, a thing she never does on Sundays. She asked a great deal about Canada. He asked the servant at what hour "*the maids*" breakfasted (meaning the maids of honour). He found out that "Lady Flora Macdonald" (as he called her) breakfasted at 9.30, and as he admired her the most he managed to breakfast with her. Yesterday was hot, only a few degrees of frost. I went to afternoon service. It had snowed all day, and the snow was very deep. After five tea, to my great delight, arrived the Cunard mail.

Tuesday, 7th.—Yesterday it rained frozen rain all the afternoon. I had a visit from Mrs. Campbell (late Speaker's wife). She is a Yorkshire lady, and married ten years ago, when she came out here; she means to go home every fourth year, wretched woman. She says when her children get older she does not know how she will manage to educate them, as where they live (at Kingston) there is not a master to be had for love or money. I drove into town in the *very* deep snow for Dick. There was a function at the Parliament House, the G. G. giving assent to the Alien Bill. They had a band and a guard of honour. This warm weather is so unpleasant. You would call it terribly cold, twelve degrees of frost; but here it is hot, as there is no wind.

Wednesday, 8th.—Yesterday I feared the "cahots" too much to drive early, but we went into town for seven-o'clock dinner at the Tessiers', and found a party of sixteen. We had Chief Justice and Madame Duval, M. and Madame Gautier, Mr. Macdougall and wife, Col. G., Mr. *O'Kill* Stewart, and others. M. Tessier took me, and Dick took Mrs. Campbell. Judge Duval ranks as Chancellor, and goes out before Dick. The people were very well dressed. M. Tessier make me talk French to him. He told me he was much disappointed with the *Lords* in the House of Lords in London; he was much disappointed to see Lord Brougham with his yellow waistcoat, and every one looking as mean as any one else. He liked Dublin better than London! He was delighted with the *Hospitals* in Dublin! Madame Tessier told me she had once twelve children; she has now five boys and two girls. After a time dancing began. I danced with Mr. Alexander, M. Tessier,

DANCE AT MADAME TESSIER'S.

Col. Gordon, and the Hon. Mr. A. Everything was a quadrille, so Dick danced away. Madame Duval told him the ladies here call him "the handsome colonel." She told Col. G. he was not so good-looking as Dick, though some people also call him "the handsome colonel." She is as full of fun as a kitten, and wore white, though she is a grandmother. Mr. A. looked at Mrs. —— with her fat red face and pug nose, and said to me, "Splendid woman that Mrs. ——; no country but England could produce a specimen like that." He praised the Gov. Gen. very much, and said they owed to him keeping so well with the States. Madame Tessier and her child played a set of quadrilles. Then a young man and a fat oldish woman in yellow played together another set. Young Canada was largely represented. You meet all the best French Canadians there. One M.D.'s wife was pretty and well dressed. In a small back room where they could not hear the music, Capt. Pem. told me a solemn set of quadrilles was being danced, no one speaking, most of them old folks. We were home by 12.30. I like both M. and Madame Tessier. To-day, to my *great annoyance*, is one of those awful wind and drift days; no chance of my getting in to the R.A. and R.E. ball; I am so angry about it.

Thursday, 9th.— Yesterday was bad all day till evening, when it stopped snowing, and the wind calmed down. Dick walked into town on snow-shoes. They laughed at my fears about the deep snow, and the G. G. made Dick "toss up" to see if I should go to the ball, and the toss said that I *was* to go, and I went in fear and trembling. Oh, the deepness of the snow! it is incredible. Some of the drifts, Dick says, must be fourteen feet; you can see over every one's walls where you could not see before. The poor horse struggled along, wading sometimes up to his knees in snow! We got in wonderfully. The R.A. and R.E. have such a nice band. The room was very large and wide, the floor capital, and the band played very well; it was placed out in the garden, in a wooden place with a stove. There were arrangements with bayonets and flags. I opened the ball with Colonel Hassard, R.E., and went to supper with Colonel ——, who amused me much by the way he went on with the mess-man. The man said, with a brogue, "This is an oyster-pie, sir; it ought to have come up after the twelfth dance, but by some mistake, sir, it has come now."

"More shame for you," said Colonel ——. "I'll tell you what, you ought to be *hanged.*" I asked Colonel —— if he was in earnest. He answered, "Yes, I am; he is the best mess-man in the world, but too extravagant; he buys up all the luxuries in the market—thinks nothing of giving any price for a wild turkey!" Then the mess-man brought me some jelly, and put it before me. I refused it. The man said to Colonel ——, "I thought I would just bring that, sir." "Try it," said the gallant colonel; "he's celebrated for his jelly." "Yes, try it," said the mess-man. I obeyed, and found it very nice. Dick danced a little, and then played whist. There were "quite a number" of pretty girls, and the dress is so improved. The snow kept crowds of people away. Most of the 25th did not come, because they sank above their knees when they tried to walk down from their Citadel. The night was like summer: so mild. Mrs. Gilmour's sister, Mrs. Smith, gave me a lovely bouquet in the cloak-room. I might always have flowers from here, but I can't bear to pick them to die in a hot room. We are invited to a musical party at Madame D.'s to-night, but are not going. Madame D. engaged Dick to go in and play whist with her. I wonder if he will go!

Friday, 10*th*.—Yesterday I drove to town in horror at the deep snow, which is now over the fences! I received three lovely photos from old Judge Day, with such a civil note, begging of me to accept of them as a souvenir of the lake scenery. They are large ones, and very clear and good. After dinner Mr. Godley came to play whist, which kept Dick and "Pem." so late that, though the "cariole" was ready, they could not go to the party. Dick was *really* quite anxious to go. You will not believe this, but it is true. We are longing for a mail.

Saturday, February 11*th*.—No mail! There must have been awful weather on the ocean this week, as not even the large, quick *Australasian*, to New York, has been heard of yet. To-day is lovely and bright, a perfect Canadian day. I mean to pay visits to-day, if I don't die of cold. The 17th give a ball, I hope, on the 22nd.

Monday, 13*th*.—On Saturday I never shall forget the cold; the thermometer was zero ; I felt as if a lump of ice had been placed on my chest, although I was covered with warm clothes; my nose felt as if it would drop off. I went to see Mrs. F. Smith ; her house is like an English villa, and is called Holland House. I went to see

PARLIAMENTARY DINNER.

"Miss Eliza Mattheson," at the hotel; she was at home. Her old father would come down with me to the sleigh, and *slipped* on the snow! (The 25th are at this moment skirmishing before the windows; they make the place look so gay.) Colonel G. came to tea. There is going to be a court-martial here this week on an officer, and many officers are coming from Montreal for it. One of the servants had his ears frost-bitten to-day, and he was jumping and dancing with agony! Parliamentary dinner. Among other people, the new Dean of Ontario dined. He had been a Dean in Ireland. He intoned a very long grace at dinner. I asked him how long he meant to stay out here, and he answered in a chanting voice, "For ev-er and ev-er, A-men." He says he knows the R. Brigade very well at Kingston, and a number of them came to his daily service. I also talked to serene and calm-faced Mr. McDougall, and others. Dear old Col. Irvine's joke *every* Saturday is the same, when introducing all these men, to finish up with, "Do you know Col. Monck?" and then Col. G. always says, "You have not introduced *me*," and then the dear old colonel is so happy. Yesterday was exquisite, but *frightfully* cold, the thermometer had been down to twenty degrees below zero the night before! too dreadful. When I went to church in the afternoon I hid myself quite under the buffalo robe. After church, to my enchantment, I found two mails, January 26 and 28. I am delighted you have ice; it must make you think of us here. I must get Nina to order me a new bonnet, to be ready when I come home, as my present bonnets look like what Mrs. Noah would have worn coming out of the ark, and I have no doubt that if I get safe home, I shall look very much like Mrs. Noah. I send McGee's eloquent speech.

Tuesday, February 14*th.*—Yesterday was most lovely, but oh! too intensely cold when you faced the wind; with the wind at your back, and the sun facing you, you could get quite warm. I only drove for Dick, and he then drove me on the Cap Rouge road. Nothing can equal the dullness of Quebec now. I am not sorry as long as the "cold snap" lasts. "Cold snap" is a trans-Atlantic expression. Mr. Alexander sent me another paper with his speech on confederation, and he also sent me Sir W. L. Bulwer's translation of Schiller's poems. "The Lay of the Bell" is beautifully translated.

Wednesday, 15*th.*—I never wrote so dull

VISIT TO THE PROTESTANT HOME.

a journal as this time; there is nothing to tell. I went yesterday after lunch and got Dick, and we drove to "The Ladies' Protestant Home." Dick would not come in; I went all over it. The matron seemed a nice kind creature. They sat down fifty-six to dinner yesterday. The "ministers" (as Mrs. G. calls them) of each persuasion go Sunday about. These "ministers" fight about their days, but otherwise the Bishop said it was very well managed, better, he was grieved to say, than our Church Home. They have a nursery where they have twenty-six children, one of them only two years old; and they have a school, a nurse and a schoolmistress; the children of a drunken father would be taken in; they don't require to be orphans. Then they have many very old feeble women; they have an infirmary for the sick, a laundry and baths for the people. It is very clean and lofty. Dissenting places are very different from Church places of this sort; there is nothing to elevate their minds in the Dissenting places, not an illuminated text, or a holy picture to be seen. I saw one wretched girl, a terrible object; she looked eight and was nineteen. Four M.D.'s attend month about, gratis. The institution is almost entirely supported by Mr. and Mrs. Gilmore—Mr. G. gives hundreds of pounds to it. The matron told me you would be surprised to see how much these old people eat. I had to write my name in a book, and to make a remark about the institution. So I said " I was much pleased with the institution." Col. G. will be so angry with me for going to a Dissenting place! Lord A. Russell was to have come to stay yesterday, but the court-martial is put off for a week, I am sorry to say! The 17th have a rink party to-morrow night; they sent to ask us through Captain Pem. Sir Fenwick comes here on March 1st to see the cone, which he has never seen. There is to be a grand fancy ball at Montreal, for which the Roses have asked us to go up with them; but this is not weather for " the cars."

Thursday, 16th.—Yesterday I had a visit from Mrs. and Miss Rose. Mrs. R. is very clever and agreeable. She told me that a lady came once to stay with her for four days, and her only luggage was a tooth-brush, which she brought in her pocket. She borrowed a night-dress, a pair of stockings, and a pocket-handkerchief, and changed none of her other clothes during her stay. After the Roses left, I drove to see Mrs. Botwood, who, of course, was at "The Falls" with her father. He has the prettiest place at Montmorençi. The snow was *very* deep, and the servant carried me and the sleigh round to turn it, before I knew where I was! I went to fetch Dick, but could not find him; at last I captured him at the rink, and we drove across the snow-covered fields, where a road is made now. I had a funny note from Col. G., inviting us to the rink; he said he would try to prevent Mrs. —— from doing the honours. I almost fear we shall not be able to go, as it is a snow-stormy drifting day. Yesterday was lovely and quite warm; only five degrees of frost. With you at home, you know, that would be dreadful, but this week we had one night fifty-six degrees of frost. Fancy that!

Friday, 17*th*.—The night was too bad, *of course*, for us to go to the rink. Fancy, the 25th are having a regular Dotheboy's Hall picnic on Monday; the officers and ladies go to it, also all the wretched soldiers, who are to march all the way to the Falls, and then be *made* to slide down the cone all in line, *on dit*. To-day is so warm. I said last night at dinner that I hoped it would not be supposed at home that I knew anything about the American war, because I know *nothing*. The G. G. advises me to say, "The *Times* is wrong," then people would be shocked for a few minutes at my presumption; then I am to say, "I have just come from America, and saw it with my own eyes." I have warned Dick never to say to me, as Mrs. —— used to say to her husband, "You are getting out of your depth; eat your beef, and hold your tongue."

Saturday, 18th. — It is thawing to-day. Thermometer thirty-four. We had the most beautiful bright aurora last night. Anything in the heavens frightens and awes me. Yesterday I paid some visits. Mrs. Adamson was at home, I was rejoiced to say; she is such a study, and so kind. How she did amuse me with her stories and her pretty little brogue, and black cap. I must tell you the racquet-court was burnt down the night before. Mrs. A. was much excited about it; and she did not know the truth till the milkman came and told it in the morning. I believe all milkmen bring servants bad news in the morning all over the world. Then Mrs. A. told me stories about "Adamson." She scolded him for over-working himself at the Parliament. She said, "You know he has never performed the service since the day he was ill in the cathedral. I must tell you he is celebrated for his reading of the first chapter of Genesis, so when he found that that was the chapter for last Sunday, he said to me, 'Have you any objection to my reading the first lesson on Sunday?' and I said, '*No*, if you'll only read that.' Well, to my horror, I found him staying through that long Te Deum about the *water and fishes*, and soon I saw him rubbing his hand through his hair, and I thought I'd have died of fright. I told him I knew he was nervous, and he confessed he was." She went on, " If you could hear 'Adamson' read the first of Genesis; three Methodists in the cathedral said it had never been the same chapter to them before." She told me that when the Prince of Wales was here, he danced with the beauty here, and I congratulated her father next day; but he seemed quite annoyed, and said, " I have no patience with that sort of thing, taking the youngest before the eldest, and Charlotte (the eldest) *being called after her mother and all*." Her face is as good as her stories, with her twinkling black eyes. She and "Adamson" are as much in love as young lovers. We had *beaver* for dinner that night; it is neither fish, flesh, nor fowl; very nasty, like a fishy, bad wild duck. Now

I have eaten all the different odd things out here except bear, which I must eat before I go home.*

Monday, 20th.—On Saturday, after lunch, I went with Dick to see Major Earle. We found poor old Mr. Forsyth there, looking so pale and sad. We had tea with Major Earle; such good tea from London, England. He is so funny and quaint. We dined at *six*, and then drove in to the music-hall. I enclose a programme. The acting was capital; but "Fra Diavolo" was too long, and rather heavy. We sat with Mrs. R. Ross and Madame ——, who came down here to look after her husband. He consequently looked sad. Madame —— is very rude; she said to poor good Mr. C——n, "You are not half so *pretty* as your brother." Mrs. R. Ross invited us to the Dotheboy's Hall picnic to-day. As the day is perfect, and as I have not yet seen the cone, we are going. Dick will drive me there by the ice. We are going about eleven, to come back after lunch.

Tuesday, 21st.—I must tell you I scarcely like writing about the second play of the 25th; after " Fra Diavolo," it was so horrible,

* I have since eaten bear; it tastes like very rich stewed beef.

and I think wicked—all about funerals; but Capt. Vivian, as the undertaker who made *vampires* his study, was as wonderful a piece of acting as I ever saw. Then, when he tried to take the girl's hand, and kissed it with *her glove on*, and when she took it away from him, he still held out his own enormous black-gloved hand, as if he forgot he was not holding hers! Capt. Vivian is always ill. Mr. Stoney makes a lovely woman, but is masculine in voice and manner. Sunday was windy and snowy. I went to afternoon service, but was so ill from the intense heat and smell of coal-oil lamps, I had to leave before the sermon. Yesterday was a heavenly day—a burning hot sun and cloudless sky; it was a day you grudged a moment passed indoors. We set off a little after eleven, and got down on the ice river at Quebec; then the horrors began! Words cannot describe my terror. We were the only fools who drove by the river. Now that it is over, I am glad to have done it. There we were, helpless and alone, surrounded by rough lumps of ice nearly the whole drive of six miles. Some ridges of ice were so high that we lost sight of the horse underneath us, while we were up on a high bank of ice all on one side, and nearly upsetting; even

Dick allowed that we lost sight of the horse! I can't express my terror; I was quite speechless from horror. I felt sure we should break our shafts and traces, and be left there helpless; this sometimes happens to people. I *prayed* that we might get safe, and, after a drive of an hour in these horrors, we arrived at the Falls of Montmorençi. The groom (a 17th soldier) was terrified, and said he had only once seen it worse. I must say that Dick drives beautifully, though Madame Gautier wondered at me trusting myself to a person so lately out from England. I was trying vainly to tie my veil at the back, when, to my intense amusement, the groom tied it for me without saying a word! I was well repaid for my agonies by the scene at the Falls, and I must say I *thoroughly* enjoyed my day except from another great fright I got before leaving the Falls, which I will relate later. The scene is too wonderful, and you cannot imagine you are looking at reality when you see this wonderful sight. As we turned into the sort of amphitheatre of rocks and fir trees, in the middle of which are the grand Falls, we saw all the 25th in their red coats, and all the R.A. in dark-blue overcoats, grouped about on the ice, and on the cone. There was a large collection of sleighs and harness in one spot, and a little further on were all the ladies of the party sitting at lunch on the frozen river at a table, with forms all round it. The officers were in undress uniform with fur caps, and were attending on the ladies. They were all very civil to us, and gave us lunch. The cone, as I told you before, is formed by the frozen spray from the Falls falling on a large rock out in the river. The big cone is about eighty feet high. There is also a "Ladies' Cone," a much smaller one. You go down these cones on "*sleds*," or little flat forms of wood on runners. We found a large party of people—the Roses, Madame Gautier, the Prices, etc. The R.A. had a large picnic also—after lunch, the two parties amalgamated, and we had great fun. A fire was lighted on the ice, I forgot to say, and we had hot soup. The sun was so hot that we did not feel the least chilled eating our food on the river! After lunch we walked off to look at the sliding down the cone. How we laughed! About twelve soldiers all held on one behind the other, and came down the cone, not sitting on sleds, but just bumping or slipping down on nothing. The terrific tumbles they got astonished us, but they did

not seem to mind; happily there were three
doctors present! The men's heads got
knocked about "pretty considerable." I saw
one head bound up and bleeding. One of
the 25th officers puzzled me much for a long
time; his own coat had got wet through on
the cone, and he wore a coachman's livery-
coat with silver buttons. He is a new
officer, and I thought he was a servant, and
wondered to see him walking with ladies.
We went to see the beautiful ice-house cut
in the cone, and the ice curiosities there.
There is an ice-sofa and table, an ice-horse,
a bird, a dog, and *two mummies*, they are
marvellously cut out of blocks of ice. A
drunken soldier there asked Mrs. Rose to
come and sit on the ice-sofa "along with a
British soldier." Just as my old friend M.
was speaking to me, he slipped on the ice,
and rolled down at my feet. I ask him if he
was hurt. He said, "It is not *agreeable;* this
is the *second* time it has happened to-day."
Mr. Serecold got a bad hurt from a sled
covered with soldiers flying up against him,
and knocking him down on his head. He
was much stunned, but one of the doctors was
in attendance, and said, "It was nothing bad."
Soon the band of the 25th struck up, and a
quadrille was proposed. Col. M. flew to ask

me to dance! The novelty of dancing on the river was not to be resisted, otherwise I should have preferred to look on at the men sliding. I got on very well, and no one fell. A ring of soldiers was made round the dancers; it looked altogether curious and novel. I looked suddenly at my brave partner, and was much amused at seeing his walking-stick stuck down his back whilst he was dancing!! I asked him if he knew it was there; he said he put it there to keep it out of his way! He implored me to go down the cone with him! Of course I refused! The bugles soon sounded; and we set off sleighwards. We met Col. R. Ross calling out to us to hurry on, as some water from a fissure in the ice was rising every minute as the tide was coming in, and we must cross it quickly. They had boards, which were getting more and more wet every moment. When I came to it, Mrs. M. was just going to cross, and when she saw me she withdrew in her stately way, and would not cross before me. This was really provoking, and Mr. Sitwell, who was helping us across, got quite angry, and called to her to go on. Then came my terrible fright. A board turned, and I suddenly saw *Dick in the water*, fifteen feet deep!! Several gentlemen rushed forward, and, thank God for His goodness, pulled him out safe. Kind Miss Price ran to tell me he was all safe. Several soldiers also fell in, and one bugler was nearly drowned. Dick was wet through, and his long boots were full of water. Mr. Sitwell wanted him to have sherry, but *of course* he would not take it. I then walked with Col. M. such a long way to the top of the gorge, while Dick went to look for the sleigh. I was so tired in the hot sun. My bones ache to-day; but I was afraid of the sleigh on such a steep place. I overheard a young Irish officer say to Col. M., with the most fearful of brogues, " Now, colonel, isn't it *ridee-clous* to think of our takin' lunch in the snow, and not feelin' cold!" All the 25th regiment were marching up at the same time with us, and I overheard a soldier say " This is every bit as bad as the Rock of Gibraltar." It turned out that the men enjoyed themselves immensely. The officers marched with them there and back. We drove back by the roads, and met the two regiments singing as they marched. The groom advised Dick to wrap his legs up in the horse-cloth, which he did, taking off his dripping big boots. For a wonder, he did not get chilled driving home eight miles.

We returned by the land road, which was very good, and such a happy change after the ice. The evening was very cold, but *beautiful*. Everything was pink with the setting sun. Dick found a letter from Gen. Lindsay, introducing to him Mr. Dudley Ryder, who also brought a letter to the G. G. from Sir F. Baring. General Lindsay invited himself and Captain Eliot here for a few days, of which we are so glad. I gave Dick a "big drink" of hot brandy and water and sugar, and forced him to drink it when he came in; and, thank God, he is none the worse. I must tell you that one of Tom's ears had dropped off from being frost-bitten that night a month ago, and she does not suffer now, but looks so ludicrous with one. The other will soon drop off also.

Wednesday, 22nd.—Yesterday was as perfect a day as Monday. After lunch, I drove to town, and found letters to my great joy. We went to the M——'s for the inauguration of the R.A. open rink. I found a large party, some skating, some sitting on chairs with bits of carpet under their feet, looking on. There were flags and the band, also a booth with tea, coffee, and cakes. It was all very pleasant. I nearly upset Gordon der Gute, by rushing across the ice holding his hand. I went too quickly for him. Mr. Coulson offered, on skates, to assist me across the ice. In a moment, of course, he was far ahead of me; he was unable to stop himself, and pulled me after him. They danced the Lancers on skates beautifully. A photographer photoed the scene; I don't know how it will turn out. Some of the ladies wore summer hats, the sun was so hot; but the fur caps looked much prettier. We had a lovely drive home; the setting sun looked like a ball of fire before us all the way. This evening some gentlemen dine here. The 17th ball is put off, alas! as the messman is ill. It will never be now, because of Lent. It was to have been to-night. A woman here wrote to complain to the G. G. of the *rudeness* of his military secretary; we suppose because he began a letter to her, " Madam," and wrote very short.

Thursday, 23*rd*.—Went out driving yesterday. The horse fell down at Quebec on his knees; we found his shoe was off, so he had to go to the forge, and we walked meanwhile on the platform of dry wood overlooking the low town and river. I was soon so hot I could walk no longer. We have summer weather now, and the streets running in wet. The Canadians hate this weather. Col. G.

came to tea. There dined Mr. Dudley Ryder, Mr. Thorold, and his brother Mr. Cecil Thorold, Col. G., Col. Rhodes, and Miss Mountain. Mr. Ryder is British Commissioner at New York. He is very pleasant; he is to spend Sunday here. His father was a bishop, and he is much excited on the subject of church architecture and church music. He asked Miss M. if the music is good at our little chapel here, and she said, "Very good," not thinking he would be here. She plays the harmonium, and leads the singing herself! He knows every one in the world. Dick heard from Major Pearson that Frank's regiment is to come here in spring.

Friday, 24*th*.—Yesterday, when I drove to town, I found that all the men were at a function at the Council Chamber, about presenting an address from the Upper House to the G. G., requesting him to present an address to the Queen about Confederation. The 25th band was playing, and there was a crowd and guard of honour, into the middle of which I drove, and listened to the band. *On dit* that the American war is to be over very soon, and that the poor South is done for. I waited at the office door for Dick, and he drove me to see the Military Asylum, which I will describe in my next. The weather is so hot now. The snow has disappeared from the streets.

Saturday, 25th.—I must tell you of the Military Asylum to which I went on Thursday. It is for soldiers' widows and orphans, and seems a great charity. There are only four old women in it now. The people prefer outdoor relief, which I wonder at, as they seem so comfortable. They earn a good deal by doing the garrison washing; that is, the outdoor relief people. They come in by the day to wash. They give relief in the shape of money all over Canada to the widows and orphans of soldiers. The old widows said they were so happy. Dick questioned them. They had a nice little attempt at flowers in their rooms—geraniums in pots. Yesterday I drove to the Hotel Dieu, the nuns' hospital, to see Fan's poor woman. No one is allowed in after two, except people from Government House. They were having an office for a dying person when I rang. I listened through the keyhole, and when they had finished they answered the door. I am thankful my visit is over; it is so unpleasant explaining who one is, and where one comes from. The poor woman was moved to a room where there were more well people than sick. It is sad to see a pretty young woman crippled from rheumatism. She is so patient, and has such a bright face. She has one little boy; her husband was killed on a railway. Her story is a very sad one, but I can't tell it now. The pretty nun, Mère St. Louis, was so glad to see me. She told me she was very anxious to see "Le Gouverneur," and asked if I could show her his portrait. I told him, and he is going to send her a present of his photo. The people adore Mère St. Louis. There was a poor sick baby; it was a sweet little thing, and the nuns were so charmed to have a baby to pet, as they rarely take babies in. Mère St. Louis said that this winter has been very healthy. The nuns are called "Ma Mère" here, not "Sœur." The hospital is so clean; but the heat was awful from stoves and sun. The day was perfect; hot sun and very cold wind—charming after the heat. I went with Dick to the rink, which was crowded with people. The 25th band was playing beautifully. Mr. A., who really never seems to have anything to do at the Upper House, spied me whilst I was talking to some one else, pounced upon me, and never left me. He insisted on my walking up the rink on his arm! There was Captain E. skating, or rather shuffling, not the least improved, but looking very proud of himself. Col. McC. was *working* round on skates. After dinner we went to the militia ball. The music-hall was beautifully decorated with artificial flowers and fir branches; the refreshments were served on the stage, with a scene at the back. There were two bands—R.A. and 25th, in the gallery. It really all looked very nice, but it was very empty. It was a great pity the G. G. would not go; it kept many away who would have gone to see him. Dick and the colonels were in uniform; Sir E. Taché was gorgeous in his uniform of Queen's A.D.C. When he entered the room, the band struck up the Canadian air, "Il y a longtemps que je t'aime." One or two of the M.P.P.'s were there, and M. Tessier and wife, also the French Consul and wife. The volunteers' dresses are very pretty. The artillery dress is just like the R.A. real dress, and they even have "Ubique" as their motto, which rather annoys the R.A., who say they go *nowhere* instead of *everywhere*. I danced a few times. There was nobody there one knew, and Dick was well bored. I think it very wrong of people, who were *asked*, not to go to please the volunteers; those who had to pay, I don't so much wonder at, as they raised the tickets half a dollar. Madame Tessier and I sat on a raised sofa, and were very comfortable. Old Colonel Sewell, who was the president of the ball, made Colonel Gordon (the commandant) take me in first to supper. There was a very good supper, and I was so hungry. Col. Sewell gave me pretty little flags for a cake. I have French, English, Southern, and Yankee flags. You know I always liked such toys! They had every sort of odd dance in the programme, amongst others, Sir Roger de Coverley, at the end, and a cotillon in the middle. It is not what *we* call "cotillon," but a sort of country dance. I did not see it; we left very early. When Col. S. saw the ball so empty, he exemplified "the art of putting things" by saying it was not often that people had such a nice clear space to dance in! I said to Conway a few days before the ball, that if she liked I would ask Dick to get her a ticket for the gallery, to look on. She said, "I thank you, ma'am, I am *invited* to the ball, and so is Félix," but she would not go, from respect to us! This day is delicious, just like yesterday. Miss N. S. skated at the rink yesterday in a bright blue dress and jacket, a scarlet *shirt*, and scarlet petticoat trimmed with black. I have just heard that our Cunard letters must be ready to-day instead of Monday, so good-bye in great haste. It is light here now till six p.m.

Monday, February 27th.—It was a great nuisance about the mail going on Saturday instead of Monday; the fact is, I believe the letters have often been late for Boston mail up to this time. They never told us of the change till a few hours before the mail was to start! Dick skated on Saturday at the rink; he went a little alone, which is good for the second trial. We then drove all about on the river; some part is very nice and smooth, but sometimes I was a little afraid. We had a broiling sun and nice cold wind; we stayed then listening to the R.A. band playing on the ice; there were crowds of skaters on an open rink. Colonel G. came to tea, also Mr. Ryder, who was to stay till to-day. Mr. Ryder was once an English barrister, but has had situations all over the world; he has lived in Ceylon, at the Havanna, in all the principal capitals in Europe, at New York, in Nova Scotia, New Brunswick, etc. He is extremely shrewd and agreeable. He loves "the little gladiators," *alias* Fuss and Beauty, and Tom with her one ear; he considers her a natural curiosity, and stares at her, saying slowly, "Curious, wonderful." Mrs. G., F. Burrowes, and I dined together that evening. There dined several M.P.P.'s. I talked to an Hon. Mr. Cockburn, an Hon. Mr. Walsh, and a Mr. Bellerose, very like the Emperor of France. Sunday was a *very* bad day: wind and frozen rain. We have not seen rain since Christmas, and it looks so odd again. Mrs. Godley was the only one who ventured to church in the afternoon. The rain poured, and the wind whistled. In the evening, after dinner, we had a discussion on mesmerism; of course the G. G. went on about the five-pound-note, etc., and so did Colonel G. Mr. Godley listened quietly and comfortably to me, and believed me. Good Dick chimed in on my side. He could speak from experience, having seen me exhibited so often in my clairvoyante state. I quoted Mr. Bob Lowe, who said he would not *dare* to disbelieve it, because we do not yet understand the mysteries of Nature, and also that "there is nothing new under the sun." To-day is luckily very fine, and all the wet is now ice. Mr. Ryder is just gone; I am so sorry. The sky is cloudless to-day, and the sun hot.

Tuesday, 28th.—I went to see Miss Rose, who is ill. I met "Adamson," who wears a military coat, trimmed with Austrian fur. He is going home in May; he has not crossed the "herring-pond," as he calls it, for twenty-five years! The day was bitterly cold, and the roads a sheet of ice. I felt as if my eyes must drop out from the cold, bitter wind. We went to the Stadacona Club ball after dinner. The ball was much crowded, but very pleasant. Some of the M.P.P.'s were there. The 25th are going to get up "Ill-treated Il Trovatore" during Lent. Mr. Ryder was at the ball; he admired the people. Many boys in jackets were there, and short-frocked good little girls. The Lord High Admiral of Canada (?), Commander Fortin, was there. He commands the *one* man-of-war of Canada, which carries two guns!!

Ash Wednesday, March 1st.—Yesterday was a most unpleasant day; we had a regular wind-storm, *so* cold. We drove to the Parliament House, as Dick wanted to speak to the Speaker. I was frozen, and much blown about. In the morning Dick and Mr. Godley were tobogganing, and Dick gave Mr. G. an upset, and cut his wrist. To-day we all went in to church to the

Quebec Cathedral, for the 10.30 service. By some mistake we had no service here till the afternoon. The G. G.'s pew is so comfortable, in the gallery, with curtains, armchairs, and stools. It was not half as hot as our chapel here. After service we were joined by Lord Alexander Russell, at the office, who had just arrived from Montreal, for the courtmartial. I left Dick at the rink to skate. Lord Alexander R. came on here to lunch. They sang the psalm, "From lowest depths of woe," at the cathedral; it is very long since I have heard the Tate and Brady psalms in church. General Lindsay comes next week.

Thursday, 2nd. — I went to afternoon service yesterday at St. Michael's; no sermon. The roads so good that I drove myself all yesterday. Miss M. went to the fancy ball at Montreal, as a rainbow. I believe her dress was composed of skirts of different colours, and flowing gauze and scarves of the same on her head, which enveloped her partners' heads when she danced. She wore very tight blue boots, and very short petticoats. One of the 60th went as Mephistopheles, but not knowing how to spell it, wrote "devil" for the newspaper account. Lord A. says that Mrs. ——'s boy is such a horrid child. Some one asked her why she never went to tobogganing parties now, and she said she never went without her husband; in fact, she could not go without him. This awful boy emerged from a corner, and said, "Oh, I like that; why, you've been out nine times with Mr. —— of the 60th." A few gentlemen dined. Dick skated for two hours yesterday. To-day is cold and windy. Lord A. is gone to his court-martial, and Mr. Ryder is coming to slide; he has never tried it, and I expect to laugh much at him. Major Earle invited me to tea this afternoon.

Friday, 3rd.—Mrs. Godley drove to town with me yesterday, and said my sleigh was so comfortable. She went to church, and I went to Major Earle's with Dick. I brought him a bouquet; only Captain Pem. was there. I looked at his photo-book; he told me when he thought he was going to die; he wrote the names under his photos, that his people might know who his friends were. It was a very windy day, and dark. A few men dined; amongst others, two Majors Warren, one in the 60th, and the other in the R.B., neither of them related to each other. To-day it is snowing, and has snowed all night. Lord A. is telling such funny stories, I find it hard to write. Mr. Ryder *rather* liked sliding, but was wet through, as Dick upset him many times.

Saturday, March 4th.—Yesterday I was so happy to get my home letters. Mrs. G. and I went to church after lunch. The snow was so very deep that we could not drive up to the church door, so we waded, and it was up to my knees. It had snowed all day, and all the night before, but it was not frozen snow, so it wetted one. The day was perfectly calm for a wonder, and the trees were covered with snow on every leaf, and even every twig where there were no leaves; it had a very curious effect, and this avenue looked exactly like a snow scene in a pantomime. I need hardly say that all the trees are firs and pines. Of course there was no sermon. I forgot to say that at the Cathedral on Ash Wednesday, just before the Communion service, the organ gave out one long *groan*, and then stopped, which amused me much. I went on to the rink after church. I promised to meet Lord A. R., to show him the beauties. Colonel R. Ross told me that they are giving a children's party on Monday, "and we have managed to *scrape* fifty children together," he said. After listening to the 25th band for some time, we drove home; it had stopped snowing. Captain P., R.A., dined; he is so odd; he told me that he *loathed* sleighing (he has only come out here lately), and gets nearly *wild* when he hears sleigh bells when he is walking in the snow. The dogs made up to him, and he said, " Now, that's very odd, for they *generally* bite me." Fancy being bitten by dogs as a *rule*. We are all invited to a musical party, at Colonel McC.'s, on Monday. The Board of Works' photographer is going to photo our sleigh and Bill Seward. There is such a snow-storm to-day, and it is so warm. I hate this weather. Tom has lost her other ear, and looks so knowing and quaint. We had longed for this event. Mr. Ryder comes to-day to stay for an official dinner-party.

Sunday, 5th.—Lovely bright day, snow very deep. Dick snow-shoed to morning service. I drove to the afternoon service, and could scarcely get on. Poor Mr. Ryder started to walk in thin boots, and when we arrived at the church door we found a mass of snow standing in the porch, and this was poor Mr. Ryder; the snow came up to his knees.

Monday, 6th.—Lovely and bright; thermometer last night eight above zero. Mr. Ryder left. The musical party at Colonel

M.'s consisted of music, a little dreary Lenten carpet dancing, and a large supper.

Tuesday, 7th.—Fine bright day. Dick saw the first crow!! Rather an event here, as it is supposed to be a sign of spring.

Wednesday, 8th, is a lovely day. Went to church, and to drive on Cap Rouge road. Colonel G. and Mr. Ryder dined.

Thursday, 9th.—Snow-storm all day. Lord A. Russell left.

Friday, 10th.—A bad day. Wind and some snow.

Monday, 13th.—On Saturday, after lunch, Mrs. G. and I rushed off to church, where I got a fright that made me quite ill. You will laugh at me, but I was terrified. There was no one in church but Mrs. G. and Mrs. Botwood, a few singers, and myself. During the prayers, I heard a great noise of sleighs, and presently the door opened just behind me, and quantities of men in long black cloaks walked in. I saw that it was a funeral and I shut my eyes in terror. Then I remembered seeing in the paper that the funeral of an old Mr. Hunter (Parliament Library) was to take place; it ought to have been over, but the roads kept them; he was Brother Hunter, a grand Freemason, and the lodges came in their badges, etc., of light riband and devices. When our prayers were over, I covered my eyes and went out, and right into a snow-drift I walked, and found myself up to my knees in snow! Mrs. G. pulled me out of it. There was a great crowd of men and horses and sleighs; the hearse has to be on runners. The snow was too deep for me to venture to town, so we drove a little on the road, and then returned to the village for Mrs. G. to visit some poor people; the funeral was still going on. A sleigh containing four men drove past me, some of the men were tipsy, and, *for fun*, tipped over the sleigh, and all four men were upset. The horse ran wildly on, frightening another horse, which ran off into such a deep snow-drift that it had to be unharnessed to be got out, and was struggling. The day was fine but cold. Funerals here are *awful*; the people *race* each other home. There was a very great noise of shouting of the sleigh-men at Brother Hunter's funeral. Parliamentary dinner. I talked to an M.P. called Jones. I found myself in a Confederation talk with him; *then* thought to myself that perhaps he was against it; but happily found he was wild on the subject, and anxious for Canada to make a name for herself. He said he was a Tory even to extremes. I also talked to Major H., from Montreal. His awful boy is at Lennoxville, and is full of Yankeeism. He says to his father, " Bully for you, governor." That is the great Yankee word. They say "a bully day," meaning a fine day. I like the expressions "A mean old cuss," and "An affable cuss," and "A gay and festive cuss" is the best of all. Yesterday it was blowing so and drifting. Captain Pem. dined in town; he says the Rifle Brigade have got their orders to come down here in June, and the 25th go to Montreal.

Tuesday, 14*th*.—Yesterday, after lunch, I plucked up courage and drove to town. The snow was piled up sixteen or eighteen feet near the Protestant Home, and we drove above men's heads, that were walking on the footpath. I met Colonel G. The 17th go home in May; they will be much regretted here. I paid a few visits, and then went to the rink, where the R.A. band was playing. Dick *would not* skate before me! I went to see dear old Mr. Price; they are such nice people.

Wednesday, 15*th*.—Yesterday turned out a very windy, snowy day. I drove to town with my hood over my head. Dick was at a function at the Council Chamber, presenting an address from the Legislative Assembly about Confederation. When we got home, we were perfectly *white* with snow; my veil was a mass of frozen snow, and the robes were quite white. You *whisk* yourself with a little whisk when you come in, and are then supposed to be dry. Mr. Le Moine sent the G. G. a most beautiful trout, a yard long. Two young Canadian sportsmen requested him to present it to his Excellency; it weighed eleven and a half pounds. The G. G. sent for it to show Mrs. G. and me; it looked so stiff—frozen, of course. To-day is wet, really *rain*. Sir Fenwick is coming to-day. So Lord Lyons is not coming back to Washington! I think it was killing him. I suppose this rain was the beginning of the end of the snow. I shall be sorry when the sleighing is over, but the green grass will be welcome.

Thursday, 16*th*.—Yesterday Sir Fenwick arrived some time before lunch. Colonel G. came to tea, and to dine and sleep. There was a hot fog. I hear General Lindsay is the life and soul of Montreal. I was ill last night, and to-day I am ill in bed. I am to be kept very quiet, Dr. B. says, therefore I mean to get up, and go in to the party after dinner! Mr. G. is ill also

THE BEGINNING OF THE "BREAK UP."

with a bad cold. Sir F. and Captain Grant, A.D.C., are gone to Montmorençi this horrid, dark, blowy day, as they have never seen the cone.

Friday, 17*th.*—I got up about five yesterday, and lay on the sofa, and after dinner went in to the party. There were only four ladies. Mrs. M. could not be made to see or understand who the G. G. was; she thought he was Colonel Irvine, and could not understand his being in plain clothes. Snow and wind again to-day.

Monday, 20*th.*—Thank God, I am much better. Everybody feels this change from bright frost to hot sun and snow, melting as it is to-day. Last Friday it rained in the morning, and then turned to heavy snow and thaw. Every one was coughing and sneezing and crying in the evening.

Saturday, 18*th.*—Some rain and thaw; wind *every* day. Parliament was prorogued in state. Dick drove Sir Kars to it. That night Sir F. and Captain Grant left for Montreal. Sir F. is so handsome and so kind; he was funny about Miss ——. He said, "I never saw such large ears anywhere out of Armenia." Saturday evening the lights were so beautiful on the opposite coast, pink and pale yellow, and a reddish tint.

Sunday, 19th.—Fine, but thawing. Mrs. G. is ill also. Mr. Rose dined, and was very pleasant. To-day (Monday) is lovely; hot spring sun, but thawing, and terrible for walking or driving. The cawing *crows* are so delightful near my windows after the long dead silence of winter.

Tuesday, 21st.—I am reading Russell's "Tour in Canada;" very amusing, and so graphic. There was a man carting away the snow before this house for hours the other day, and Sir F. looked out after he had been here, and said, "Dear me! the snow is disappearing fast; it has already sunk a foot and a half." He likes to think everything wonderful is always happening where he is; his imagination helps him *much*. The summer session is to begin in June, *on dit*, and to last six weeks. Old Mr. Price came to see me on Saturday in an *enormous* otter-skin coat and yellow mocassins.

Wednesday, 22nd.—Mrs. B. told me that the people here are terrified at the idea of the G. G. going home when everything is unsettled, and Lord Lyons gone. They will be relieved to find he is not going for a while yet. I went out to drive in my sleigh after lunch, but found the melting roads too un-

ARRIVAL OF GENERAL LINDSAY.

pleasant. I was going to turn back when I happily met Dick, and he took me a drive on the Cap Rouge road, which was not so heavy, and we saw a bit of grass (!!) round the bottom of the trunk of a tree. Twice the horse tried to run away; he took fright, and was very fresh, and splashed the wet *brown* snow all over me. The day was nice and mild. We had a storm of wind last night, and to-day it is raining and blowing, but will be fine later. At breakfast-time this morning arrived the charming General Lindsay and Capt. Eliot. They were upset in the sleigh crossing the river, and the general fell out *on* Capt. E., who was wet through, in the pools of water. The 25th have theatricals to-morrow night. I long to go, but fear the roads. Everybody in this house has a cough, so it sounds cheerful.

Thursday, 23rd.—Yesterday the gentlemen went to town early. I walked in the verandah with Fuss, and the Prices' enormous big dog Boatswain, who chooses to reside here. It was blowing and raining terribly. A few officers dined. A great clap of Thunder came whilst we were sitting talking after dinner. I was so afraid, it sounded like very odd Thunder—*one* clap, and so sudden. To-day it was snowing.

Friday, 24th.—Captain Eliot amused us at lunch yesterday, by telling us that the priest at Montreal preached since Lent began against *officers*, and discouraged young ladies from associating with them. Last Sunday our Bishop Fulford of Montreal preached a great sermon *at* the ladies: spoke against their seeking and loving admiration, and particularly warned married women against setting the bad example. The General said it was a very powerful sermon. After lunch, I ventured to town. The roads were *awful* half the way. I felt exactly as if I were at sea in a small boat; you could not conceive it unless you saw it. I drove to look at the ice-bridge from the platform; it is getting very dangerous, and will soon give way. It began snowing and blowing, and I was glad to bump home again in safety. Some of the gentlemen dined in town with the 17th, and then went to the 25th plays; after which they had supper at the barracks, and were not home till one. The Godleys, the G. G., and I dined together. Mr. G. and I argued and fought the whole night together about officers and civilians, etc., etc. He said he liked "sharp snobs" better than "gentlemanly fools." I tried to find out from the G. G. if there is going to be *war*, but he would not give me a direct answer. They hope it won't come till summer is over. As long as the Americans fight together they will leave England alone. The General was delighted with the 25th acting.

Saturday, 25th.—Yesterday Mrs. G. and I went to church, and then I went on to the rink, where I was soon joined by Dick and the Gen., who had been to the Falls. The 25th band was playing. Mrs. —— (25th) was there, and again told me about her little "dot" of a baby, and how her nurse had lived with "two other little dots" before she came to her. We saw a lovely new girl skating, dressed in black silk and bright large scarlet belt, and scarlet petticoat; she was a French-Canadian. The gentlemen found Colonel Rollo at the cone, who photoed the group. They went in to see the ice-house with umbrellas up and mackintoshes on. The Gen. drove me home, Dick sitting up behind. Some officers dined, amongst them Gordon the Good, and Col. H., R.E.; the latter amused me much. He told me he had been quartered at the four Channel Islands; only one man lives at Sark, called Mr. Le Pelly, who makes every one who lands there pay one shilling. Alderney is three miles long and three broad, and the principal street is all grass. He made me laugh about Wymering; he and Mr. Nugee were like tame cats there. He said "the major" was a nice woman, and another sister was "a jolly party." The peacock belonging to the Sisters used to eat Mr. Nugee's rosebuds, and Col. H. advised Mr. Nugee to hit it on the head with a stick if it came again. Col. M. was thrown from his horse a few days ago, and rolled in the wet puddles. No letters this week at all. On Saturday, after lunch, I drove into town, and thought I should have been upset in the "cahots." I was nearly run over by a horse in the town; it ran off from the stand, and knocked its sleigh against mine, and very nearly put its head in my lap. Dick drove me home; the holes are not so bad returning, as you go *up* first instead of down, and that is less sickening than *first* down, then up. We had our usual fun at five-o'clock tea; Gordon the Good was there also. There dined M. Cartier, M. Brown (President of the Council), Col. Rollo (Mil. Sec. at Montreal), Col. Rhodes (the mighty hunter), and Col. Reeves, who was once in the 79th, and married and settled out here. The Dean of Christchurch's wife is Col. Reeves's sister;

he is a fine-looking man, and mad on the subject of homœopathy. He carried a bottle of pills in his pocket. M. Cartier was very amusing; he abused Col. Gordon for being so *cold* to the Quebec ladies. He said, " His face was like marble, and his lips moved not." Cartier and some others go home on the 12th about Confederation. He says that he and I must *correspond* when he goes to England. He always talks English. Once in Parliament he made a speech for seven hours in French and seven hours in English.

Sunday was very fine and warm. Cunard letters, but no Canadian ones yet! Gen. Lindsay went to see Mr. Price after lunch. The Gen. said he thought he *never* heard a more prosy sermon than Mr. B.'s; he said it in a sort of decided way that amused me much. Capt. E. told us some quaint things. He says that when Col. C., at Montreal, is acting, and does not know his part, he walks up to the prompter, and says in a *very* loud hoarse voice, " What is it ? " He acted an admiral, wearing his moustaches, and walking with a cavalry strut. To-day all are gone to town but the Gen., who will drive me in later; I am so dreading the holes. He and Capt. E. leave to-night, I am sorry to say.

Tuesday, 28th.—Yesterday the General drove me to town in my sleigh. Mrs. G. had frightened me so about the holes, that I persuaded the General to let me walk part of the way. The holes were, however, less than usual. At the office door Sergeant Lambkin gave us all a terrible account of the dangers of crossing the ice-bridge; he was three-quarters of an hour crossing it (it is about a quarter of an hour's drive), and his horse went through the snow up to its shoulders. No one will venture across after dark. I was so sorry to say "good-bye" to the General and Captain E. I went to the rink after paying visits, and then home. Mr. Sitwell has coloured a photo for me of the day we all went to the cone picnic; it is from a drawing of his, and is so pretty. Dick dined at the club with Colonel Rhodes; six other men dined, and he does not know who one of them was! It was a whist dinner. We were much surprised to receive our letters of the 9th after dinner.

Wednesday.—Yesterday was a perfect day, cold wind but very little of it; cloudless blue sky, and broiling sun. I drove to the platform to hear the K.O.B. band play. Several " muffins " were there. It was nice to have the band out of doors again. All the girls now wear blue veils with their fur caps, as the hot sun tans. The drift at the Protestant Home was in the act of being cut down when I drove in, and I found myself perched up on a step of snow, and driving regularly down snow-steps; I was so afraid. Tom the cat is offended if you call it "Puss." Whenever any of us look out of the window, Tom rushes and looks out also, looking so quaint and wise without ears.

Thursday.—Went to church after lunch. Had a talk with the Botwoods. He leaves St. Michael's on May 1st for a church in Quebec, which Mr. Hall, his father-in-law, is going to *buy* for him. After church I drove to town. It was a long business, as the snow is almost gone inside the toll-gate, and you bump along through pools of water. I got out and walked down and up the *stairs* of snow at the drift. Dick laughed at me so. I was proud to hear that the G. G. walked also. To-day we have rain and a thick fog.

Friday, 31*st.*—Yesterday cleared into the most perfect day of hot sun and cloudless sky, but was so very hot I felt quite ill. The smells on the roads are very oppressive, and no one could feel well at this time.

They say in eleven days we shall have to take to wheels. Alas! for my dear sleigh. I asked the groom if we could drive with wheels now inside the toll-bar. He answered, "Yes, ma'am; but at the first cahot the springs would break." I took a long drive on the Cap Rouge road, nearly asleep in my sleigh. I drove myself all the way home, and first bumped my sleigh so hard against another sleigh that we hopped off the ground! Then I banged up against a riding-horse, and pushed it on, and I very often let the horse slip through the snow! So much for my driving; but I was nearly asleep, and the snow was so dreadfully soft. I visited two families in the village. In one house seven people sleep in one very small room; all of them ill but the father. Another woman whom I went to had a goat called "Nelly" walking about the room. When I returned home, I got a bundle of welcome letters. Mrs. Rawson wrote to me, and begged me to tell her something about Confederation; as her husband was in England, she knew nothing, and feared it would now be at an end for years! I must confess to you that I am a little changed since I thought well over the Protestant Home. I don't know that they are right to let in other ministers Sunday about ; it is different if they only visited them ; but they hold service Sunday about. We are all reading Sala's book on Canada and America. It is very amusing; far more amusing than Russell's book.

Saturday, April 1*st.*—Yesterday I went to church, and to the village to see how the sick poor were, and then to town, meeting Dick *en route.* The roads were quite decayed, and worse than ever, and the horse tumbled about in a most wretched way. I must give up my dear sleigh now, as it is too heavy in the present state of the roads. I got out at the town, and walked to see Major Earle ; we walked for a long time with him in the sun. We saw a *wheeled* vehicle, it looked so *high* and odd after the sleighs. Major E. amused me as much as usual. He was really angry because he had a long letter from Captain de Winton, "not a *note,* but a long letter, and all about the American war, I won't answer it," he said. We had tea with him. We met Cartier whilst we were walking, and he said his wife had rheumatism at Montreal, and it was the first time a doctor had entered their house for fifteen years ! I don't believe it. I walked half-way to Spencer Wood, and was half-dead with fatigue, as I had on two pairs of stockings, two pairs of boots, and a seal-skin; but there happily was some east wind, which cooled the air. I have nothing to say, so will amuse you with some Canadian advertisements. Every one now sees the word "Sozodont" written in chalk letters on the walls of Quebec. I will copy you an advertisement about it. "In everybody's mouth. *Praise* and *Sozodont* — greatest luxury of modern times—beautifies and preserves the teeth. The repulsive breath is rendered as fragrant as a rose, and coldness by friends or in business will now no longer be noticed. Sold by druggists everywhere. March 23rd, 1865." "*Sozodont.* This word, which has been staring everybody in the face for the past few weeks, is now getting into nearly everybody's mouth; it is a preparation for cleaning, beautifying, and preserving the teeth, and arresting the progress of decay." Here is another advertisement— "Who is N. H. Downs? He is, or rather was, a public benefactor, a philanthropist. He is now dead; but he has left behind him a monument more lasting than brass and marble. His memory is enshrined in the hearts of a grateful people, and his Balsamic Elixir is, or ought to be, a household treasure in every family. It is a certain cure for coughs and colds." Here is a very good one—"*Time will Tell*. Yes, that is the sure test; that which does not appear plain to-day may be thoroughly cleared up in a short time; our certainties or uncertainties are all to be decided by time, which never fails to bring out the truth or falsity of any matter. For five years the Vermont Liniment has been before the public, and their verdict has always been steadily in its favour. Use it for pains both internally and externally. It is warranted." Mr. F. C. turned up again yesterday; he was dressed in a light-grey dust suit, grey gloves, and a fur cap! A Yankee bishop was here once, and when asked if he would have some coffee, said, "I am not *through* with my tea yet." A Yankee expression I *love* is, "Shall I saloon you?" It means get you refreshment. A waiter at a Yankee dinner was once heard to say, "They are not through with the Charlie Rush yet"—*Anglice* Charlotte Russe. I am ashamed to send a letter with nothing in it.

Monday, April 3rd.—The thermometer on Friday last, at night, was twenty-eight above zero, and on Thursday it was nearly fifty. Saturday (April 1st) was very fine, but we have a little east wind every day now. After lunch on Saturday the photographer of the Board of Works came to photo our sleigh. It took ages of waiting on the approach, and when at last he was ready, he told Dick to move the horse and sleigh round a little. Poor Bill Seward fell into a drift, and struggled sadly down in the snow. We were nearly upset, as the horse fell quite down ; at last it was got up again. The photo is a very pretty one. It is taken near the house, with a lovely view of the river and shore opposite. Dick had a note from Col. Rollo, in which he said that the *Himalaya* was going at once to Malta for Frank's regiment. Dick also heard from General Lindsay, who had a letter from Mr. Ryder, from New York, in which he said that Lord Palmerston's speech about Canada and America had produced a great sensation among the Yankees. Sunday was very fine. Got my Cunard letters of March 18 before lunch. Col. McMurdo, who was to have come out here, to be over the militia, is not coming, because of his wife's health. It is said that perhaps Col. Macdougall is coming. He lately wrote a " Life of Sir C. Napier." Sala's book is very funny, and his description of Boston *very* good, " like a toy city "—just what I thought when I saw it.

Tuesday, 4th.—Yesterday was a heavenly

day, but I feared the roads too much to venture to town. I read the debate in the English House on Canada. I drove out in the red "cariole" to see the sick family in the village. To-day is most beautiful also. It froze ten degrees last night. It looks just like summer now, were it not for the snow. Now is the time for tapping the maples, to get the sugar. Frost at night, and hot sun by day, makes the juice come.

Wednesday, 5th.—Drove in the "rough weather sleigh" to see the Botwoods. I told them the news of the fall of Richmond, which was great excitement to Mr. B., as he had not yet seen the papers. He is a warm Southerner, and we lamented together the power of the South being broken now, and gone for ever. Mrs. B. has many cousins in the Southern army. They both told me how very kind the Southerners are to their slaves. They said they are just as we are with our servants, and till lately a Northerner would not *speak* to a black. Mr. B. told me that "Uncle Tom's Cabin" had done much mischief. One can't believe what Mrs. B. Stowe says, as she was only a short time in the South. He showed me the curious Labrador snow-shoes, and made me come and look at his birds—six or eight canaries, two of which he had dragged from Labrador, and one of them was dreadfully sea-sick on the voyage! He showed me a photo of the coast of Newfoundland (where he also was)—very arid, bare rocks, with an iceberg in the distance on the water. I also saw a photo of the new cathedral at St. John's, Newfoundland, which when finished will be the handsomest cathedral on this side the Atlantic, both inside and outside. It is beautiful. There is a very good Bishop there; Field is his name. Mr. B. is going to run down to Labrador some summer, to see his people again. He loves them so, and they are very fond of him. He says the people are so hearty and hospitable down there. On the road to church, where the snow is now gone, and stones are put down, you grate along on the ground in your sleigh, your teeth on edge all the time. I met a wheeled waggon on the road. The day was like summer. Mr. Godley and I had agreed to go out and tap maples together to-day; but it is very wet, so we can't go.

Thursday, 6th. — Adamson and D'Arcy McGee are going to Ireland as commissioners for the Exhibition. McGee expects the Fenians will make a row when he arrives in Ireland, as he *was* a rebel, and now is a loyal subject. Such a funny pair to go together, Adamson and McGee! There is a great London fog here to-day.

Friday, 7th.—Dr. B. came to see me. I have such an inflamed eye I can scarcely write. I spoke of how I dreaded heat, and he said, "But you never went *below*." I told him how ill every one was on our Saguenay trip. He said it was from drinking St. Lawrence water. Quebec is now supplied with St. Charles Lake water; the St. L. water used to make every one ill here. Every stranger was sure to get ill. 'I will tell you a story from Sala's book. The Yankees say they are "hell" or "death" at a thing, when they do it well. A child once had the small-pox in Yankeeland. When the M.D. was called in, he looked attentively for some time at the little sufferer, and then said, "This here babe has got the small-pox, and I ain't posted up on pustules; *we must approach this case by circular treatment.* You give the little cuss this draught, that'll send him into fits. Then you send for me; I'm hell on fits." Did you ever hear such a story? No wit amuses me half so much as Yankee wit. When they speak slightingly of a person or thing, they call him or it "a one-horse concern." If they talk of two people sleeping in one room, they say "they *roomed*" together. Mind you teach Cecil all these things by the time I get home! To-day is rather wet and dull and dark.

Saturday, 8th.—I have scarcely one word to say to-day. Yesterday cleared up into a beautiful day, so hot and bright. Mr. G. *rode* to town! My throat was too bad to go out at all. Dick went to see the volunteers shoot cannons at the citadel, and found the 25th band playing there. I had a visit from Colonel M. He stayed from five till six. I showed him the greenhouse. He is a great florist, and knows so much about every flower. He told me all about the Queen's visit to them at Freshwater, when he was quartered there. She picked wild flowers, and gave them to her maids-of-honour, who each pressed them in little pocket-books. He took the Prince Consort to show him the fort, etc. Mrs. M. gave the Queen tea. Colonel M. went to a picnic last Monday to see maple sugar-making, and there were two upsets in the deep snow at the sides of the road. One was Colonel H., whose sleigh remained in the deep snow, with him and Miss Irvine in it, whilst the tandem and shafts went on alone!! The other upset was an R.A. officer and Colonel M.'s niece. McLaughlin sent out the photos of the sleigh so beautifully mounted. The G. G. was delighted with them. Last night Mr. G. told us a story of a boy, aged thirteen, who has been brought up in such a way that when he was asked how he was, said, "I have a slight threatening of a cold." This boy's mother made her husband one night get into one of the children's beds to warm it for the child, because it was cold!! No mail but the China had reached New York.

Monday in Holy Week (Evening), April 10th.—This journal will be dull to a degree, as you can fancy. There is nothing pleasant going on till after Easter; besides, I am duller than usual, as my cold is very bad, my throat and eyes are both so painful, and I am so very stupid. On Saturday I was alone all day. Dick and Capt. Pem. went with Madame Duval to the organist's concert at the Cathedral. Dick said he played very well. All the "muffins" and lovers were there, and every one was decorous. No one paid to go in. Col. G. and F. B. came to tea.

Sunday, 9th.—At lunch-time, to our intense joy, came both mails, March 23rd and 25th.

Tuesday, 11th.—I was interrupted yesterday by Dick coming home and telling me about poor Lee's army having capitulated. Dick, Capt. Pem., and I are in despair, whilst the exultation of the G. G. and Mr. Godley drives us mad. All the nicest and bravest men belong to the South. What cold weather you seem to have at home, and what hurricanes. I have not been out for a week. Though Dr. B. has desired me not to go out, I mean to go to-day; the weather is so exquisite. Sunday was very cold, and at night we have eight and ten degrees of frost. Yesterday we had snow like home snow, that melted instantly. The church will be lovely on Sunday. People have given flowers, and Mrs. Godley has made beautiful decorations. I helped her a very little yesterday to cut out letters.

Wednesday, 12th.—Yesterday I walked out a little on the gravel. It is odd to feel gravel under one's feet again. I wore a velvet bonnet for the first time, and missed the heat of the fur cap on my forehead. I will tell you what sort of pain the cold here gives your forehead. Don't you know, when you eat ice fast, the pain you feel in your throat and mouth? It is just that pain you feel in your head. Had a visit from Mr.

Sitwell and Mr. Cecil Thorold. We had a moan over the South. Mr. S. says that quantities of R.E. officers are coming out here about the fortifications. I hear now that it takes only a few weeks to learn to fight, so I fear the Yankees would sweep us away if they come here. Mr. Godley always says to worry me, "There's going to be *a bloody war.*" It is a great thing Lent is nearly over. The Lowest Church people here don't go to balls in Lent. Captain Eliot told me that there was a dance in Lent at a Roman Catholic house at Montreal, and he danced for *self-denial*, as he hated dancing on a thick carpet after a big dinner! You know having a carpet on makes all the difference here in Lent; it is not thought a *ball* with carpet on! I read such a funny story in a paper of Captain Pem.'s. I must tell it to you. A doctor told Sydney Smith he must walk every morning on an empty stomach. S. S. asked, "Whose stomach?" They drove to church on Sunday on wheels for the first time, and now they drive in a waggon every day. One or two flies and a gnat have appeared, and the snow is nearly gone. The cat and the dogs here attend prayers, and are very particular in rushing down when the bell rings. Mrs. G.'s maid hates the dogs, and one day, after petting one of them, was heard to say *fervently*, " I wish there was no dogs in the world."

Thursday.—Yesterday was very wet all the morning, and cleared late.

Good Friday, April 14*th.*—Canadian mail in. As I was reading my letters and talking them over, into my room rushed the G. G. and Captain Pem. to say the ice-bridge was breaking up—a great event! Pem. thrust an opera-glass into my hands, and in we flew to the G. G.'s sitting-room, and watched it breaking asunder in the middle, and being carried slowly down by the tide; a most curious and interesting sight it was, to see this enormous bridge that had carried so many hundreds of people for three months, breaking in two. It is going *very* slowly, and above this is not broken at all. The blue river looked cheery again after the dead ice. The day was very cold and windy, but fine. After lunch, our fate was decided. Dick and I are to go home in May! Of course I am *enchanted* to see you all, and my pet Cecil again ; but at present I am thinking too much of the horrors of the passage to realize anything else; don't be angry! I spent a bad, excited Good Friday; it had to be settled, as the mail was going. How dreary an English winter will be after a Canadian one! Yesterday was fine, but rather cold north wind.

Saturday, 15*th.*—The news has just come in of Lincoln's death by stabbing; it took place in the theatre last night!! Is it not too horrible? What will happen next? He kept off war with England always. We were just saying, two days since, that he was about the cleverest Governor anywhere. What will become of America?

Easter Monday, April 17*th.*—We had just heard the horrible story of Lincoln's assassination when I wrote on Saturday. The day was dreary, cold, stormy, and snowy. Mr. Godley lunched with me, and after lunch he drove me to the church in the phaeton, to help Mrs. G. to decorate. The church was lovely with roses and green and illuminations. I helped about the font, and cut green things for the wreath-makers, and my hands were as black as a sweep's when I had finished. I could not help telling about Lincoln. I stayed only an hour; it was oh, so cold—thermometer twenty-nine above zero—and it was snowing hard; winter again! I believe we go home in the *Hibernian*, May 20th, for two reasons, viz. she is not the first ship from home, and also I trust

I shall see F. Captain Pem. told me the 25th think I am the cause of F.'s regiment staying here; one of them told him so, and he denied it. Colonel R. R. is gone to remonstrate; I thought of writing also to Sir Fenwick, but I will trust him. It is nice to see the snow back again, and it is bitterly cold; last night the thermometer went down to eighteen degrees, that is fourteen degrees of frost. F. Burrowes arrived after tea, bringing an "extra" with more horrors — fifty people drowned near this, from floods, and all the property destroyed—the most heart-rending stories, like that water disaster in England last spring. Mr. Seward and his son were also both stabbed at Washington, but are not dead. The wind was blowing a hurricane, and everything felt so mournful and awful. We are so comparatively near the horrors here. Colonel G. and F. B. came for Easter. Whilst we were at dinner, a letter came in to Colonel G.; of course we expected more horrors. This was to say that an officer of the 17th was on board the *Moravian* at Portland, unable to land; because he had no passport, he was kept in the ship. The wind was blowing a hurricane and *crying*, and the night was the blackest ever seen—

just the night for horrors and everything dreadful.

Sunday was a miserable-looking Easter Day, snowing and blowing and bitterly cold; the ground white with snow. We drove to eight-o'clock service in the cariole, bells and all! It was very good sleighing, and I enjoyed it after the stupid wheels. At the four-o'clock service it was so dark the lamps were lit. Mrs. G. and I drove after church to inquire for Mr. Price, and were *all* but upset on a drift near Mr. P.'s house. To-day is lovely, though bitterly cold. The *Hibernian* is a very good ship; she was built as a model of what an ocean steamer should be. The *Himalaya* is expected on May 15th.

Tuesday.—Yesterday Mrs. G. drove to town with me in the phaeton. The drift at their gate was so bad their waggon could not be got out. The old drifts along the road are marvellous; they have been cut through, and I can't describe the height of them. You pass through a narrow defile of snow. We went first to the rink to see Dick skate; he is getting on very well. Mrs. G. and I went to Col. Gordon's, by appointment, to drink tea. We had good tea and cakes. Dick joined us after tea.

To-day is so warm and lovely. Yesterday was very fine, but cold.

Wednesday.—Yesterday, after lunch, it was blowing much, with violent showers. Mrs. G. lent me her waggon, which shuts in even the servants with waterproof curtains. I went to say "good-bye" to Mrs. Adamson. She told me "Adamson" preached a beautiful sermon on Lincoln's death on Easter Sunday. Her talk is so filled with parentheses that I always forget what the beginning of it was about. The evening cleared up so beautifully, and was so warm and nice. I sat all the evening at the window watching the *débris* of the ice-bridge at Cap Rouge floating past; we saw bits of wood, supposed to be *débris* from the mischief done to houses by those terrible inundations. After dinner we drove to the 17th ball. The hurricane was awful. There were lines of spectators about the room watching a young ensign just arrived from home. That was Dick's great amusement at the ball. I must try and describe this boy: Rather short and fair, with a big head and high shoulders, with a mouth that looked as if he was laughing at everything in a sly way. Every time he danced, out went his tongue, his eyes opened and shut, and he twisted his head;

in fact, he danced with his tongue. He did not do one step in time, and he and his partner twirled in the middle of the room, knocked and kicked on all sides. Every one laughed at me because I said I begged of the G. G. not to go to the theatricals, as *on dit* that Booth is in Canada, and, knowing that the G. G. is a Northern sympathizer, Booth might try and shoot him, or "dagger him," as the Yankee papers say.

Thursday.—Yesterday was very fine, with such a cold wind. I drove myself to see Mrs. Gilmour. She told me that at the Protestant Home all the well people are supposed to go to church, and no one is ever forced to attend any service of any other sect. Some officers dined here, among them Gordon the Good and Major Brice (17th), *alias* "Tito." He is at present looking out for a happy home for Paul, his dog.

Friday, 21*st.*—Yesterday, soon after breakfast, I set off with Dick to be photoed in our furs by McLaughlin. He made me laugh by saying suddenly, "By-the-by, you may wink." What do you think the Quebec people did? They wanted to do much honour to Lincoln, so they meant to shut all the shops on the day of the funeral; but they shut them yesterday, and the funeral, after all, happened the day before. We dined at 6.30, and went to the theatricals after. I must tell of them to-morrow. I was accused on all sides about the 25th going.

Saturday, April 22nd.—Now about the plays! The first play, "Aladdin, or the Wonderful Scamp," was very well done; but the second one, "Little Toddlekins," I liked much the best. The puns in the first were almost too marvellous to understand. The man who acted "Barney Babbicome," in the second play, once forgot his part, and, pretending to talk to Amanthis, said, "Speak louder," meaning the prompter. They all acted beautifully. The women were done by a drummer and Mr. Stoney (25th). The room was crowded to suffocation. Col. M. accused me about the 25th going, and said I might have saved Col. R. Ross the journey, as I knew he would not succeed. During the epilogue, which was about their leaving and saying "Farewell," Mr. G. whispered to me, "Do you want a pocket-handkerchief? Take mine; it's as dry as a bone." The applause was tremendous, as it always is here—a great thing for actors. The band was so beautiful, and they sang part of the "Farewell Valse," the men with broad grins on their faces. Yesterday was wet, blowing and hailing, and dark. The steamer from Montreal arrived here yesterday—a great event. Col. M. invited me to a party at his house to hear glee-singing, but it was too wet to go. Mr. Godley recommends my giving medicine presents to all at home—"Radway's Ready Relief," to one; "Are you in Agony?" to another; and "Time will tell," to a third. This day is so wet and horrid.

Monday, April 24th.—I am writing twelve rules of etiquette for "Gordon the Good." I tell him he is to make use of them when he goes into English society! On Sunday we had snow, sleet, rain, and wind. It froze six degrees of frost last night, and the ground was covered with snow this morning; but it is all gone now. The Rifle Brigade come here on May 2nd, and General Lindsay and Captain E. come May 7th for inspections. Yesterday I drove to town; it was bitterly cold, and dull, and dark, with many little snow-showers. I went to the Ursulines Convent, to see Mère St. Charles. She told me they all get up at four a.m., and go to bed at nine p.m. They dine at 11.30 a.m., and have good meat very coarsely cooked, as she says there are too many of them to be able to have a carefully cooked dinner. They have wine if they are ill. They have coffee or tea for breakfast, with dry bread, and those who like have butter. Their sermons are on the subject of their three vows, " Poverty, chastity, and obedience ;" they call it all a sacrifice of themselves for God ; but she sees no sacrifice in it, and says she does not understand the meaning of that word. She teaches music for four hours a day. They meditate four times a day. These sad women may only talk to each other on holidays! I happily came on a holiday, when there was no *prayer* at four! We talked about Lincoln's death, and I explained to her that Dissenters go about on Good Friday like any other day. I think the nuns thought he was "daggered" as a judgment for going to the theatre on Good Friday. It seems an odd day to choose for a visit to a theatre. After the convent, I went to see Dick skate ; he is making progress. This morning Mr. Godley sent me a newspaper to read, with a French speech about slavery. If the accounts are true, the cruelty to the slaves is awful ; they say their masters' names are branded on them with red-hot irons, and they are beaten worse than horses, and one was burnt alive for killing his master! I should much like to hear the other side of the question from a reliable eye-witness. I must prepare my arguments for Mr. G. to-night. We had seven degrees of frost last night; to-day is lovely, but cold; not a bud has appeared yet.

Wednesday, 26th.—Mrs. Godley and I drove yesterday by appointment to see the St. Bridget's Asylum for old Roman Catholic Irishwomen and orphans. It is an excellent charity; there are thirty-three very old women, two blind girls, and twenty-four orphans. The priest met us—a most "jolly" old Irishman. The matron and schoolmistress are volunteers, and are sorts of ladies. They took us to the chapel, and the priest said, "This is a very common place; the only good thing in it is the holy-water pot," which was made of marble from Ottawa. We went up to see the inmates, and we had to speak to *every one* separately. The priest was a play in himself. The women were all between eighty and ninety, and one was a hundred; the younger ones were about seventy! The priest said to one, "Oh, you old *coon*, are you not dead yet?" "No, your riverince," she said. They were all exhibited by their ages, like shows. "This one was twenty-five in the rebellion of '98," and so on.

Most of them came from the south of Ireland. They are allowed to smoke their pipes twice a day. The matron told me, "We have so little room we are obliged to use this large room as dormitory and re*frec*tory." The 25th band acted for this asylum, and got £30 or £40 for it. We went to a loft where were two blind girls and several old women, and one poor little orphan baby. One old thing said she had seven cousins who were priests in Ireland. "They don't do you much good now," said the priest. His rough grotesque jokes seemed to suit them, and amuse them. We then went down to the cellar, where the children were being taught near a stove. They were made to sing "God save the Queen," curtseying the whole time at us. I suppose they thought any one who had to do in the slightest degree with the G. G. ought to be treated to "God save the Queen." *How* amused we were. I then went to see Mrs. M. She told me about her mothers' meeting, where she teaches the soldiers' wives to sew and help themselves. To-night we have the Stadacona Club ball. To-morrow we dine at the Godleys', and Friday at the Gautiers' (French Consul).

Thursday, 27th.—The Stadacona Club ball

was very pleasant. A Mr. T. (a Canadian) asked to be introduced to me, and made out in some inexplicable way that he and I were related through "his lordship," who I discovered was Lord Castlemaine.

Friday, 28th. — Went yesterday to see Mrs. ——— (25th); she told me there was a lovely view from her back windows — "mountains, and those sort of things." I went to the Hotel *Jew*, as the St. Bridget's priest calls the Hotel Dieu, to give the G. G.'s photo to the pretty nun, but she was *en retraite*. The Godleys' dinner was very pleasant; only Capt. Leslie (25th) and Mr. Botwood. We told Mr. B. about Booth having been shot, and this good clergyman said, "I'm sorry he did not die a more lingering death." He told us all the odd things he ate at Labrador. He ate ravens, owls, seals, foxes, wild cats, beaver, and musk rats; he liked the rats *much*. He said, "I liked the taste of all these animals, but the smell was sometimes unpleasant." The first owl he ate was very tough; but the second owl he hung up for six months, and it was excellent.

Saturday, 29th. Fancy, to-day we have snow again and great wind, and now rain. Nearly every Saturday since September we have had bad weather. The ground was white this morning, and last night we had a great fog, and it was pitch dark. Yesterday it rained terribly in the morning, but cleared up after lunch. I drove to town, and through a most horrible side-road deep in snow. I was nearly upset. The groom had to walk behind the phaeton and *hold* it, for fear of upsetting. We dined at M. Gautier's. After dinner a lady sang a song called, " The Ivy Leaf." Col. R. R. was there, and asked me to write and ask Sir Kars to let the 25th stay here now, instead of Frank's regiment! When nearly every one was gone, M. Gautier entertained us with an account of Col. G.'s auction, at which he had assisted. He said that the auctioneer pretended that everything had been with Col. G. in the Crimea, so as to make the things more interesting to bidders! He sold a tea-pot at a high price, as having been in the Crimea, and it was bought here. An old wooden box, bought here, was called a " divan " that had been in the Crimea, and sold *very* well. Col. G. had given his servant an old white hat, covered with crape to make it look cleaner ; the servant, in his zeal, sold it by auction ! One grand instance of mistaken zeal the servant showed by selling a cozy made for Col. G. by one of his lady friends, and highly prized by him. Madame Gautier showed me a photo done at the Sandwich Islands, of a lady and her baby, so odd and pale-looking, and they had big heads!

Sunday.—Very windy, but pretty fine. If F. comes soon, I shall have to go in the first ship, which I don't much like; but I know it is not really dangerous; it goes on the 13th. We have three ships now near this on the river. It is lively to have ships once more.

Monday, May 1.—To our surprise, we got our Canadian mail letters of April 19th this morning, per *Peruvian*—a very quick passage. Saturday was a very bad day—hurricane and great rain, so I stayed at home all day.

Tuesday, 2*nd.*—Yesterday, before lunch, I got a note from Captain Ballantine (*Peruvian*), sending me a fine large *turbot* as a present. They made the passage in nine days and twelve hours. Drove to town. There was a very cold wind and hot sun. I am in all my winter clothes still. Mrs. G. and I went to see " Les Sœurs Grises," and left the phaeton, which was to come for us to St. Matthew's Church at 5.30. We were kept waiting an age at the door, and had to tell that we came from the Government House. Two very nice English nuns took us over the convent. It is very interesting; but so sad to see so much suffering. Sœur Ste. Marie was exactly like an English *Sister* at home, with such a gentle voice. Their dress is quaint! Light-brown with black hoods, and a silver crucifix hung round their necks, and check aprons. Out walking they look so odd; I feared the horse would shy at them. They wear light-brown cloaks and hoods over their heads. They may go out and visit the poor and sick. There was a little *tin cross* at *every* door, with a "bénitier;" and the tall English "Sœur" crossed herself every moment; the other did not. We were taken to a room full of objects— quantities of *old* women, *blind* women, two or three *idiots*, and one girl of thirty, with the falling-sickness, who was the impersonation of Little Mother (in "Little Dorrit"), in a short frock, pinafore, and close cap! She frightened me, and so did one idiot; and she was also thirty, and could not speak, but made horrible noises, said Mrs. G. was a "chen" (chein), and wanted to pull her. It struck me it was the seal-skin coat; so Mrs. G. went over, and the idiot gave her a great grasp, and frightened her; the girl laughed the whole time fits of wild laughter. I then produced my eye-glass, which quite excited her. She instantly *smelt* it. I held it to her eye, and she was nearly wild with delight and excitement, and made worse noises than ever, so we left her, poor thing. She has two sisters idiots also. She was the saddest sight there. One poor thing, with no eye in one socket, and only half an eye in the other, said, " I'm longing to die, but I can't die ;" and the nun said she must be patient here till God took her. She told them they would be rewarded in Heaven for their sufferings here. The idiot and a very old paralyzed woman sit together, and adore each other. When the old woman told me her sufferings, the idiot laughed *loud*. Their supper was laid so nicely—a napkin in a ring at each place, also a bit of bread, and the infirm ones had little tables to themselves. Every bed had check curtains. We then went on to see where the nuns make flowers so beautifully, and then to the chapel—rather pretty for this country—and then to the place for the orphans—girls in one room, and boys in another. The girls were made to sing a song for us about " *Shamrogue* for Ireland." They were clean, pretty children. The boys were at their prayers, and were making faces and laughing. The Sœur said, "They can stop their prayers; it will not matter; they can go on afterwards." We also saw where they make the patten for the Holy Sacrament. They stamp it with moulds with the Crucifixion, and "I.H.S." on it. These nuns make it all; also the candles for all the altars of the churches. One of the school children asked that we might be shown their Oratory, a queer little place, with a wax doll on some straw in a glass case, meant to be our Saviour when an infant. "La Sainte Vièrge" was standing up in a glass case, with a straw hat on, with a wreath of flowers round it in the schoolroom, supposed to be a child reading. After *living* at this convent, we went to church, and were very late, which annoyed us much. To-day I had letters from General L. and Mr. R. General L. told me about Lincoln's funeral at New York, which he had seen. The ladies in the carriages wore the brightest colours, and were drawn by horses draped in black and white! They played slow marches in quick time. Mr. R.'s letter was very amusing. I had asked him to get me the song of "John Brown's body lies a mouldering in the grave." He said, "John Brown's mouldering body leaves this (New York) to-day, honourably escorted by Gen. Lindsay." He also said, "The men roar here, and the women scream for blood; let us hope that the shooting of Booth will act like a sop to Cerberus."

Wednesday, 3rd.—Yesterday I drove to see the 25th off. First, I nearly ran over a 17th soldier; it was *his* fault, for he stood with his finger in his mouth in the middle of the road. Capt. Pem. and Dick met me in town, and went with me. We did not go to the wharf, but looked over the cliff; the crowd was too great below. The R.A. and 17th bands were playing. It was rather sad to see them go; they played "Auld Lang Syne," having been here ten months. There was much cheering and waving of handkerchiefs as they slowly moved off. I then went to church, and was in time this time! To-day, at 7.30 a.m., Lord and Lady A. Russell and boys arrived. She is so nice, and the boys are both handsome and quiet.

Thursday, 4th.—Yesterday, after lunch, Lady A. and the two boys and I drove to Quebec. We went to the Citadel, where Lady A. and the boys went in to see their rooms. I was much amused, sitting in the carriage at the Citadel, and looking "around." There dined last night Mr. Godley, Col. G., Mr. Fitzgerald, and Capt. Seymour (Rifle

Brigade). We were so glad to see Capt. Seymour again. Mr. F. is very amusing. To-day I believe we all go to the 17th band. We have the most lovely weather; the wind is very cold, though the sun is hot.

Friday, 5th.—We went to the 17th band on the esplanade. The "muffins" were all there, looking very pretty. Many of the R.B.'s were there. Lord E. Clinton, Major Brice, and Capt. King dined.

Saturday, 6th.—There is not very much to tell since yesterday. Lady A. and I drove out in a wind and dust storm. The footman's cockade was blown off his hat! I went to see Mrs. ——; she is a regular Mrs. "Fairbairn;" her three gigantic children came into the room. I could happily say they were "magnificent," though they were plain to a degree, which I did *not* say. The boy was asked to say his letters, but happily ran out of the room. The dust was terrible; we were quite black. Mr. Wilson Patten and Mr. Somerset (R.B.) dined. Lady A. walked lame into dinner, and Lord A. said that *I* had kicked her so in the carriage that I had lamed her. "I left her quite *sound* this morning," said he, "and I found her lame after her drive."

Monday, 8th.—I found out too late on

Saturday that the mail goes out on Monday this week, so I can add a little to-day. Saturday was a very bad hurricane and much rain. It partially cleared about four. Sunday was dull and dark till evening, when it became most lovely, but cold. Before breakfast arrived Gen. Lindsay and Capt. Eliot. Sir Kars had gout too badly to come. To-day the General and Capt. E. are gone in early to inspect the 17th. I am in a fuss about the *Himalaya*, knowing nothing about our plans.

Tuesday, May 9th.—Yesterday, after lunch, I went with Mrs. Godley to see the Church Home; Lady A. had too bad a cold to go, as it was raining. We saw over the old men's and old women's place. One old man had been Sheriff of Gaspé once; he was bedridden for eleven years. We talked a great deal about American politics in the two minutes we were with him. He said the Yankees were so mad for blood that they were accusing every one, and it would be the Gov. Gen. who would be accused next of being an accomplice. I am not very clear what he was talking about. The old women were mostly disagreeable old Englishwomen. They have Sunday and week-day services there. We then went to the boy place. The boys were away at school; the atmosphere was stuffy to a degree. I had seen the girl place before. It is a nice enough Home. The people did not look very happy; but they were English most of them, and seemed *farouche* and unpleasant. After tea, I got my Canadian mail letters of April 28th; a very quick passage the *Hibernian* made! The gentlemen all dine to-night with the 17th, and Lady A. and I have "severe" tea together. Yesterday evening cleared up so beautifully, and everything looked so lovely, though we have not one bud out yet. We had a very pleasant dinner-party last night; I send a list. I sat between Lord A. Russell and Lord E. Clinton; both were very pleasant, and they were very good in not talking "shop." Mrs. M. and Madame Gautier entertained us after dinner with terrible stories of earthquakes; and Mrs. M. said, "*The third shock is sure to bring the house down!*"—in a most *measured, marked* way she said it. Col. M. gave us a long account of his animals. His present cat, Jack, meets him on the ramparts when he returns from parties, and rubs itself all over his face; then it asks him to come to the kitchen and give it some food, which he does; then, in his room, first he washes his teeth! and then gives the cat some water in the glass; then he takes off his clothes, and throws them into a portmanteau, and then in jumps Jack on the clothes. He had another cat, "born in Jamaica, died in Newfoundland;" it was buried with military honours. "Jack" he has had "since it was a *youth*." I told about "Tom" having kittens in my wardrobe; he said, "My cat never has any; *he* is quite above those things."

Wednesday. — I drove Lady A. to town; we went to the Hotel Dieu. I wanted to give the G. G.'s photo to the pretty nun, and Lady A. wanted to see the Hospital. The photo gave intense pleasure; the nun *kissed* it! and carried it about like a child with a new toy, showing it to every one. The poor thing had been *en retraite*, and was so glad to get out again. The hospital amuses her, she says, like "Little Mother." The sunset last night was so lovely it almost made me cry. First the opposite shore was all pink, while the river was deep blue, and the grass so green; there were also brown tints from the earth, and patches of white snow about; and then the exquisite colours faded to mauve and grey tints. I never could describe it all; the eye cannot satisfy itself enough in looking at such scenes. I had a tradeswoman with me this morning, half Yankee. She was told to wait in the *hall;* to my surprise, I found her in the *drawing-room*, quietly rocking herself in a rocking-chair! It is very interesting to us here reading about the feeling England shows about Lincoln.

Thursday, 11*th.*—I left Lady A. at the Citadel. She showed me her rooms; they are very nice. All the military ladies here, except the 25th Dr.'s wife, are too *grand* to live in barracks! Went with Dick to see dear old Mr. Price, to thank him for some very fine watercresses he sent me. He was in his bedroom in a dressing-gown and a blue-and-gold skull-cap. One side of him is quite dead; but he is much better. Of course we do not sail now till the 20th. I get ship panics at night. There are to be cheap trips to Ireland, to see the Dublin Exhibition.

Friday, 12*th.*—It seems too wonderful that this is my last letter but one, home. Yesterday, after lunch, I drove to hear Miss Mountain play the organ, which she did most beautifully. Last night dined Captain Ballantine, Col. G., Major Brice, and the Godleys. Capt. B. amused me much; he would inspire any one with confidence, and I wish we were going to cross with him; he says he thinks no more of crossing than of *eating his dinner!* The General leaves to-day; I am *so* sorry. The papers say that the citizens are to give a ball in a few days to the 17th.

Saturday, 13*th.*—I find I must write to-day instead of Monday, as the post people are so stupid. Yesterday Gen. S., Capt. E., Capt. Pem. and I drove to town together after lunch. We dropped Capt. Pem. in town, and we drove to see Lady A. Russell, but she was out. We met Lord A., however, who told us that the *Himalaya*, with the 7th Fusiliers, had been telegraphed from Father Point, twelve hours from here! Lord A. pretended to read out the telegram, and said, "Much sickness on board." He never forgets to worry me. It was not true; but it made me feel quite ill. We left the Gen. and Capt. E. at the Montreal boat, and had a talk with our dear little friend, Capt. Labene, who saved such quantities of lives during the inundations. I was so ill last night, I thought I had the Russian plague! and sent for Dr. B., who relieved my mind by saying it was only hearing suddenly of the *Himalaya's* arrival after a week of waiting. Lovely day. *Himalaya* arrived about twelve noon. She had been detained by fog. Drove to town, and brought Frank back to stay at Spencer Wood.

Tuesday, 19th. — Very hot, thermometer seventy-eight degrees in verandah. Went to a very bad concert for the sufferers in the inundation.

Friday, 19th.—Cricket-match at Spencer Wood. Farewell ball to the 17th Regiment, given by the citizens.

Saturday, 20th.—We embarked at ten a.m., in *Hibernian*, sailed at eleven a.m., passed Father Point at a quarter to eleven p.m.; rather foggy.

Sunday, 21st. — Rainy day. Attended service, and saw a whale spouting. Went 320 miles since yesterday.

Monday, 22nd. — Fine day. Made 270 miles. Passed Cape Rae at noon. Sickness coming on.

Tuesday, 23rd.—Made Cape Race at noon. 260 miles. Fine day.

Wednesday, 24th.— 272 miles. Passed icebergs. I saw none; ill in my cabin; much terrified. Effort to keep the Queen's birthday. Fireworks and a concert! *Rough!*

Thursday, 25th. — Rough. 276 miles.

Ship on one side for three days. A steep hill outside my cabin door.

Friday, 26*th*.—Calmer. Got up, and went into the saloon to hear the steward sing comic songs. 275 miles.

Saturday, 27*th*.—255 miles.

Sunday, 28*th*. — Rolling a good deal. Went to evening service in the saloon. 276 miles.

Monday, 29*th*.—Fine, with showers of rain. Went on deck for the first time. Horrified with the look of the ocean. 260 miles.

Tuesday, 30*th*.—Arrived at Greencastle at seven a.m., and in Dublin about six p.m. Fine day.

THE END.

www.ingramcontent.com/pod-product-compliance
Lightning Source LLC
Chambersburg PA
CBHW020314240426
43673CB00039B/800